Standing
on the Sun

Standing on the Sun

HOW THE EXPLOSION OF CAPITALISM ABROAD WILL CHANGE BUSINESS EVERYWHERE

Christopher Meyer
with Julia Kirby

Harvard Business Review Press

Boston, Massachusetts

Part opening illustrations by Don MacDonald

Library of Congress Cataloging-in-Publication Data

Meyer, Christopher, 1948-
 Standing on the sun : how the explosion of capitalism abroad will change business everywhere / Christopher Meyer with Julia Kirby.
     p. cm.
  ISBN 978-1-4221-3168-8 (hardback)
 1. International trade. I. Kirby, Julia. II. Title.
  HF1379.M493 2012
  330.12'2—dc23

                               2011032402

The paper used in this publication meets the requirements of the American National Standard for Permanence of Paper for Publications and Documents in Libraries and Archives Z39.48-1992.

Chris Meyer

To my teachers:

Emily Alford

George Norton Stone

Philip Wagreich

Otto Eckstein

Peter Temple and Carl Sloane

Stan Davis

Stuart Kauffman

Kevin Kelly

Julia Kirby

To my family:

Alan, David, Jane, and Ted

Contents

Introduction

The center of capitalism?

I n the central market in Phnom Penh, the smell of sweet pork sausages on street vendors' grills hangs in the humid air, and the sound of merchants and motorbikes is a constant buzz. Inside the huge, domed bazaar and surrounding awning-covered stalls, it's easy to lose your bearings; around the next corner you might find silver jewelry, vibrant silks, $20 knockoffs of vintage Movados with movements made in Russia. On a recent visit, Chris, traveling with family, edged past an eight-foot pile of hoodies and was confronted by a table of Hollywood films at roughly 50 cents per DVD.

He wasn't surprised; it's what one has come to expect in a country that is not itself a significant producer of intellectual property. Chris thought of the usual prediction: that as such nations' economies mature, they begin to see the light and devote the resources to protect intellectual property rights. As grown-up capitalists, surely they'll live by grown-up capitalist rules. But in the midst of that buzzing Cambodian hive of capitalism, it was hard to hold fast to the belief. He had to wonder, Would emerging economies really adopt a two-hundred-year-old approach to intellectual property? Or would their rapid ascendance give them the chance for a do-over so that they might concoct a new way of conducting business more aligned to the realities of the digital age? And then, as they gradually overtook the first world in vitality and sheer size, would a new global norm take shape around their practice?

A few months later, we started researching this book. Its thesis, in a nutshell, is that capitalism itself is a system and that as the environment that hosts capitalism changes—in particular, as the better part of global economic growth begins to occur outside the mature economies of the West—the capitalist system will evolve.

This is a high-level argument—and a tough one to counter. Like any "ism," capitalism is a social construct; *capitalism* is only a term for what capitalists tend to believe and do. Beyond a few fundamentals—that it puts faith in markets as the best way to allocate resources, that it depends on private ownership of property, that it features mechanisms for accumulating capital to fund endeavors larger than individuals can undertake alone—very little about it is set in stone. This is why we often hear phrases suggesting different styles of capitalism: "capitalism with Chinese characteristics," for example, or "Northern European social capitalism." No surprise, then, that capitalism is subject to change.

And what's behind that change? Again, at the theoretical level, it's easy to surmise. Like any adaptive system, capitalism is nested in an environment, so any substantial change in that environment alters what it takes to thrive. It's the same basic phenomenon as in nature: when the insect population of the Galapagos moves on to new flowers with a different shape, the beaks of the finches evolve in turn.

That the environment of global commerce is undergoing major change is no secret. Advancing technology, for one thing, constantly reinvents the context in which commerce operates. Demographics, too, have an effect, as the generations raised with new technological capabilities begin to fill positions of power. Most strikingly, the very geography of capitalism is shifting. With each passing year, emerging economies account for a larger proportion of global GDP; from 2004 to 2009, they accounted for almost all of the world's GDP growth. Patterns of consumption are being upended as global standards of living rise; India's middle class is now bigger than the entire U.S. population. Americans and others in the developed world have long fretted about job losses and other social implications of this huge and ongoing shift. But the impact of emerging economies will go beyond what anyone is talking about. It isn't simply that capitalism will increasingly happen elsewhere. It's that, taking root in different soil, capitalism itself will grow into something new.

Capitalism doesn't evolve only in theory. The most cursory review of economic history shows how much it has changed in practice. The rules shift constantly. For example, when Great Britain was the epicenter of industrial capitalism, it was understood that a business founder who borrowed capital and then went belly-up should be shipped off to debtor's prison—or worse, Texas (before air-conditioning). But U.S. capitalists more disposed to second chances later rewrote those rules, creating bankruptcy laws that encouraged entrepreneurial risk taking. The system morphed again with the introduction of limited liability, which allowed firms to shoulder the risk of large-scale manufacturing and, in doing so, gave rise to monopolies (an eventuality no one had worried about before). Even rock-solid assumptions—such as the assumption that currencies must be backed by precious metals—have been tossed aside as trade marches on. These are only a few, top-of-mind examples of ideas that cropped up locally, took hold, and changed capitalism globally.

At a more fundamental level, when production shifted from agriculture to industrial production, the theories of economics changed profoundly, because financial capital gradually overtook land in importance. As information—inherently *not* a scarce resource—becomes the most productive resource, economics will change again.

We're convinced therefore that we're on firm ground with our thesis: capitalism evolves, and even now it is evolving into something new. The question is, Into what?

To know that, it's necessary to question some seemingly central capitalist aims—because it was the old environment that gave rise to them—and look at things from a new vantage point. That is what we hope to provide in this book and why we chose the title for it that we did: "standing on the sun" is a reference to taking a new perspective. The phrase comes courtesy of Richard Morley, an MIT physicist who has made so many original contributions that a prize awarded by the Society of Manufacturing Engineers has been named for him. Once in a conversation about how innovation happens, Morley said to Chris, "In order to see the solar system as it is, Copernicus had to be standing on the sun."

Morley meant to underscore how hard it is reexamine a model in which you are situated and one that you believe to be working quite well. Standing on Earth, it was easy for pre-Renaissance scholars to believe they occupied the center of the universe and to persist in believing so even as evidence mounted that should have compelled them to rethink that position. As the instruments used to study the night sky became more and more powerful and as astronomers began to communicate across larger distances and share their observations, that central assumption forced their calculations into contortions. Planets showed themselves to be capable of anomalous retrograde movements, frequently deviating from the paths that mathematicians had plotted. But rather than question the basic model, astronomers added layers of complexity to it, positing epicycles and deferents within orbits—whatever it took to give their geocentric model the power to predict the movement of heavenly bodies.

Then came Copernicus' hypothesis, and workings that had seemed impossibly complicated suddenly became elegant.

By analogy, today's capitalists look around them, see anomalies, and struggle to incorporate them into the model they have embraced as true. What are some of the messy parts being shoehorned into this Ptolemaic version of capitalism? The value of corporate social responsibility (CSR), for one thing, is an idea few can bring themselves to deny but one that clashes uncomfortably with theories of capital markets. Open source initiatives, for another, seem to flout all the physics of economic motivation but continue to gain force. Still another anomaly: venture philanthropy, which can't be reconciled with the laws of profit pursuit. Nonetheless, happening.

Our argument is that, with a shift in perspective, such phenomena cease to seem aberrant and instead align with the logic of the system. It requires only a belief that capitalism can evolve and center on new pursuits. Imagine, for example, that something most people consider to be the core of capitalism—competition—is actually not so central. Shift your vantage point so that *innovation* holds that pride of place, and suddenly initiatives like Wikipedia don't seem so unlikely. Competition, still very much part of the system but unseated from its central point, moves over to allow for collaboration. Likewise, what if the pursuit of financial gain is not really the heart, much less the soul, of capitalism? What if it's really centered on the pursuit of *value*?

That's a formulation that, again, does not reject financial profitability but allows it to sit easily beside the pursuit of other kinds of gains.

We're hoping to provide a vantage point that not only does not have to resort to epicycles to explain the recent past but also provides a better basis for predicting what comes next. It might challenge many capitalists' allegiance to the "planet" on which they happen to stand, but, in providing a logic more hospitable to emerging reality, it might also strike them as a more comfortable home.

We're speaking in abstract terms here about what stands at the center of capitalism and what is peripheral to it. Now let's return to the concrete sense of geography. As a new version of capitalism begins to emerge based on the commercial environment of the twenty-first century, we see it taking hold first in the economies least invested in the status quo. It has been mainly in our travels to places like Dhaka, Dubai, Mysore, Shanghai, São Paulo, and Tel Aviv that we've seen businesspeople going about their work in surprising but effective ways. As we study the actions of today's frontier capitalists, we ask, Why is their new way succeeding? And does that mean it is likely to spread?

We learned, for example, about a curiously structured firm created to provide 9-1-1–style ambulance service in India. It consists of a for-profit dispatching service yoked to a charitable concern that receives donations of ambulance vehicles. Setting it up wasn't easy. Sweta Mangal, who cofounded Dial 1298 for Ambulance, joked with us, "In India, all the rules are there to make sure you cannot start a business." But the enterprise she and her colleagues cobbled together is doing so well that it suggests that the bright line capitalists traditionally draw between profit seekers and social benefit providers will get murkier.

In Brazil, we saw aircraft manufacturer Embraer taking on a responsibility that no Friedmanesque (Milton, that is, not Tom) capitalist would embrace: improving public education. Embraer reportedly spends $3.6 million a year on the secondary school it runs near its San Jose dos Campos facility. That's not only an investment in its own future workforce or a retention strategy for the parents it employs. Embraer considers it a pilot for developing better teaching methods and materials that can then be transferred to São Paulo's public school system. That might sound awfully altruistic to managers in the

United States, where the burden of improving public education falls primarily on public servants. But there's little consensus around the world on how business and government should between them serve the public. (In the United States, for example, the burden of health insurance coverage has been borne by employers.) Why should the arrangements set up by yesterday's superpowers go unquestioned?

Meanwhile, in China, capitalism is flourishing but with a heavy cost to the environment. When Walmart arrived with a plan to build eco-friendly, LEED-certified facilities relying on local contractors, the idea was met with great enthusiasm. As it became clear that those subcontractors lacked the engineering knowledge to deliver, however, Walmart didn't trim its ambitions; instead, it devoted resources to teaching the Chinese construction companies what they needed to know at its own expense. Under old-school capitalism, firms don't work this hard to keep from polluting unless the law forces them to. Environmental impact is what economists call an *externality*, and not something that must be factored in to one's own profit-maximizing equations. But we think that many more capitalists, sometimes because they're forced to but sometimes because they want to, will start internalizing the costs of externalities.

Let's underscore the theme here: we're seeing much of this rule-breaking and rule-reshaping activity (though not all of it) outside the world's most mature economies. Like the Americans who redefined capitalism in the nineteenth century, emerging-economy capitalists have the advantage of designing enterprises on a cleaner slate. They are building institutions to take full advantage of today's capabilities and conditions, unimpeded by any vested interest in sustaining the obsolete.

The "capitalism abroad" part of our title, however, doesn't assume only one definition of "here." Our point is that wherever you are, you need to attend to developments elsewhere. If you're an American, watch the emerging economies for cost-slashing innovations. If you're in India, Africa will be leapfrogging your payment systems. If you're in Singapore, look at how Brazil is exploiting bottom-up initiatives. The degree of connectedness and diversity of the global economy means that no island is an island.

Wherever you are, as capitalism takes new forms, the ways to succeed in the capitalist system will change, too. Firms will rise and fall according to how well they have tracked the shifting territory. You—your firm if you are a manager, your constituency if you are a politician, yourself if you are all you need to protect—will prosper according to how well you adapt. As the environment around you moves on, you must know how to move with it. It's no good to be a finch with an unevolved beak.

What to Expect from This Book

In the past two years, plenty of books have been published about the recent financial crises, with many suggesting policy moves for avoiding them in the future. This is not another entry to that particular library. Rather, we focus on economic change drawn on a larger canvas and the ways it is ushering in a whole new future for capitalism. But the 2008 credit crunch and 2009 recession are not irrelevant. By casting serious doubt on the status quo, the crisis has given an extra push to the changes already under way. Alarm about the financial system has made the forces of inertia less potent and given people who already want to see change more reason to push ahead. Since the Great Recession, new-style capitalists have seen less risk in departing from established models, and defenders of the briefly unassailable "Washington Consensus" are no longer in a position to bully them.

We are also eager to offer a caveat: we describe here many positive stories about capitalism in the emerging economies. But we spend little time on the many shortcomings that exist there. We understand that corruption, crime, and greed exist abroad, too, and that every economy will have to continue to deal with them. In fact, we see no greater threat to the developments we describe than cronyism in capitalism, which as far as we know damages the performance of every capitalist country. But that is not our subject.

This book presents in three main parts our version of what will come next. Part I, Capitalism Adapts, explains the dynamics of the coming change. Chapter 1 describes the most important ways in which the landscape of commerce is changing, and chapter 2 explains just how a complex system like capitalism adapts.

Part II, Runaways and Renaissance, identifies two major ways in which today's dominant form of capitalism misses the mark, explains how solutions to these problems will evolve, and shows how a new form of capitalism will reorganize economic sectors. The first problem, explored in chapters 3 and 4, is the form of value that capitalism is tuned to produce. A powerful system that formerly pursued financial returns relentlessly but narrowly will change to one that just as relentlessly pursues value measured more broadly. The second problem, covered in chapters 5 and 6, is its modus operandi. We show how a shift from cherishing competition in its own right to cherishing innovation will allow more innovation to occur, sometimes through intense competition but often not. When these excesses are overcome and when value and innovation occupy center stage, capitalism's fixed belief in the strict separation of the public and private sectors gives way (as described in chapter 7) to a world in which business, government, and NGOs no longer need to be adversarial.

Finally, in part III, Moving On, we take our vision of transformed capitalism and imagine how actors within the system might in turn adapt. We do this at a macroeconomic level in chapter 8, and at the more micro level of the firm in chapter 9.

One final, framing point: our conclusions arise out of analysis, not advocacy. The demotion of financial profit as one of many kinds of value, and of competition as a useful tool rather than an unquestioned dogma, arise from the trends emerging around the world and capitalism's vital property: adaptability.

At the outset, we can assure you: the patient lives. That's not what you were told in the midst of the downturn. You saw the analyses in the business press: the *Economist*'s cover story "Capitalism at Bay." The *Washington Post*'s editorializing: "Is Capitalism Dead?" As recently as August 2011, Nouriel Roubini asking again, "Is Capitalism Doomed?"

We agree that capitalism took its knocks. But it can rise to meet the challenge. It won't look the same—but in some lights it has never looked better.

We like the way playwright Tom Stoppard put it. His *Rock 'n' Roll* is set in the former Czechoslovakia and explores, among other themes, the fall of communism. In the play, an Oxford professor muses on the "beautiful ideas" of Marx and wonders how it could be that the revolution didn't succeed. It's another character, Stephen, who explains:

> "Marx read his Darwin but he missed it. Capitalism doesn't self-destruct; it adapts."

We're interested in your reactions to the ideas we present in this book, and we're always fascinated by fresh examples. To make it easier for you to share them with us, we're relying on a Web site and social media. Please visit us at www.standingonthesun.com, or post notes on Twitter using the following hashtags:

Chapter One Ideas:

#newlands   *#newhands*

Chapter Two Ideas:

#runaway   *#coevolution*   *#greenfield*

Chapter Three Ideas:

#happiness   *#triplebl*   *#ROE*

Chapter Four Ideas:

#externality   *#scale*   *#sensor*   *#sensibility*

Chapter Five Ideas:

#PseudoComp

Chapter Six Ideas:

#InvHandshake

Chapter Seven Ideas:

#fourthsector   *#CapitalismsR&D*

Chapter Eight Ideas:

#UtilitySector   *#InnovSector*

Chapter Nine Ideas:

#NewDupont   *#MNCvector*

Early in the chapter we remind you of these. We hope this device, admittedly an experiment, will not prove a distraction to your reading.

Capitalism Adapts

PART I

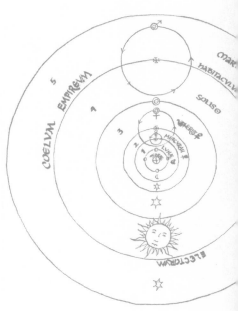

Capitalism is not immutable. It has changed before (remember industrialization?) and will again.

Darwin explained how change comes about in complex systems. Writing about the finches of the Galapagos Islands, he observed that the shapes of their beaks adapted to alterations in their environment, in particular to fit the forms of the flowers that provided their food. Likewise, capitalism will adapt to changes in the broader world of global commerce in which it is situated.

What changes? Two big ones: the world's growth will no longer come from today's high-income economies (they now consume 77 percent of world GDP—but only 32 percent by 2050). Second, just as industrial technology gave form to the fast-growing economies of the twentieth century, information technology will shape the emerging economies of the twenty-first. As some businesses thrive and others struggle in this new low-income, high-growth, globally connected, digital-native environment, the rules will evolve for everyone.

In chapter 1, we survey the new world, contrasting it with the one in which today's capitalists grew up and formed the assumptions that guide their actions. In chapter 2, we draw on the science of evolution to understand how systems change, paying particular attention to one dynamic that can be blamed for capitalism's worst excesses: the runaway effect.

CHAPTER ONE

Capitalism's New Center of Gravity

The shifting environment of the global economy

> *In the 21st century, history will unfold in the exact opposite direction of what Western intellectuals anticipated in 1991. Then they all assumed that the end of history is the triumph of the West. Instead, we will now see that the return of history is the retreat of the West.*

> —Kishore Mahubani, author of *The New Asian Hemisphere: The Irresistible Shift of Global Power to the East*, April 2009

It was 1997, and Chris was visiting Beijing for the first time. He was lucky to have a guide, the son of a Chinese colleague, who was both bilingual and bicultural; the twenty-something entrepreneur had spent his teenage years in California. On the tortuous drive to the Great Wall the two of them passed a curious neighborhood—a cul-de-sac of supersized faux-Tudor homes, the kind of ersatz splendor usually encountered in wealthy American suburbs. Surprised to see such conspicuous construction in a land still firmly ruled by the Party, Chris asked how people felt about it. Wasn't it decried as the ultimate in capitalist folly? The young man grinned as he offered an explanation: "In China, we're very pragmatic: if it works, we call it Communism and move on."

The ensuing years have underscored the power of Chinese pragmatism. But in retrospect, why should we have expected otherwise? No law of nature dictates what communism must be. Karl Marx might

> **To discuss these ideas on Twitter, use these hashtags:**
>
> *#newlands*   *#newhands*

have thought he was being definitive when he wrote, "The theory of the Communists may be summed up in the single sentence: Abolition of private property," but like all *isms* communism remains socially constructed: only what its adherents make it. Over time, if their attitudes and behaviors change, they can make it over.

The same goes for capitalism: it's only what capitalists believe and do. And it changes when the bulk of capitalists start doing something different.

Or when different people start doing the bulk of capitalism.

That is what this book is about: the fact that capitalism is now being practiced by a new set of people—in terms of geography, demography, and ethnography—and that as a result, capitalism itself is changing. Just like the young man Chris met in China, today's capitalists can expect to see changes in our own system that violate the prior orthodoxy. And if we are pragmatic—and we're accustomed to thinking that there's nobody more pragmatic than capitalists—we will move on.

In slightly more detail, here's the thesis we advance in this book. First, capitalism is an adaptive system, which is to say that it evolves when its environment changes. Second, we are now in a period of dramatic change in the environment in which capitalism is situated. Businesses follow the money, and we're in the midst of a dramatic shift of the economic center of gravity to different regions of the globe. It's not only that the growth of demand is coming from new markets; it's also that the societies hosting this economic efflorescence are markedly different from those that capitalists focused on in the second half of the twentieth century.

In this chapter, we talk about change along five dimensions: geography, demographics, technology, the nature of goods being traded, and the global span of activities. We hope it will become clear that the trends in any one of these areas are powerful enough to force changes in prevailing economic rules. Before we proceed to examine them separately, however, we should point out the important interaction among them. The emerging economies, characterized by low income per capita, are experiencing rapid growth; the level of capitalist activity in them will continue to rise rapidly. At the same time, the populations of emerging-economy nations, in stark contrast to the West, skew toward the young. This means that just as the geographical shift is happening, the reins of capitalism's course are also being placed in the hands of the first *digital-native* generation. The first populations that are majority-born into a world of powerful and inexpensive information and communications technologies, and most comfortable applying them to new areas, will be those of emerging economies, just as the United States gave rise to the first generation dominantly raised with industrial mass production, even though its enabling technologies originated in the then more developed United Kingdom.

As the demographic shift lends power to the geographic shift, change may come fast. Capitalists schooled in the old environment will have to find ways of working suited to a landscape they've never seen before. Businesses following the money will find themselves in unfamiliar territory, and will adapt, individually. The approaches they take will collectively shift the practices we think of as capitalism.

As we talk about the importance of the first digital-native generation, we also stress that the technologies its members are comfortable with are, in themselves, a huge changer of capitalism's environment. This is not another book telling you about the transformational potential of information technology (IT) at every scale, from a village in Africa to continental electrical grids to global disease detection and containment. Nor is it another book discussing the way people will work in networks. Both are rich and important topics about which we know less today than we think we do, because these forces are nowhere near mature. What's important for our purposes is that the emerging economies get to build their infrastructures with spanking new technologies. Remember Y2K? It was a yawn in India, China, and Brazil. The surplus from these economies' rapid growth pours into the seemingly instant creation of infrastructure that has more intelligence, higher efficiency, and more ubiquitous connectivity than what came before.

Economies built on this infrastructure will be taking on board some new economic realities with it: that many forms of value can be shared without limit; that tools and processes can spread almost instantly, at minimal marginal cost; that physical capital may be more anchor than asset; that human and capital resources can be accessed around the world. These are not merely complicating developments to integrate into today's capitalism like epicycles being added to a geocentric model of the universe. These are fundamentally different assumptions. They subvert many of the basic tenets of economics like scarcity, competitive advantage, the power of wealth, and the importance of location. Net: we can expect two decades in which the shape of capitalism will be in the most rapid flux in history.

Set in New Lands

At any given time, there is a dominant form of capitalism that feels more or less definitional. Capitalism does have a center of gravity, and it's determined in a very simple way. It's wherever the most wealth creation is taking place. Spain and its conquistadores, Britain with its East India Company, the United States with, at one time, Detroit, then Hollywood, then Silicon Valley. The players in the economies marked by the most valuable entrepreneurial activity lay claim to the concept. They call the most shots and set the overall tone. Other forms of capitalism are talked about with reference to the version practiced at the epicenter. And the epicenter for a long time has been the United States.

The United States has been the colossus of capitalism for more than a century—ever since the term gained currency, really. (The word didn't even exist in English, claims the *Oxford English Dictionary*, until William Makepeace Thackeray used it in his 1854 novel *The Newcomes*.) But the center of the action is gradually drifting to what are called the emerging economies: Brazil, India, and China in particular. (Russia? Intentionally left blank. More later.) Goldman Sachs also likes to talk about the "next eleven" countries with the greatest economic potential in the twenty-first century: Mexico, Nigeria, Egypt, Turkey, Iran, Pakistan, Bangladesh, Indonesia, Vietnam, South Korea, and the Philippines. When we speak of the emerging economies, we most often refer to these fourteen nations.

You'd have to have been living in Outer Mongolia to be unaware that the emerging economies are rapidly gaining in almost every measurement of economic importance. (Oh, wait—our point is that if you were living in Outer Mongolia, you probably *would* know.) A few facts help underscore both the magnitude and the immediacy of the phenomenon:

- In 2000, 77 percent of world GDP was produced by the rich countries. By 2050, this number will fall to 32 percent.

- Today, as Yale's Jeff Garten has pointed out, the globe hosts six billion people, one billion of them living in rich countries. By 2050, there will be nine billion people—and *still* only one billion in today's rich countries.

- It used to be that the rapid growth rates of emerging economies were dismissed because they started from a small base. No longer. In 2005, China alone accounted for no less than 33 percent of the growth in *world* GDP. We've already seen how much difference that makes in the global economy in this decade's commodity price run-up: new demand from emerging economies drove the prices of iron ore, shipping hulls, copper, and the like to Himalayan levels.

- Of the world's twenty-five hundred largest publicly held companies (based on market capitalization), nearly half are now based outside North America and Western Europe. The proportion from emerging economies has grown at a compound annual rate of 14 percent, to the point that in 2010 the headquarters of more than a quarter of these twenty-five hundred companies were in emerging economies.[1]

- Whereas in 2000, the U.S. GDP was about eight times that of China, by 2008 the ratio had shrunk to about four: $14 trillion versus $4.3 trillion.[2] Jim O'Neill, Goldman Sachs chief economist, has estimated that China could lead the GDP league by 2027.

We could go on, but here's the real question: why are economists like O'Neill so certain the trend will continue? It's because the conditions exist for both growing consumption and growing production in the emerging economies.

The world's consumption engine for decades has been the acquisitive American middle class. But the planet's population growth has occurred mainly in its poorer countries. As economic conditions have improved in the less-developed parts of the world, whole new middle classes have arisen that, though not proportionately huge in their nations, represent prodigious numbers of eager new consumers. Goldman Sachs analysis claims that roughly 2.4 billion income earners globally will attain middle-class status in the decade 2010–2020. The ratio of those in the BRIC countries (Brazil, Russia, India, and China) to those in the G7 (Canada, France, Germany, Italy, Japan, the United Kingdom, and the United States), it says, will be 2 to 1.

At the same time, it's been recognized that consumption is not only a middle-class activity. There are the upper classes, of course, and it is not immaterial to mention that there are already more than a million Chinese millionaires. Barclays Capital recently released a report showing that China buys 12 percent of the world's luxury goods, and its consumption of them is rising by at least 20 percent per year. (Extrapolating, the country will be snapping up one-third of such goods by 2015.)

But more importantly there are the lower classes to consider. The 2.5 billion people in the world said to live on less than $2.50 per day—the group famously named by C. K. Prahalad "the bottom of the pyramid"—may individually make minuscule purchases, but collectively they represent an enormous demand for basic goods and services. With virtually all the growth of global population occurring outside the high-income world, the fastest-growing segment of consumers is the have-nots, and capitalists increasingly will target that segment.

Income per capita is surely a different-looking number in most of the world than it is in the mature economies of the West: in 2007, India's GDP per capita was $1,050, for example, whereas in Germany it was $40,320. To put this in purchasing power terms, the average Indian has 6 percent of the income of someone living in the United States, and the German counterpart has 76 percent.[3]

When capitalism is practiced by the comfortable—wealthy managers catering to the tastes of wealthy customers—it takes on a certain character. Priorities and practices may change, however, when capitalism focuses on the bottom of the pyramid. At a macro level, business will perceive that there is less and less money to be made selling diamond-studded cell phones to the elite few, and more and more to be made selling practical provisions to the many. (It was William Randolph Hearst, responding to someone's disdain for his "yellow journalism," who declared, "If you write for the classes you will eat with the masses. But if you write for the masses you will eat with the classes.")

Here's our suspicion: when the prototypical capitalist is someone selling cheap cell phones to struggling millions, as opposed to David Yurman watches to the affluent, the nature of capitalism itself changes. Indeed, even if you've been in the business of selling basic cell phones to millions of ordinary folks but in rich markets, your tried-and-true approaches may fail you. Vodafone, the world's second-largest provider of mobile services (after China Mobile Limited), discovered this when it ventured into India and found it could not be profitable with the same business model that had served it well in the developed world. Geared to produce profits at an average revenue per user (ARPU) of about $50 per month, Vodafone foundered when revenues from Indian consumers proved to be less than 10 percent of that, and falling, as new low-usage segments signed up.[4] Its need to charge 8 cents per minute minimum to cover costs was wildly out of line with a population whose demand would be almost insatiable at 2 cents per minute.

Tellingly, even as Vodafone was concluding that the market simply could not be served profitably, a homegrown firm called Bharti Airtel was doing just that. Its approach to fulfilling the same basic market need that Vodafone had recognized differed in almost every conceivable respect. Bharti was the first mobile company to outsource everything except marketing and sales.[5] It obtained network operations services from Ericsson, business infrastructure from IBM, and transmission towers from an independent company that had grown up to build infrastructure for all the mobile competitors. Bharti also discovered a great way to lower the costs of managing customer relationships: get rid of them, by marketing prepaid phones. By eliminating much of the cost of billing and customer support, by using shared infrastructure, by paying Ericsson by the minute for network operation, and by buying rather than building business systems, Bharti was able to serve customers—131 million of them as of 2010, compared with 427 million for Vodafone across thirty-one countries—with about one-tenth the capital investment of Western providers.

No one would call Bharti's business anything but capitalist. But at the same time, no well-trained and well-practiced capitalist in first world mode would have created it, because it dispenses with scale, capital intensity, and customer loyalty as sources of competitive advantage. Serving large, low-income markets is just not the same.

Grameenphone, a business founded by Iqbal Quadir in 1999, underscores this point. With a mission and model now broadly celebrated, Grameenphone brought phone service to the poorest corners of Bangladesh, today distinguished by the world's lowest ARPU—and did so profitably. Grameenphone is our first case of a *mixed-value* company, an idea we take up in chapter 7. This means that even though it was designed to turn a profit, it was founded to produce social value. "In Bangladesh, a cell phone is like a cow," Quadir has said. "An essential piece of capital equipment." His underlying motivation was to provide a key component of the infrastructure that could help some of the world's poorest people improve their quality of life and begin to lift themselves from poverty.

To do that required the invention of a new distribution system and a new financing apparatus. Quadir created a plan that brought together Telenor, the Norwegian national phone operator, to invest in the network, and Grameen Bank to provide microfinancing for the handsets (not an obvious strategy in 1999). No developed economy provided the model of the "village phone lady," an entrepreneurial entity on the most humble level imaginable. And none offered the tools of microfinance, which made it worthwhile for lenders to dispense the tiniest of loans for capital equipment, probably because no one with global-scale capital to lend conceived of the handset as a piece of capital equipment. Once you have that perspective, you can imagine that the phone will produce income, reducing the financial risk; that the buyer has an incentive to grow usage in her village, increasing ARPU; and that financing is as appropriate at this scale as it is for any business's capital equipment.

The growth and character of consumption in the emerging economies are only half the story of why capitalism will increasingly be rooted in their soil and compelled to adapt. Production skills and capabilities to meet that demand domestically are also rising rapidly. Pundits love to cite the masses of engineers being churned out by Indian and Chinese universities, and sometimes those numbers are disputed given uneven interpretation of what really constitutes a trained engineer. But less arguable is the trend of Western multinational corporations establishing R&D centers in emerging markets. And still more convincing is the rising number of multinationals headquartered in emerging economies. Every year, the *Financial Times* publishes its *FT 500* of the world's largest multinational firms. Between 2006 and 2008, the BRIC representation on this list more than quadrupled, from fifteen to sixty-two.[6]

What does the repotting of capitalism in new territory mean for the shape it takes? It means quite a bit, because geography is a matter not only of longitude and latitude but also of history and culture. The various societies of the world have their different ideas of fairness, social equity, the value of transparency, and the role of government. Traveling in 2009, Chris had a fascinating reminder of this in the space of one day. He picked up a newspaper as he left Mumbai to go back to Boston, and read about one implication of the Indian Congress Party's election triumph: the fact that the new administration would need to reshuffle federal ministries out of obligation to its coalition partners, because certain ministries offer richer opportunities for bribes. (Bureaucrats dealing with the telecom industry, for example, enjoy access to particularly deep pockets.) This transitional challenge was reported without a trace of opprobrium, essentially in the way one might find an American business page story reporting on negotiations of acquisition terms and conditions between Hewlett-Packard and Palm.

Ten hours later, having endured the forced march through high-end retail that is Heathrow's terminal 5, Chris picked up a London paper and saw a very different tolerance for governmental grubbing. The news was full of the expense scandal in Parliament, some MPs having crossed the line in terms of which personal expenses could be considered to have been incurred in the course of their work and charged to taxpayers. Still later, having arrived on U.S. soil, he saw a news report in which strenuous objections were being made to U.S. oil industry executives' even being present in meetings focused on policy making.

In short, different attitudes prevail toward government and the state, the desire for wealth, and the rule of law. All these things vary with the cultural heritage of a society. This is why the R in BRIC has turned out to be silent: Russia's cultural heritage turns out to be a major impediment to its economic progress.

We have a theory as to why Western managers have been slow, in general, to recognize the implications of the emerging economies' growing scale and sophistication: it's because they set the changes in motion, first, in the offshoring wave, and then in the outsourcing wave, for purposes of their own. If you look at the business press coverage of the 1980s, it is clear how managers regarded these economies then: simply as sources of cheap labor. This was the decade of Ross Perot's "giant sucking sound"—the noise he perceived as jobs rushed out of the United States into post-NAFTA Mexico.

It wasn't until the 1990s that the role played by emerging economies expanded in the eyes of Western managers, and, even then, it was only to see them also as markets: buyers as well as makers of Western goods. Multinational consumer goods companies cast a hungry eye on those tens of millions of new middle-class consumers, whose numbers, as a direct result of offshored production jobs, were rapidly swelling.

It is only in the past several years that we have seen leading multinationals shift their perspective on emerging economies as themselves sources of innovation, much of it better suited to local markets and some of it destined to take on the world. *Fortune* 500 companies now have ninety-eight R&D facilities in China, and sixty-three in India. GE's health care group built its largest facility in Bangalore.[7] When Hewlett-Packard opened its newest research center in June 2011, it chose to put it in China. HP CEO Léo Apotheker told reporters, "It is in China, for China, but also for the world because the R&D capabilities here in China we want to leverage for other markets as well."

The old mental model has persisted in some quarters, long after the BRICs were declared to be rising powerhouses. In many minds, the mature economies of the West remain at center stage; other nations are the cheap labor to produce its goods, the new markets to buy its goods, and the new adherents to the Washington Consensus. Practitioners of capitalism in these countries have their own perspectives, though, and it does not consign them to such minor supporting roles.

This, in fact, is the big news about the emergence of those economies—news that most managers in mature economies are missing. They have a sense of foreboding that we are entering some kind of new epoch, which some like to call "post-American," in which the lion's share of global wealth creation will no longer be accounted for by the United States. They worry that U.S. firms, as their nation loses its 800-pound gorilla status in the global economy, may see their dominance threatened. They suspect that worldwide manufacturing and marketing will no longer revolve around the tastes of the U.S. consumer. But they haven't pondered the higher-level effect: the vibrant economies of new global players like China, India, and Brazil will not simply win more hands in the increasingly global game of capitalism. They will also rewrite its rules.

Placed in New Hands

Sweta Mangal is a Mumbai entrepreneur. When Chris asked her about leaving Pratt & Whitney to found her business—about which more in a moment—she had this to say:

> While I was working in the U.S., I thought life was so mechanical. The economy is already developed. You'd find everything was exactly the same, every day . . . and everything worked like magic.
>
> I'm a person who comes from a country where *nothing* works. I missed that! I missed the traffic jams, I missed that the lights go off, that when you go someplace there's always confusion. In the U.S. I never thought I could create something, because everything is already there. That's what got me thinking: maybe I can do something better in India, because India has so many opportunities.

Mangal gave us a few glimpses of how a fresh kind of capitalism might be cultivated by new hands. When Chris met her in 2009, her business, Dial 1298 for Ambulance, was being celebrated as a success—and it still is one. But to our eyes it was a curiosity. Chris is a longtime strategy consultant to *Fortune* 500 firms, and Julia is a veteran *Harvard Business Review* editor. We've spent our time around the thoroughbreds of capitalism and know how to size them up. This thing looked like part donkey, and maybe part monkey. Throw in a duck for good measure. As Mangal explains the challenges she and her colleagues faced bringing 9-1-1–style ambulance service to Mumbai, all the individual decisions they made sound perfectly reasonable. It's impossible to bootstrap such a service, for example, because the ability to respond instantly across a wide geography is a necessity on Day 1. You can't start with one ambulance and grow from there; you need a fleet of ambulances. But who will invest on that scale when the business has never existed before? Will there be sufficient demand at a price people can afford? Will cost control suffer if money is invested as philanthropy?

To obtain the funds without losing discipline, the founders of "1298" created a second entity: a nonprofit foundation that could accept charitable donations to fund the purchase of the vehicles. Then that foundation provided the services of these ambulances to the company, charging only for hours of actual use. Lacking the operational expertise to run an ambulance service, they partnered with the London Ambulance Service to learn how it's done. What's more, India lacked a pool of emergency medical workers, so Dial 1298 persuaded educational institutions to start training them.

To the eye of a Western capitalist, accustomed to keeping its sectors neatly compartmentalized, all this looks jury-rigged—a business model constructed of baling wire and tape. But it works, and more important, once you set aside Western preconceptions, it looks as if it could even be a model for others: find a source of patient capital—the donors accessible to a foundation—yoke it to a for-profit business that can survive only if it's efficient, and access know-how wherever you can find it. And oh, yes, while you're at it, create a new category of jobs and persuade universities there's a financial opportunity in training people for them. Dial 1298 has expanded into other cities, and others are copying its model.

By the way, Mangal mentioned another obstacle people pointed out to her—the objection that no one in Mumbai would pay for ambulance service. "So I went to the emergency room and asked people, 'How did you get here?' They told me, 'By taxi.' So they are already paying—they need these services." It is always difficult to measure demand for services that haven't existed before, but that doesn't mean it isn't there.

In some ways, entrepreneurs are the same the world over, but Mangal and her colleagues strike us as a new force to be reckoned with. Whose hands have firmly held the reins of capitalism until now? It has been not only the capitalists of developed Western nations but also, within them, a certain cohort of people. The baby boom that followed the Second World War created an unprecedented bulge in the demographic tables. Baby boomers have dominated not only the markets served by consumer goods companies but also the boardrooms and managerial ranks of businesses of every kind.

That can't last forever. The exploding markets for concierge medical care and designer half-glasses tell you that the boomers aren't immortal. And the next cohort of capitalists looks quite different. Increasingly non-Western and less moneyed, on average, they are a new generation whose attitudes and aptitudes differ markedly from their parents'. Recall our earlier observation that the generation now sliding into the driver's seat of capitalism is the first digital-native generation.

Alan Kay, inventor of the mouse and much of the rest of the computer interface even the elderly now take for granted, once offered the following definition of *technology*: it is anything invented after you were born. (Presumably even for Kay, then, the touch screen is pretty whiz-bang.) None of us thinks of cars, let alone trains, as technology, but they were certainly newfangled in their day. Now consider this: if someone is younger than twenty-five, is the World Wide Web something she thinks of as technology? Or is it only an accepted part of the world, the existing foundation on which one builds? Doug Adams offered this answer in a short 1999 article for the *Sunday Times*: "We no longer think of chairs as technology, we just think of them as chairs. But there was a time when we hadn't worked out how many legs chairs should have, how tall they should be, and they would often 'crash' when we tried to use them. Before long, computers will be as trivial and plentiful as chairs (and a couple of decades or so after that, as sheets of paper or grains of sand) and we will cease to be aware of the things."

Putting business into the hands of those born into the connected economy has implications at three levels at least. First, of course, is the facility, efficiency, and thus enhanced capability displayed by digital natives in using the information vehicles of the global economy; for example, we've seen many imaginative uses of mobile phones spawned in Africa. Second, business practices and capabilities will change even more rapidly than in the past as the method of making changes in systems evolves from the titanic corporate project of the pre-ERP 1980s to the continual downloading of new widgets of the post-ERP 2010s.[8] These changes in operations will seem natural to a generation raised on the Web.

Third, the environment of the Web seems to be raising a worldwide generation whose personality has been influenced by social media and the economics of information. Don Tapscott, who prefers to call that group "Net Geners," claims they live by new norms, learned in their online lives and transported to their offline ones: freedom, customization, scrutiny, integrity, collaboration, entertainment, speed, and innovation. John Palfrey and Urs Gasser, who lead research on digital natives at the Berkman Center for Internet & Society, say the differences run even deeper—as deep as identity formation. In people who came of age on social media, that process involves experimentation and reinvention, as well as different modes of expression. "It would be too simple to say that the Internet age represents only an amplification of the trends that began to emerge in the industrial age," Palfrey and Gasser argue in their book *Born Digital*. "In fact, something quite new is happening: The use of new technologies by Digital Natives— the most sophisticated of wired young people—is leading to changes in our understanding of identity."

Here's a story that could never have happened to a boomer—in part because the technology didn't exist, and in part because no one born in the 1950s could conceive of it. It's just . . . too weird. Kyle MacDonald, a twenty-six-year-old blogger (in 2006, when this happened), set out to trade a paper clip for a house. (Why?) He started off on Craigslist, announcing his intent in the Barter section, and promptly found someone who was willing to give him a fish-shaped pen for it. Posting that in turn, he was rewarded with a ceramic garden gnome. The incremental trading up continued through a camping stove, a generator, a beer keg . . . all the way, one year later, to an eleven-hundred-square-foot home in Kipling, Saskatchewan.[9] Along the way, MacDonald departed from the physical barter model; as the Internet discovered his quest, the established media seized on it, putting him on *Good Morning America* and equivalent shows in Canada and Japan. At one point he was trading a year's rent in Phoenix for an afternoon with rocker Alice Cooper.

Here's the point: if you're a blogger, for whom the open source development of Linux or other software, the free provision of Web-based apps in exchange for a little attention to ads, and the media culture in which an item gets picked up and amplified by the media the way a planetary probe gets slingshotted around Jupiter to get to Saturn are all just part of life, why *not* try to trade a paper clip for a house? There are implications here for capitalism on a larger scale. It shows how social capital can be fungible with financial capital. That the marginal cost of trading is so low that Ronald Coase's assertion of the fundamental reason for the existence of the firm needs a new look. That the "gift economy" concept spawned by free value available on the Net may be a real economic phenomenon that changes our ideas of trade. In sum, digital natives will see possibilities for reorganizing economic activity that wouldn't occur to the previous generations.

Again, the youth story turns out to be tightly bound up with the emerging-economies story, because the populations of the fastest-growing economies are on average younger that those of the indus-trialized world. If it's significant that capitalism will increasingly reside in the hands of digital natives, then it's significant which nations are richest in that resource. Let's think about the part of the global popu-lation that is less than fifteen years old. Going back to Alan Kay, by the time this cohort was born, the first graphical Web browser had been released for a couple of years, so the Web doesn't count as tech-nology for them.[10] That group, in India, made up 31 percent of the population in 2007. In the euro area, it represented only 15 percent. The United States and China are both at 20 percent. The average age of the population of the G7 countries was forty-two years in 2009; of the emerging economies, only twenty-eight. And although we're not ready to write the book about the not-yet-emerging economies, it's worth noting that if we rank all nations according to this metric of youth, thirteen of the top fifteen are in Africa.[11] And now let's think about the population over sixty, for whom stereophonic LPs count as technology. That group represents 7 percent of India and 12 percent of China, but 18 percent of the United States and 24 percent of the European Union. (Japan? Ichiban, at 30 percent.)

It's predictable, then, where nations will first become dominated by their digital natives. So what happens when some parts of the world have digital native societies?

Built on New Machinery

On May 6, 2010, Jack Ablin, a Chicago-based investor, sat stunned as he watched the price of his Procter & Gamble holdings drop more than 40 percent within half an hour, from the mid-$60s to $39.97. It was part of a larger event that came to be known as the flash crash; in those same few minutes, the Dow Jones Industrial Average plunged almost 1,000 points, losing nearly one-tenth of its value. Ablin told a reporter he quite literally fell out of his chair; it was not only the biggest drop he'd ever seen during a trading day, but it was also the biggest one (in absolute terms) the Dow had ever experienced. Even more amazing, no one seemed able to determine exactly why it had happened. Early theories centered on the possibility that a trader who meant to sell $16 million worth of futures made a typographical error and placed the order at $16 billion. In any event, something kicked the sell-off into motion, and, as automated orders were activated, it quickly snowballed.

For us it was a dramatic reminder of another way that capitalism's environment has changed. It is now situated in an electronic world of ubiquitous, fast-moving information, increasing transparency, and strong feedback effects.[12] Technology is always advancing, of course, and that doesn't usually spell fundamental changes for capitalism. But sometimes, it does. Futurists like to say that when an important technology arrives, "we expect too much in the short run, and too little in the long run." We've been through the former. The dot-com bubble was an expression of faith that "The Internet changes everything"— a belief that proved premature. It was succeeded by a Dark Age. Following the 2000 dot-com bust, there was a certain amount of relief on the part of those who chose to believe that the Internet was much ado about nothing—until Google's phenomenal stock performance, starting in 2004, turned geeky talk about "Web 2.0" into an "eyeball bubble," driven by social networks, with investors eager to buy in to the new world of advertising-supported business models.[13]

Now the long run is arriving. It's not about better targeting of marketing. Rather, it's about the democratization that was promised at the dawn of the Web, because, as promised, information technology is empowering smaller economic entities—including individuals.

Three current developments really do have that power. Cloud computing is one, because it changes not only the economics of data storage but also the risk profiles and capital requirements for new businesses. The mobile Internet device is another, because it allows rich information not only to be received but also to be created and transmitted by anyone, anywhere. And what has been referred to as "the Internet of things" is a third, because it allows remote and dispersed phenomena to be sensed and reported and because it automates another class of labor. Each of these trends can be and has been explored at book length, and there's no need to do full justice to them here. We're interested only in the ways they change capitalism.

Cloud Computing

Cloud computing gets its name from the fact that the computing power that firms rely on to operate needn't be on the ground at their own facilities. It can be "out there" somewhere, accessed via the Internet and purchased on demand from vendors like HP and Amazon.

If this were just outsourcing to take advantage of scale and specialization it would hardly be a new story for capitalism. Two benefits of cloud computing are more subtle. First, it lowers the barriers to innovation. If you have a new, information-based business model, to have to set up an IT infrastructure to prepare for customer number one is a big burden. To be able to buy computing power economically "by the sip" removes it. Before electric utilities, every company needed its own source of power. After they arrived, companies could use electric equipment without that investment. In 1982, when Xerox invented Ethernet, it had print ads showing a jack in the wall labeled "Information Outlet," illustrating that someday you'd plug in (how quaint!) to a network and get all the information power you needed. Now it's happening.

The second benefit cloud computing brings is illustrated by Salesforce.com, one of the first apps to run in the cloud. Its experience shows how the cloud can bring true Web 2.0 value to apps; the many companies who use its sales management tools not only pay for the privilege, their usage helps to extend and improve the software's capabilities. Salesforce.com learns from everyone and makes that learning available to all. In general, shared information systems not only cost less than a population of proprietary systems, they encode more knowledge, and learn faster. This continuous, cloud-based learning takes us a long way from the architectures installed in the 1990s by big systems integrators, whose strategic mantra was "design, build, operate." When the firms for which they used to deliver their walled-garden solutions opt for the cloud instead, few are able to gain a proprietary advantage through IT, but all benefit from a more rapid diffusion of innovation.

We'll return to this theme—the creation of platforms for continuous learning—in chapter 8, when we look at firm-level implications of capitalism's evolution. For now, let's move on to another technology with transformative power.

Mobile Internet Devices

Mobile Internet devices are important because they represent a tipping point in the world's access to shared information—and they produce a lot of it as well. The idea of providing everyone on Earth with a laptop has been superseded by the explosive growth of smartphones; Gartner reported that third-quarter 2010 sales of the devices were 96 percent higher than in 2009. Internet-connected phones have been a cool development for technophiles in developed economies, who can now layer browsing and snapshooting onto their calling and texting. But it's been a crucial development in emerging economies, where the value delivered previously had not reached the threshold to justify the purchase. The breakthrough performance of mobile Internet devices ensures that they will become ubiquitous and that ubiquity in itself will become the story as the network they combine to create becomes the prevailing information infrastructure.

Already, cell phones have become the safest and most convenient means for individuals to transfer funds in many parts of Africa, simply because the devices have the capability and are at hand. In Bangladesh, entrepreneur Kamal Quadir has created CellBazaar, a market along the lines of Craigslist, to connect buyers and sellers, and has chosen to base it on a mobile device platform. (Yes, Kamal is Iqbal's brother.) In Katine, Uganda, farmers use phones to check prices, and, armed with market information, they band together to eliminate predatory middlemen.

What does this mean for capitalism? If gaining access to functioning markets is as simple as using a handheld device, a whole class of potential entrepreneurs who were sitting on the sidelines will now be in the system and helping to shape it, at the expense of those who have used their capital advantage to extract value. The economic value of this connectivity is conveyed by this statistic: although the emerging economies' income per capita is about one-ninth of the G7's ($3,000 per year versus $28,700), the penetration of mobile phones is effectively the same—76 phones per 100 people, versus 76 per 109. As ubiquitous mobile devices increasingly promote transparency and inclusiveness, expect them to have an impact on many industries beyond banking, including media, medicine, and education.

The Internet of Things

The advent of a new *Internet of things* is a third, fundamentally important change in capitalism's environment. Using a combination of miniature connected sensors and radio frequency identification (RFID) tags, inanimate objects become collectors and transmitters of data. If you put the right kind of sensor on a bridge, for example, it can detect movement that falls outside acceptable parameters and is therefore a sign of deterioration. If you give it the ability to transmit that data to the Internet, the need for maintenance can be spotted by engineers remotely. As we explore in chapter 3, that ubiquitous sensing capability changes the rules for capitalists because it makes the effects of their activities visible to the broader society. Impacts they used to think of as externalities become increasingly measurable and attributable.

If capital is defined by ownership and markets, it seems technology is changing both. Already 5 billion of the world's 6.9 billion people have cell phones. The next generation of IT will be cheaper again.[14] So markets will become much more connected, arbitrage more challenging, bottlenecks more difficult to create. We've seen this in the case of labor markets, where connectivity has shifted demand for everything from radiologists to call center operators from the United States to India.

And for some people, IT will take much of the need for capital out of capitalism. More efficient use of equipment, pay-by-the-seat information systems, access to intellectual capital that used to be a corporate asset—all these trends favor and empower the small business and individual. It appears that the revolution is finally arriving—and it's profitable!

And back to poor Jack Ablin, our Chicago investor. Happily he's not poor any more: P&G recovered fully from its share-price tumble. But the rollercoaster ride he took is another property of the new world. Its intense interconnection makes for unpredictable volatility. It creates the preconditions for an explosion of innovation, and that's what we expect. But it also creates the risk of other kinds of cascades, some of them potentially catastrophic. The cascading power blackouts in the northeast United States in 1965 and the one-day Dow Jones Industrial Average loss of 23 percent in 1987 were both the results of connected system components (in one case circuit breakers, in the other programmed trading instructions). The Internet of things, meanwhile, is an ideal host for an Ebola-strength computer virus planning its leap from the information world to the physical one. This book isn't about that—but don't say we didn't warn you.

Trading New Goods

There's a related fundamental development in capitalism's environment: the source of value has changed. What people pay for in markets is increasingly intangible rather than tangible. This has been a long-term trend—perhaps as long as human history—and it shows up markedly in the shift every developed economy has experienced from product manufacturing to service provision. But it's also about products. The price of a product like Apple's iPad has very little to do with the cost of the plastic, metal, and silicon that go into its manufacture. What customers value is its design, its connectedness, its intelligence.

When the source of value changes, it has big implications for the economic system. And information has unique economic properties. As a simple example, land doesn't depreciate—but property, plant, and equipment do. Thus the shift from an agrarian to an industrial economy called for new capitalization solutions, accounting rules, and financial instruments. Likewise, as we move from an industrial to an information economy, we must deal with a new fact of life. Although mass-produced, tangible goods have substantial marginal production costs, information goods have essentially zero marginal costs. Once someone has paid for the first recording or software solution or essay to be created, any additional copies are almost cost free. In a world where many goods cost nothing, it is meaningful to talk of a gift economy—and new approaches must be devised to fairly fund the creation of new goods. Insisting on retaining the old models—copyright and patent systems, for example—as they are is a rear-guard action.

When we refer to information goods we are talking about much more than the media and entertainment offerings that consumers buy. We're also talking about the "machine tools" of the information economy: CAD/CAM software, spreadsheets, website designs, instructional videos. In the industrial world, both tools and offerings were tangible: behind the manufacture of a physical tube of toothpaste was a physical toothpaste-making machine—and it was, and remains, expensive. Consumers didn't pay for the machines, but through their consumption of toothpaste they funded them. Today, the media industry is in turmoil because the marginal costs of the goods they produce is zero, and so people readily give them away (try giving away your used toothpaste). But increasingly, the capital equipment of the information economy is also information goods, and these production tools are also being shared freely.

When Linux appeared and then succeeded, the self-organized network of volunteer coders was remarked on, but few observers outside the software industry—and not many within it—considered it of great importance. When Wikipedia appeared and put Microsoft's Encarta out of business, commentators began to see Web 2.0 as a mode of production. Now SourceForge.net, a product of Geeknet, Inc., is a superstore of open source software and a hangout for volunteers who want to work on it, a kind of global *souk* for free machine tools—230,000 of them.

The ability to freely share capital equipment undermines some of the most well established ideas about barriers to entry. It challenges the very meaning of terms like capital and ownership. It also suggests the rate of innovation will continue to accelerate. Thanks to free sharing, innovations become instantly available everywhere. Imagine how rapidly the Industrial Revolution would have progressed if machine tools had been free.

Spanning the World

One last fundamental alteration in capitalism's environment is something we would describe as a phase change. After centuries of becoming increasingly international, the context of trade suddenly has become truly global. Picture an historical map of the world, with pinpoints of activity in the earliest commercial centers. Now think of how those points of commerce began to interact regionally, the lines between them multiplying and broadening to the point that they became saturated splotches of trade. Now consider the current economic interdependence of the world; the pinpoints and lines have filled the screen to the point that there is no white space remaining. When the scope of one's economy grows from the tribe, to the village, to the city, to the nation, to the sphere of influence, and finally to the planet, that is not simply a linear progression. Rather, the world is reordered in important ways.

We're just now teetering on the point of that phase change. As we write, in the summer of 2011, the Greek debt crisis has placed the future of the euro in some doubt. The debates raging in European capitals make it clear that we're still at the point of tension between nation and sphere of influence, held back by the strictures of nations. But at the same time, the reality of one global economy is dawning.

That's a new reality that will certainly force capitalism to adapt. For one thing, we predict it will create the stage for multinational corporations to rise in global influence. We should note that multinationals will no longer be a Western club; the United Nations reports that there are now 21,500 of them based in the emerging world. Wherever they hail from, we'll see multinationals routinely achieve scale larger than many political entities. As early as 1992, former Citibank chairman Walter Wriston predicted what he termed the "twilight of sovereignty." His book by that name portrayed a world wherein a new electronic network—made of advancing information and communications technology—had unified the world into one global market of ideas, data, and capital, all able to move with lightning speed to any corner of the globe. International financial markets, he noted, had outpaced the ability of governments to control national economies and old political borders. A "global conversation" was now possible that could, among other things, advance civil and democratic rights.

More recently, and far more darkly, Prem Jha (in his similarly titled book, *The Twilight of the Nation State*) describes globalization as "a sudden explosive expansion of capitalism, one that is now breaking the container of the nation state to encompass a large part of the globe." For good or for ill, in a planetary economy many former functions of the state will be exercised de facto by multinationals; at the same time, certain regulatory functions—police, health, and monetary authorities among them, we hope—will feature international governance. We'll spend more time contemplating the evolving role of the state in chapter 8.

No Embedded Base

Back in the days when competition was coming to the U.S. telecommunications market, the new entrants were rapidly deploying modern digital technologies to give them an edge over the established regulated monopoly. Bell System executives, faced with having to write off and replace their aging physical plant, encoded their predicament with a rueful joke: "How did God create the world in six days?" they asked. The answer: "No embedded base."

We started our survey of environmental changes with the growth of emerging economies, and we end there as well. For although the changes we've described will create a new setting for capitalism worldwide, not every part of the world will be equally positioned to capitalize on it. The emerging economies, by virtue of their rapid growth rates, their youth, and their delay in entering the global economy, are the fields in which new practices will flourish.

There is a precedent for this pattern. In the eighteenth and nineteenth centuries, it was the British economy that was the engine of innovation. New industrial technologies were pouring out of its workshops. Inventors in England and Scotland came up with the theory of electricity and magnetism, steam power, dynamos, and Bessemer steelmaking. They invented the telegraph, Bakelite, and pasteurization. Steel replaced wrought iron. Mass production using interchangeable parts and division of labor unseated artisanal fabrication. The Scots even invented a fundamental doctrine of market capitalism—the invisible hand—to explain to the foot-draggers why they, the British, were being so successful. In light of Great Britain's standing and continued innovation, the Victorians had every reason to believe that their empire would remain the leading global power. The reason behind all this innovation was obvious: as the world's richest economy, Britain could afford the universities, the time devoted to study, and the private laboratories lords liked to have in their castles. (Birr castle in Ireland, where the dynamo was invented, also for a time housed the world's largest telescope. Yes, cloudy, rainy Ireland.)

But a strange thing happened on the way to hegemony. Another nation, geographically larger but far poorer in its stock of intellectual and financial capital, also embraced the new technologies. And precisely because it had no embedded base and no establishment to speak of, these technologies became the foundation of the new society that was rapidly growing there. As the new industrial systems presented challenges, the impulse was to respond to them and not to see them as proof of the innovation's limited value. Need massive amounts of capital to build mills? Create a national banking system. Need to get more productivity out of that investment in a plant? Institute a third shift—and while you're at it, build a company town to ensure your labor supply. Need a bigger market to absorb the output of efficient-scale factories? Build a transcontinental railroad system to open up far-flung territory. Need workers capable of operating machine tools? Make high school mandatory.

Even plagued as it was by missteps and misdeeds—from gold price manipulation and railroad stock fraud to the excesses of robber barons and labor uprisings—the United States by World War II had become the dominant military and economic power. It succeeded almost in spite of itself because it had built its economy and society around the newly available technologies of the Industrial Revolution. And because it had room—physical, mental, emotional, commercial—in which to grow.

The parallel today is inescapable. We've all read the statistics about the upside potential of the Indian and Chinese markets, and we know they are only now embarking on their own phenomenal growth trajectories. We know there are not well-developed industries in these emerging economies that will resist the disruptive innovation; those with enough juice to play are desperate to move forward. We know there is little now to hold back the entrepreneurial talent and ambition of literally tens of millions of people, to whom it is now abundantly clear that economic growth is possible.

Meanwhile, this time around the United States has that inertial challenge to overcome, the unattractive prospect of dismantling the massive institutions and entrenched interests built up in the industrial age. And the other G7 countries, having just caught up with the United

States, don't have it any easier. It will be the economies that lack an embedded base that can get right down to building what makes sense given the new rules of a changed world.

We had a bench-scale preview of this situation in the 1980s when Japan had the opportunity to do a "release 2.0" on the world economy and beat the United States at its own game as an industrial power. U.S. auto companies were startled to find that Japanese competitors had surpassed them on both cost and quality dimensions, and even when they understood the logic of that breakthrough performance, it was a tremendous struggle for them to retool themselves. And in that case, it was mostly just a change of technology. Executives had to swallow only one power-shifting idea—that customers, and not manufacturers, got to define the meaning of "quality"—and the rest of the challenge was sucking it up and investing what was needed to replace outmoded production techniques. This time, fundamental ideas about capital, competition, and collaboration and the roles and purposes of government, the financial industry, and corporations are all subject to rethinking.

John Maynard Keynes once observed, "The difficulty lies not so much in developing new ideas as in escaping from old ones." In the coming decades brilliant ideas for business, economic, and social innovations will come from everywhere, but it will be in the green fields of the rapidly growing emerging economies that the next generation of capitalism will take hold. Will the institutions of the developed world—corporations, governments, and citizens—react in the way the U.S. automakers did to the Japanese innovations of the 1980s? Will they be a little late to wake up but willing to learn, adopt the innovations, and fight back? (Note that even then success was elusive, or the U.S. wouldn't have had its bailouts.) Or will they mirror the stagnation of England, which took fifty years to adapt to its loss of leadership? It's a question of how quickly their capitalists can escape their old ideas.

CHAPTER TWO

Cambrian Capitalism

Runaway feedback, the peacock's tale, and the evolution of capitalism

One hundred years from now economists will look back and say the father of the profession wasn't Adam Smith—it was Charles Darwin.

—Robert Frank, 2011 Aspen Ideas Festival

n 1992, Chris was facilitating an annual strategy offsite for the senior management team of MicroAge, one of two *Fortune 500* companies in Arizona at the time.[1] The discussion turned to a new class of competitor and its possible effect on MicroAge. After ten minutes of increasingly concerned discussion, the VP of sales exploded: "It's a war out there, and these guys are getting ready to attack us! We have to be ready to hit them first, before they can build momentum." The President, Alan Hald, responded, "Maybe, but could we consider another way to think about it? What if it's not a war of us against them, but more like an ecology, in which they're a new species with a niche distinct from ours, and we're both better off by coexisting?"

Chris was startled. He'd been following the literature of complexity theory (more formally, complex adaptive systems), which often suggested parallels between biology and economics. And he had tested some of the ideas with businesspeople, most of whom reacted with bemused skepticism. Now, for the first time, he was hearing a corporate executive try to sell this concept to his team. (To be honest, though, it didn't

> **To discuss these ideas on Twitter, use these hashtags:**
>
> *#runaway*   *#coevolution*   *#greenfield*

get much uptake, except from Hald's equally innovative Chairman, Jeff McKeever. The VP of sales responded with an ostentatious eye roll.)

Complexity theory went on to enjoy a vogue in the mid-1990s after which much of the punditocracy considered it passé. But in the fifteen years since, the idea of business as biology has only grown stronger, to the point that businesspeople employ the jargon without giving it much thought, as when they say, for example, "That's not in our DNA" about a corporate capability.[2] Books have been written, the ideas continue to be diffused, and biology-inspired techniques have been developed, applied, and proven fruitful. The eye rolling stopped long ago, and complexity applications don't go by that name any more; they're called things like *agent-based models*, *genetic algorithms*, and *nonlinear search algorithms*, or accepted as a subset of analytics. Practitioners have taken on these ideas, developed new tools, and proved their capabilities. The methods are in ever-broader use, and the power of the parallels between economy and ecosystem has only begun to be exploited.

This is not another book about biology and business, but it does build on what has been learned about systems that evolve, be they ecologies or economies.[3] In chapters to come, you will find us invoking a few concepts about feedback, selection, and evolution that are valuable to understand at the outset. It's not that you need a glossary to read this book, but our use of some terms draws on meanings they might not always carry in common parlance.

Chapter 1 already provided a specialized definition of the word "environment," explaining that the environment in which capitalism is situated is not only geographic, but also demographic, technological, and cultural. This chapter moves from the "where" of capitalism's evolution to the "how"—providing the language to discuss the process by which a system adapts to its environment. If we're going to convince you that capitalism can change its spots, we need to be clear on the process by which that transformation will happen.

A Theory of Change

In the world of NGOs—the nongovernmental organizations that work to make the world a better place—a phrase has caught on in recent years. It's the observation that one must have a "theory of change." The point in the social sphere is that it is often easy to get broad agreement on a desired end-state—for example, to reduce homelessness or eradicate malaria—but the hard part is outlining for donors and others how you think the movement will happen from point A to point B. Often the most effective route is not the one that seems most obvious and direct.

In writing this book, we didn't start from a point B; we had no consensus target for capitalism to move toward. We do, however, have a very definite theory of change: that capitalism is made up of rules practiced by capitalists; that in different environments capitalists will adapt, generating new rules; that the new rules will be taken up wherever they work well; and that some of the existing rules will not be favored in new (and increasingly influential) environments. In the jargon, capitalism is an *adaptive system*.

Not to get too Discovery Channel, if you were watching the evolution of *homo sapiens* and got to the part where the monkeys came down from the trees, you might notice that they were using their limbs differently on the ground and imagine that someday they might look like tailless, upright apes. That would happen because the monkeys with capabilities best fitting their no-longer-arboreal environments got to pass their genes on to successors more frequently than those that didn't. In the same way, capitalism will end up optimized for a new world not because of policy or revolution but because of adaptation.

To state it all but redundantly, adaptive systems come to reflect the features of their environments. In chapter 1, we explored how capitalism's environment has changed broadly, deeply, and rapidly. Knowing that, one could adopt one of two points of view: either this shift has no feedback on capitalism itself, or it does. If the economy is like a machine, a change of environment will mean nothing to it. It will go through all the same motions it did in the old environment, even if they prove less productive. But if it's more like a natural, organic system, made up of individuals who can figure out new ways to make a living, the system will discard things that are not working out well in this new world, and adapt.

Capitalism Is a Set of Rules

What is it exactly that changes when a system like capitalism evolves? Economist Paul Romer addresses this question in the theory of history he is developing. A new theory of history sounds awfully ambitious, and it is, but Romer brings it down to two forces. Change in human society, he says, is the result of fresh ideas, and those come in two flavors: technologies and rules. "Technologies are just ways to rearrange physical objects to make them more valuable to us," he explains, and "rules are just ways to structure the interactions that people have with each other, to get the most value out of those interactions."[4] Ideas of both kinds are easily spread, and they often go hand in hand. The constant quest to gain value on both fronts propels civilization forward.

At the level of an economy, a rule might be a matter of law or it might be less formally stored in culture, values, and norms. Romer cites, for example, the social repercussions that followed as people in communities got past their sense—their internalized rule—that if they were harmed by someone the right response was to exact vengeance. When a new rule took hold—that instead of meting out retribution they should seek compensation—civilization advanced. "If a man is wronged and retaliates by burning his antagonist's house down, there is a net loss to the economy," Romer explains. "If he instead sues for the value of the house and prevails, there is a transfer with no overall cost." (Legal costs were presumably de minimis at the time.)

We're in full agreement with the emphasis Romer places on rules in his theory of history. The march of technology is stunning and constantly commented upon, but it is only half of the force that advances civilization. The new possibilities created by technological progress must be navigated with new rules. This, we think, is appreciated on a very deep level, even if it is rarely articulated as well as it has been by Romer. It's why many people relish what John Maynard Keynes said about the power of new mental models:

> The ideas of economists and political philosophers, both when they are right and when they are wrong, are more powerful than is commonly understood. Indeed the world is ruled by little else. Practical men, who believe themselves to be quite exempt from any intellectual influence, are usually the slaves of some defunct economist. Madmen in authority, who hear voices in the air, are distilling their frenzy from some academic scribbler of a few years back. I am sure that the power of vested interests is vastly exaggerated compared with the gradual encroachment of ideas.[5]

So let us point out that capitalism is nothing but a set of rules, some explicit but most implicit. The rules dictate the conduct of exchanges, economic and otherwise, among owners, managers, citizens, and the state. Some of these rules turn out to serve society better than others. For example, in the introduction we mention the question of how a capitalist society should deal with an entrepreneur whose venture fails. If a business goes bankrupt, it might be considered fair to hold its founder completely accountable for the loss. Those who can't repay their investors or vendors might justifiably be sent to debtors' prison. On the other hand, throwing a borrower in jail, in addition to the costs of incarceration, removes the possibility of repayment—and meanwhile deprives society of whatever business venture that bold risk taker, now wiser, might have pursued next.

Developing bankruptcy protections as an alternative to debtors' prison is one of the steps in the more general shift Romer noted from vengeance to compensation. It was logical to realize that treating debt as a sin meant taking potentially productive assets out of the labor force and paying to imprison them. In a society that prized innovation, it made more sense to acknowledge that debt happens and devise a system for dealing with it productively. The rules changed, and capitalism adapted.

Coevolution

Did a less punitive stance toward capital squanderers mean they got off scot-free? Ideally, no. Easing up on bankrupts threatens to create what economists call *moral hazard*—a situation in which someone has an incentive to make bad choices because others will pay for them. For the rules to serve society well, they must achieve a careful balance that encourages reasonable risk taking while discouraging recklessness and free riding. And note that some of that balance can be achieved by rules other than laws. For most of the twentieth century in the West, moral hazard was contained by the social stigma of bankruptcy; debtors' prison or not, "going bust," becoming a "deadbeat," and declaring financial failure were sufficiently painful that no non-sociopath would choose them.

But after leniency regarding bankruptcy became the norm, some borrowers responded to that change with new behaviors. A century without debtors' prison eroded society's aversion to bankruptcy, and it became a tool of management. Frank Lorenzo, former CEO of Continental Airlines in the United States, embraced bankruptcy in the 1980s to restructure its labor agreements, even though Continental was not in such dire balance sheet straits that Chapter 11 was necessary. Lorenzo shocked business commentators but also earned their admiration for the creative use of the law. In that case, moral hazard was not an issue: there's no suggestion that Lorenzo's predecessors considered the bankruptcy strategy when negotiating raises with pilots in earlier years. But when Lorenzo didn't burn in business opinion hell, it inspired a truly bankrupt use of bankruptcy law: land speculators in the 1990s observed that in Florida and Texas, the law allowed them to walk away from deals gone bad, and thus they began buying high-risk properties. The deals looked bad to anyone who feared bankruptcy, but to those immune to its stigma, it was an attractive "heads I win, tails my creditors lose" opportunity. Since then, Florida has evolved its bankruptcy statutes to close this loophole, as community shunning was no longer a sufficient deterrent. Indeed, according to the Web site of a Florida bankruptcy lawyer, "There are no good or bad reasons to file for bankruptcy . . . There is no shame, stigma or embarrassment in filing bankruptcy anymore."

Yes, this should put you in mind of bailouts, whether in the context of AIG or Greece, and yes, it's been a similar story: Anglo-American capitalism has so strongly rewarded financial innovation, and has been so averse to letting financial institutions take their lumps, that moral hazard has moved from a curiosity of economists to the editorial page. And yes, we have lawyers, in many cases holding public office, who defend those institutions as doing their jobs as society needs them to. But that's not our point here.

Our point is to introduce you to the key concept of *coevolution*. This is the phenomenon by which changes in one species spur recip-rocal changes in another, in a sort of arms race of adaptation. As computational biologist Stuart Kauffman says, "When the frog gets a sticky tongue, flies get Teflon feet." The growth of digital networks and the changes in the music distribution industry are an economic example. The rules and technologies beget innovations in behavior; the new behaviors induce changes in the rules (in this case, both social and legal).

The behavior of capitalists coevolves with social values and the law. A qualifiying phrase we used earlier—"in a society that prized innovation . . ."—speaks to the reciprocality involved. Society's needs and values, and the conditions created by current technology, con-stitute the environment in which competing rules are judged. When one set of rules replaces another, it's a matter of fitness for that environment.

Fitness and Selection

We've already described (in chapter 1) the different world in which capitalism now finds itself. It's a world of values, needs, and technolo-gies that certainly have not been prominent in the past. So striking is the difference that capitalism's critics, and some of its adherents, fear it will never be equal to the challenge. These are the people who, whether they would put it this way or not, see capitalism as a machine.

They imagine something like a car, designed for paved roads, now having to perform in an ocean. Unable to retool itself, it will engage its gears, spin its wheels, and sink.

A Buick in the Pacific exhibits a disastrous lack of fitness for its milieu. But an AquaBuick's inventor might notice that internal combustion engines work in boats, and tires could serve as life preservers, and find another way to make a living. And in nature, when species find themselves in changing environments, some of them indeed do adapt.

The ones that have the best chance of responding to change are those that have a lot of variations in their gene pools to start with. Individuals that had quirky, even hampering, features in the old world find themselves relying on those features to survive. And if they live long enough to produce offspring, they pass down those newly useful features.

The perhaps depressing fact is that this is the whole purpose of sex: to ensure that there are always enough innovative designs with the potential either to improve on the previous solutions or to suit a newly changed environment better than the old model. Nature arranges to take two sets of instructions for making an organism from the current generation—the parents' DNA—and recombine them in a structured but somewhat random way to make a new set of instructions.[6] Then the new genotype grows the phenotype, as a new blueprint gives rise to a building.

Next, of course, the environment, through selection, decides whether this new variant was a good idea. The phenotypes that work well in the environment are fit, and the fittest survive and get a preferential opportunity to breed the next generation. The elements of its genotype get a chance to "radiate," or show up in multiple successor species. (It's the same basic phenomenon when a product thrives that has a certain characteristic, and then that characteristic gains prevalence. This is why, post iPhone, touch screens are becoming ubiquitous.) Evolution is the outcome of new ideas presented to the environment by recombining old ideas and waiting for selection to operate.

If the environment is unchanging, the same genes will prove fit again and again. If something suddenly changes, though, the chance of survival is increased if there's a reservoir of alternatives to fall back on.

This is why the U.S. Department of Agriculture, noting that farmers favor only about half a dozen strains of very productive corn, maintains a pool of other corn varieties; it is hedging against the possibility of a new blight, climate change, a new fertilizer or pesticide, or some other shift in the environment. Diversity provides insurance against change, as any financial advisor will tell you. When nature is left to its own devices, sexual recombination preserves a level of diversity in any species' gene pool.

If genetic variation is the most important trait that improves the odds of successful adaptation, then second most important is speed: the more often the available variety of genes is recombined, the faster change can occur. There's a new flu virus every year because influenza can respond to last year's vaccine by changing its shape—so flu survives. Dinosaurs' long gestation periods reduced their ability to survive a sudden climate change.

More depression: sexual recombination is a process that can be precisely described mathematically and is therefore not at all limited to biology. In the 1990s people like Melanie Mitchell (then at the University of Michigan) demonstrated this by taking lines of computer code and "breeding" them to produce new versions that were then tested for fitness for a task—essentially treating binary code as if it were DNA code. DNA is a code with four letters; digital code has only two. But it's not hard to imagine starting with two equally long strings of ones and zeros and creating different ways of taking half the code from each to make a new string. Then that string's fitness to do its intended task can be evaluated and it can have the opportunity, or not, to breed a next generation. The Wikipedia entry on genetic algorithms, as such processes came to be labeled, now lists sixty-two realms, from "artificial creativity" to "wireless sensor/ad-hoc networks" in which they have been applied.[7]

Let's suppose the digital strings a genetic algorithm started with comprised the blueprint of an online ad, for example. And let's agree to define the fitness of an ad as its success at attracting clicks. The Web users who see it are its environment; they do the selecting.[8] The marketer doing the advertising might produce different versions featuring various combinations of images, copy, and promotional offers. Then by sending these different versions to samples of its market, it would discover which versions were most fit. So far, a pretty standard procedure: this is how marketing is done, whether it's testing alternative magazine covers or tweaking product descriptions in catalogs.

But now imagine that, like a horse breeder, that marketer took the highest-performing ads and applied a genetic algorithm to produce new lines of code for new ads, recombining the different elements (images, copy, offer) that were part of the mix in the first-round winners. Those new genotypes would yield new phenotypes: different-looking ads that might or might not outperform their parents. Now it's time for a round 3 competition—a trivially easy exercise in an online setting—after which the winners produce another batch of progeny. In no time, the marketer has the Triple Crown winner of ads.

This is not a product of our febrile imaginations. We've just described part of the business of Affinnova, an award-winning Massachusetts company that lists Procter & Gamble, Walmart, Diageo, Microsoft, and many other consumer marketers among its clients. Affinnova's strength is in translating recombination and selection to mathematical formulas applying them to design tasks, and executing these inexpensively on the Web. As the company describes it, "Affinnova's technology mimics the process of evolution, but at a greatly accelerated rate."[9]

Acceleration is the key, given the number of permutations that end up being produced. In one assignment, for example, office-supply company Staples wanted to create packaging for a line of recycled paper products that would appeal to customers. It was flexible on the choice of colors and fonts, and also had certain words it could alter (such as changing *multiuse* to *multipurpose*). Affinnova proceeded to serve up design options, in each round asking 750 consumers to choose among three packaging designs. As winners begat more options, increasingly fit designs emerged. In short order, Affinnova analyzed some twenty-two thousand different designs and declared one most fit.

In an impressive proof-of-concept project, the same approach allowed the company to predict political preferences. Applying its "evolutionary optimization technology" to arrive at a winning strategy for the 2008 U.S. presidential election, it asked thousands of likely voters months before the election to react to different combinations of platform issues and vice presidential candidates. The project revealed that the economy would be the key issue with voters, and the Iraq war would not.

The genetic algorithm approach has been applied to dozens of business problems by numerous companies. In one of the most surprising cases, GE used it to design the engine it was building for the Boeing 777. Engineers were startled by the "creativity" shown. Beyond optimizing the parameters of the engine in its standard seven-stage compressor configuration, the software made a leap to a six-stage design, leading to a material improvement in the weight of the engine.

Our main reason for describing these tools, however, is that they vividly illustrate how better solutions can emerge when complex systems are broken into their defining parts, the parts are recombined and subjected to fitness testing, and the process is iterated many times. If you translate this to the notion of capitalism adapting, the defining parts are its current rules and technologies, in all their rich variety. The combinations are tested every day, in diverse environments. NeuroSky CEO Stanley Yang tells us that the empowering, consensus-seeking approach he must employ in Japan would be regarded as wimpy by his team in China and would lose him his employees' respect. What is considered crony capitalism in Israel is legalized as lobbying in the United States. As the landscape of commerce changes, some of these local variants will prove to be valuable genotypes—differences that confer a fitness advantage. Some elements that formerly seemed secondary, or even hampering, may take on central importance.

We should quickly add, too, that we don't expect any single form of capitalism to prevail globally. The mutations will continue, and variation will persist. We return to this theme in chapter 8 as we address the expectation of convergence we've encountered in some quarters. Yes, it's true in genomes as well as social systems that some really good ideas—say, the way the cells of all vertebrates convert food to chemical energy—can become universal. But it's not a contradiction to say that some ideas will prove fit only in some locales. If you took Anthro 101 you likely learned about the sickle cell, which brings with it improved resistance to malaria and therefore is selected for in geographies where malaria is common. Thus it became a common component of the human genome in Africa's lowlands. In another environment or in another time, it serves no good purpose; quite the opposite, sickle cell anemia is a terrible disease. Hence over time the gene becomes less prevalent in the pool.

By analogy, there can be rules that confer advantages in some business environments and not others. Risk aversion, for example, might be an attribute associated with high performance in the heavy industries of the Industrial Revolution. In a steel or chemical plant, a slipup can kill people.[10] In another industry more dependent on constant innovation and on manipulating only bits, risk-aversion DNA could be hobbling. We can't help noting what seems to be a persistent cultural variation in attitudes toward risk in the U.S. auto industry versus the software industry, and it makes sense: the consequences of "crashes" in the two industries are quite different.

And consider what happens when these risk attitudes collide, as in software for medical devices. New attitudes breed at the intersections. Such recombinations are an example of the yeasty, distributed process by which the overall system changes, one rule at a time.

It's an important and fundamental point that the rules of capitalism are selected, not derived from first principles. Whether intentionally, by the World Trade Organization, the U.S. Congress, or international financial regulators, or unwittingly, by the choices made by customers, investors, and executives, the rules continually change and coevolve. A case of fraud induces enforcement of the Sarbanes-Oxley Act, which in turn, as a matter of self-protection, may drive greater collaboration in the accounting profession. And when capitalism finds itself in a new environment, the choices change, because they are made by people having different criteria, living in different circumstances. What is privacy? How should digital property be protected? What corporate behavior should be regulated, and what constitutes monopoly power? What are the rights of different stakeholders in society? There are many possibilities for the answers, just as there are many layouts for an ad.

Perhaps we prefer to think that we decide these questions by rational political debate or judicial processes. But these are only two of the tests of fitness among the interlocking feedback loops of coevolution. And more often than not, they follow practice rather than lead it.

Feedback and Dynamics

Having reviewed the essential concepts of environment, coevolution, breeding, fitness, and selection, we should now turn our focus to *feedback*. The effect of what happened yesterday on what will happen tomorrow is a powerful force in any ecology, biological or economic. Performance reviews don't only describe what happened in the past; they affect how individuals will behave in the future. Market acceptance is a form of feedback that determines what will get made.

The powerful operation of feedback has not been, in the past, a force recognized in economists' models.[11] The academic scribblings of most of the twentieth century have assumed that systems remain static and have focused on creating the methods for optimizing within them.

We are in a moment now, however, when the underlying ideas of economics are in flux, and the focus has moved to understanding changes in dynamic systems. It's been a gradual encroachment of ideas, to recall Keynes's language, but it has already managed to influence the thinking of practical managers. One fundamental work was Brian Arthur's *Increasing Returns and Path Dependence in the Economy*. Arthur described a particular positive feedback loop and the dynamics of increasing returns in network businesses, and the phenomenon of *lock-in* became self-evident to technology executives, if controversial among economists (a classic case of an idea working fine in practice but not in theory). The idea of first-mover advantage, not an unknown thought in business of the 1980s but rarely relevant (and often subordinated to the fast follower strategy), grew in importance.

No doubt it is true that static analysis wasn't always as inadequate as it is today; the world changes faster now. Inventor Ray Kurzweil maintains that the rate of technological change doubles every decade. But the criticism of it has deeper, older roots than you might imagine. As early as the 1890s, Thorstein Veblen used the term *evolutionary economics*. He introduced it in an 1898 article called "Why Is Economics Not an Evolutionary Science?" that combines the mid-nineteenth-century thinking of Marx with that of Darwin. Its first line: "M. G. de Lapouge recently said, 'Anthropology is destined to revolutionise the political and the social sciences as radically as bacteriology has revolutionised the science of medicine.' Insofar as he speaks of economics, the eminent anthropologist is not alone in his conviction that the science stands in need of rehabilitation."

We leave most of the history of these ideas for a different kind of book—namely, Eric Beinhocker's *Origin of Wealth*, which gives a full account. Briefly, though, as the twentieth century wore on, economics was influenced far less by evolutionary science than by engineering. It became a discipline focused on questions of optimizing prices, processes, and resource allocation in a world assumed to be in stable equilibrium. If you've studied economics—and probably even if you haven't—you've been introduced to a picture of a supply curve and a demand curve meeting at a market-clearing point defined by a price and a quantity. You might have spent the next semester studying what happened when you perturbed this equilibrium—say, by raising or lowering price. Your exam probably asked you to calculate the new equilibrium, given something called the price elasticity of demand.[12]

As Beinhocker writes, "The notion that the economy has a balancing point to which it naturally progresses is a theme that stretches back well before Smith . . . and remains a core concept of Traditional Economics today." Analysis comparing such stable situations, called *comparative statics*, certainly can be useful—to estimate, for example, whether your current price is the profit-maximizing one, assuming that the costs of suppliers, the prices of competitors, and the availability of substitutes stay the same. Michael Porter's Five Forces model deals with this kind of thinking. Many managers, however, embraced that model as a kind of "Comparative Statics for Dummies," enabling strategic thinking without the heavy lifting of equilibrium economics.

In the real world, when a business changes the pricing of its offering, for example, that action creates ripple effects. It puts other changes in motion—for example, in the prices offered by competitors and makers of complementary goods, in customers' expectations, and in the availability of inputs. Those reactions in turn create their own ripples. In real life, the water never returns to a glassy calm—the equivalent of that notional new equilibrium you calculated. Instead, the ripples and reactions continue forever. Sometimes, those changes create such disequilibrium that a market ceases to exist. Comparative statics would treat, say, digital modems as a substitute good for analog modems, but the field offers no help in understanding innovation and change—not to mention the ripple, or tsunami, of the digitization of the economy.

Robert Lucas at Carnegie Mellon deserves much of the credit for introducing another way of thinking. Around 1970, he began explorations in two new directions. First, he proposed that in principle, macroeconomics should be describable by building up a picture of the economy from the set of microeconomic decisions. That is to say, he posited that a picture of the whole should be able to emerge somehow from an understanding of the individual parts. At the time, economic methods afforded no way to incorporate this insight; you might describe individual choices, but there were no tools for aggregating them except to look at averages. Our GDP and other national statistics, developed during the Depression, could do no better. Today, though, cheap computing power has made it practical to simulate individual decisions and the effects of their interaction. You don't have to be a well-funded economist to run such simulations; this is how games such as SimCity work. The Sims are the agents, each Sim has a "personality" made up of a set of rules to live by, and the properties of the population (its overall happiness, for example) are the net results of all their choices and interactions. Such *agent-based modeling* (ABM)—understanding the macro-scale picture that emerges from the interactions of many individual decision makers—has become a foundation of adaptive systems research.[13]

Second, Lucas introduced recursive methods to macroeconomics, meaning that what happens next year is driven in part by what happened last year—in effect, acknowledging that last year's ripples cause this year's decisions. Ecologists use these methods to explain variation over time in the numbers of species in an ecology: last year's rain kept the hunters at home, so fewer grouse were shot; this year there are more grouse. The good hunting draws out hunters, so the year after that, fewer grouse, and the population exhibits a "business cycle" for no endogenous reason. Lucas won the 1995 Nobel Prize in Economics for his work and paved the way for others. Ideas that seemed far out in the early 1990s won Nobel Prizes in 2004 and NIH Pioneer Awards in 2009.

Economists call this way of thinking—assessing how one economic action creates a force that acts on others—*dynamic analysis*, in contrast to comparative statics. And, consistent with Lucas's first insight, it applies not only to a single market. According to Edward Prescott, who won the 2004 Nobel Prize in Economics, "The revolution in macroeconomics was to use dynamic economic reasoning."[14] Prescott carried Lucas's work on agents forward in the late 1970s, developing models of economic cycles incorporating these individual-driven dynamics.

In 1988, a landmark event took place: Kenneth Arrow and Philip Anderson, Nobel laureates in Economics and Physics, respectively, pulled together interested academics—including biologists and computer scientists—at the first of three conferences at the Santa Fe Institute (SFI) called "The Economy as an Evolving Complex System." Reflecting on the relative states of the social sciences and physical sciences, one of the physicists in attendance compared economics to his recent observations of cars in Cuba, shut off from the modern world for forty years. "The mathematical Packards and DeSotos were the . . . techniques that the Marginalists had plundered from physics textbooks a hundred years ago."[15] The impatience for progress seems to be spreading; in 2010, George Soros pledged to spend $50 million over ten years to fund the Institute for New Economic Thinking.

The SFI conferences signaled an understanding that if economies were dynamic systems, there was some new thinking to do. At its core, SFI was devoted to the idea of generalizing from biological evolution to all systems that adapt. In this framework, any system made up of groups of interacting agents—decision makers, who might be birds in a flock, traders in a market, or individuals in a bar—behaves according to a set of rules, and these rules, properly applied, govern the evolution of all systems that adapt. What calculus did for physical sciences— allow lots of confusing data about falling cannon balls, magnetic fields, or chemical reactions to make sense by applying the same powerful toolkit to all of them—complexity scientists are trying to do for the social sciences. And because the biosphere is the adaptive system that has been studied most, some of this thinking involves observing how biological evolution works, abstracting those observations into mathematics, and then seeing whether the rules apply to other systems.[16]

It's not hard to see the parallel: the market is an environment in which certain goods and services thrive and, having been selected, shape a new generation of an industry's participants. And coevolution—the adjustments going on between the shape of finches' beaks and the forms of the flowers they feed on—is a fact of economic life: when Intel makes faster chips, Microsoft's code expands to fill them. Social scientists are at work modeling growth, innovation, economic coevolution, mergers and extinctions, and other economic phenomena to prove the parallels at deeper levels. A new economics that conforms to the facts of life—faster adaptation, variation of practices in contact with one another in a global economy—is on the way. But business needn't wait for the previous generation of economists to be defunct to take advantage of this perspective.

The Peacock's Tale

One special case in biology turns out to be unfortunately common in economics: the *runaway* effect. As the term implies, this is what happens when a feedback loop gets established that reinforces a trait beyond all reason. Like a runaway horse, it's hard to rein in.

The best way to describe this effect is with reference to the classic example: the peacock's tail. How has it come to be so extravagant? Well, because peahens are partial to males with long tails. This means that if you're a peacock, size matters: more tail, more offspring.

If you live, that is. The challenge is that growing and hauling about that large ornament is as expensive as owning a Ferrari; it costs the peacock energy, meaning it needs more food. Worse, unlike a man with a Quattroporte, the peacock is slowed down by that attractive appendage, making it more difficult to elude predators. In nearly every species of bird and beast, females select males based on visible attributes, but in the vast majority of cases, those attributes are legitimate signifiers of survival strength. In the case of the peacock, sexual selection fails to align with fitness selection. So the peacock lives a shorter, if perhaps happier, life, but the net is that there are fewer peacocks in the ecology. You can see why experts on evolution also like to call this phenomenon *biological suicide*.

Nature has had billions of years to sort out this problem, so it's rare in ecologies. Human society is newer to the game, so the potential for runaway effects is higher. Indeed, R. A. Fisher, the British scientist who first described the phenomenon in the 1920s, was quite aware of its applicability to social matters. According to Mary Bartley, a student of his work, Fisher "often contrasted sexual selection with its well-known counterpart, natural selection, and used both of these brands of 'selection' to discuss fundamental problems impeding the progress of British society." He was fond of extrapolating to worst-case scenarios; using the analogy he would warn that, if certain problems were not corrected, their runaway nature could lead to the nation's demise.

Picture the financial trader in the role of peacock, incented by short-term profits to undertake behavior that increases systemic risk for the financial species. Or the manager selected for the extravagance of his return on equity rather than for the ability to generate value on many dimensions. Or the CEO told incessantly by Wall Street analysts that quarterly profits are the essence of running a company. Runaway effects happen when a single criterion governs resource allocation—the economic equivalent of sexual selection—without balancing other criteria that determine the overall value of the choice to society.

Readers who have spent careers in management might think of this as a special class of *unintended consequences*—those logical but somehow unforeseen effects that often take place following bold managerial interventions. A common example is a new incentive system that aims to motivate some narrow behavior and does so at the expense of the overall health of the system. Steve Kerr, a longtime colleague of Jack Welch (Kerr led the creation of GE's management training facility in Crotonville, New York, and now serves as a dean of the online MBA program Jack Welch University), wrote about such cases in a classic management article, "On the Folly of Rewarding A While Hoping for B."

Unintended consequences happen all the time in human rule making. Our favorite recent example is the legislation in Indonesia designed to reduce its awe-inspiring traffic jams. Perceiving that carpooling would make a difference, the government created new traffic lanes that could be used only by vehicles carrying more than one occupant (such lanes are common in many urban settings). But in a land filled with poor people with time on their hands, the main effect was to create a new industry: passengers for hire. A sort of inverse to taxi stands started to show up: lines of people at entrances to highways willing to hop in any car that would hire them as its ticket to the high-occupancy vehicle lane. The net effect was not only an unintended consequence but also an outright negation of the original goal to improve traffic flow.

Often, organizations or societies rely on cultural norms to rein in a runaway incentive. But a strong enough selection for the incented behavior can actually change the norms. (Recall Frank Lorenzo and the Florida home flippers.) Without law enforcement, regulation, morality, or some other form of social code to represent the nonfinancial interests of society, the combination of runaway selection and moral hazard can lead to something like "social suicide." This is a line of thought we return to in chapters to come—and a crucial thought in understanding the forces that drive the selection of rules in the capitalist system.

The Rain Forest of Capitalism

We began this chapter by putting forth a theory of change by which capitalism would evolve as a complex adaptive system. Now we offer a corollary to that theory: that this process of adaptation will happen more readily in the rapidly growing emerging economies, and the emerging shape of a fitter form of capitalism may first be spotted there.

Remember Paul Romer's theory of history based on technologies and rules. When he talks about it, he makes an important point that we haven't yet mentioned: that it is very hard to change rules once they have taken hold. Brian Arthur, having thought so thoroughly about lock-in, would agree: because networks depend on standards to make efficient connections, the standards they begin with end up being nearly impossible to walk away from once the network is functioning. Others would describe the difficulty of changing rules in terms of stickiness or inertia.

For all these reasons, rules have a self-perpetuating quality. Once everyone is driving on the left side of the road, good luck to you if you're trying to get them to drive on the right—even if the rest of the world is doing it. Even when the decision is not so arbitrary and there is a strong argument for a new approach, change is not embraced. Just ask an American about the metric system.

Romer's notion of how to get past that rule of stickiness in a society is to give people a good look at how well a different system can function, and even to let many of them put a toe in the water. Romer proposes doing this with *charter cities*—cities created from blank slates to operate according to different principles than their underperforming neighbors. The reference is to the charter schools set up in U.S. cities to test alternatives to public school methods. Romer is getting some traction for the idea; it was packaged as a very popular TED talk, and *Harvard Business Review* called it one of the "breakthrough ideas" of 2009. Romer is persuasive in arguing that there are in fact still large enough greenfields left in the world on which to plonk down new cities.

And to a degree, it's happening: Mazdar City, in the United Arab Emirates, and the city being built around Prince Abdullah University in Saudi Arabia are both being built as Petri dishes in which to culture new rules—sustainability in the former case, and gender equality in the latter. But while they may get their rules right, it will be a long, long time before they have enough economic mass to promulgate them. They may also simply lack enough diversity of rule ideas to create a vibrant ecology.

We're looking instead to emerging economies to be the disruptive influence. They are richly, chaotically packed with activity. And because, as noted in chapter 1, their growth collectively equals in size, and far exceeds in speed, the growth of the rest of the world, emerging economies are attracting every capitalist idea on the planet. Thus they have the diversity and speed of breeding to try everything. And their digital native populations and the falling costs of connectivity reinforce both of these strengths. They will be to the information economy what the United States was to the industrial—the source and integrator of the new rules.

But their influence may be even greater, for three reasons. First, in a connected world (OK, fine, "flat" if you must), ideas encounter other ideas much faster than ever before, breeding more novelty. Second, of course, the new ideas spread around the globe in no time. There are private equity funds in China that invest only in copies of new U.S.-based Internet businesses for the Chinese market and do so with no perceptible lag.

Third, connected systems are different. The parallel between these two observations about politics and evolution, written almost a century apart, is striking:

> World history, with its great transformation, does not come upon us with the even speed of a railway train. No, it moves in spurts but then with irresistible force.
>
> —Otto von Bismarck

> Instead of a slow, continuous movement, evolution tends to be characterized by long periods of virtual standstill "punctuated" by episodes of very fast development of new forms.
>
> —F. Heylighen, *Principia Cybernetica*, 1999, referring to Gould and Eldredge's Theory of Punctuated Equilibrium

Innovation doesn't proceed in a linear fashion or even, as Ray Kurtzweil's analyses suggest, log-linear, accelerating constantly but predictably. We're headed into a period of *punctuated equilibrium*, or period of intense evolutionary activity. One such period was the Cambrian Explosion five hundred million years ago. Scientists believe new species appeared and disappeared across an eighty-million-year period at a rate ten times greater than usual.

Why should this be? There is controversy about both the theory and its explanations, but one that is intriguing as an analogy with the current world is that during periods of equilibrium, genetic diversity builds up but little of that diversity is expressed, because dominant species occupy all niches in the ecosystem. Only when something dramatic happens to unseat those strong occupants—such as an asteroid that changes a world seemingly made for the dinosaurs—does room open up for the expression of all those suppressed "ideas."[17]

What would this logic say about the present moment in economic history? We believe that the leap in connectivity among the world's cultures and economies presents precisely a radical increase in the rate at which business ideas encounter other business ideas, creating the opportunity for innovation; and simultaneously an enormous increase in the number of niches in which their fitness will be evaluated. Whatever happens will send ripples to the next round of recombination.

It is inevitable that we will see a rate of economic coevolution comparable only to the effect of the technologies of the early nineteenth century—which spawned a set of revolutions around 1848—but much, much faster, because software spreads much faster than machine tools.

The technologies of globalization are like an instantaneous land bridge between continents, allowing the exchange and recombination of ideas at an unprecedented pace. No one society, Western or Eastern, will be dominant. We will all be struggling to keep up with a rate and a strangeness of innovation never experienced before.

Requisite Variety

Around the world, there are different species of capitalism and capitalists, displaying myriad mutations of rules, beginning to interact more intensely with new environments and each other. In Israel, the venture capital industry was started by the state and then devolved to private ownership, as an element of economic policy. In India, the partnership of public and private, for-profit and nonprofit, is a major source of growth. In Brazil, private companies are taking responsibility for improving education and for providing the human capital needed for growth. In the United Arab Emirates, the government is pursuing a hybrid of Singapore's strong and enlightened approach to government, with the use of oil wealth to import the expertise needed to train the next generation. In China, energy policy is being used simultaneously to ensure an infrastructure for growth, to prevent further environmental catastrophe, and to develop a new world-class industry. And in the United States, the digital natives are exploring open source models of collaborative production and the gift economy, while venture philanthropists are propounding theories of patient capital.

In every locale, capitalism exists as a set of rules selected by its practitioners to serve their various interests. As they are confronted by changes in their opportunities and constraints—and by each other's examples—they will begin to choose new rules. This doesn't constitute advice on our part but merely a factual observation: when an adaptive system finds itself in a new environment, it evolves. The new rules need not be chosen consciously, any more than an evolving species chooses its form. Feedback reinforces some rules positively, and others negatively.

We don't anticipate everything's changing; many rules of today's version of capitalism will remain in its genome, reasserting the logic that made them instrumental to its fitness in past eras. But some evidence is emerging that suggests that other rules are changing. These changing rules equip capitalism to perform in a new world of digital abundance, broad value expectations, and constant innovation—and may even spring us from some barreling runaway effects. That's what the next part of the book is about.

Runaways and Renaissance

PART II

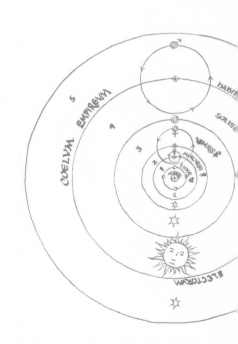

The medieval model of the solar system put Earth in the center and then found the data didn't agree with its predictions. To accommodate, astronomers made the model more and more complex, until Copernicus saw that moving the sun to the center created a model that was both simpler and more accurately predictive.

Capitalism has similarly put some things at its center, the relentless pursuit of which has led it off course. Part II identifies two ways in which this model misses the mark and explains why aiming more squarely at the proper goals is more possible now.

First, in chapter 3, we look at the possibility of bringing the same discipline and accountability to the pursuit of nonfinancial value that already characterizes the pursuit of shareholder value. Chapter 4 exposes the danger of instead focusing narrowly on profit maximization: the imposition of externalities on society. We conclude that with greater measurement of an organization's impact on its environs, the proper internalization of such costs will naturally occur.

Next, we look at the runaway obsession with competition, thought by some to be the one aspect of capitalism that defines it most. In chapter 5 we expose the dangers of mistaking competition for the central concern. The thing to be encouraged and protected, instead, is innovation. It's not a 180-degree difference, but it's a substantial enough change in perspective that suddenly it becomes clear how new forms of collaboration—the subject of chapter 6—can be just as important to the system.

We conclude this part with a reconciliation. Both runaways are checked when we rethink the bright-line separation that U.S.-style capitalism draws between the major sectors of the economy. Chapter 7 shows how limiting it is to believe that the private sector, the public sector, and the NGO sector must each stick to its respective knitting and describes how the new pursuit by businesses of value defined broadly makes it inevitable that they will weave together.

CHAPTER THREE

Capitalism in Color

What doesn't get measured . . . needs to be

If we know money doesn't buy happiness, why are we optimizing for money?

—Adam D. I. Kramer, creator of the Facebook Gross National Happiness index

On May 25, 2010, one Lilybeth Cope chose to update her Facebook status with the following pronouncement:

> Lilybeth Cope is going to enjoy this life NO MATTER WHAT! ordinary days are the best, they go fast and they never repeat themselves . . . so find the silver lining and keep up.

In posting to her friends on Facebook, Lilybeth was, of course, doing what millions of people do every day—letting her network know how she was feeling. Apparently she was having a perfectly ordinary day, and she was OK with that.

She wasn't alone. Facebook's index of Gross National Happiness shows that May 25 virtually *defined* an ordinary day. The index is Facebook's barometer of the mood of its subscribers. Each day, a software program created by the company's data scientists scans every status update typed in by users, looking for certain words that generally denote positive or negative sentiments. Then it does a quick calculation, essentially subtracting the negatives from the positives, to produce that day's happiness score. May 25 came in near the baseline

> **To discuss these ideas on Twitter, use these hashtags:**
>
> #happiness   #triplebl   #ROE

zero, nowhere near the 16 score on Mother's Day—much less the soaring 28 on Christmas Day—but also a far cry from the low point of the past twelve months, when it dipped below –2 (on June 25, 2009, when Michael Jackson died).[1]

Given that Facebook (at the time of this writing) claims more than 500 million active users, each with an average of 130 friends, the happiness index might not be a mere gimmick for Facebook junkies; it might be a credible reading of society's pulse. The company claims that people spend 700 billion minutes per month on their accounts. Within the United States, Facebook's 120 million users constitute more than one-third of the population. With that level of statistical sampling, one could sense zeitgeist and not just site geist. Knowing that, Facebook has proclaimed the index a measure of gross national happiness.

We could quibble with the methodology behind Facebook's index; probably some of the words produce too many false positives, and probably those spikes on holidays are in part due to pro forma greetings rather than deeply felt sentiment. For that matter, words plucked from context might not constitute reliable data. On the same day that Lilybeth Cope was finding her silver lining, another Facebook user offered this status update:

> went to doctor. He removed bandages and brace (yea) and said I could begin bending my arm some and to come back next week. The best news is that all test came back negative and it was as he thought. A plain ole ordinary every day fatty tumor.

Picture a software package seizing on the words *negative* and *ordinary* (let alone *tumor*) and treating this update as one more for the dreary-mood pile. Now think of the giddiness the man must really have felt. In measurement, methods matter. And a part of the answer to Adam Kramer's question at the beginning of this chapter is that measuring what does buy happiness is damnably difficult.

For now, though, let's look past the methodological queries. The bigger question is this: is it even important to try to measure happiness at an aggregate level, whether for an economy, a city, or a firm? If, in some hard-to-quantify aspect of well-being, we're better off now than we were a year ago, would it be useful to know that? Would it guide our decisions and policy making? Should it?

That's the question we explore in this chapter, as the first major challenge to the orthodoxy of capitalism. We explore new forms of measurement, all of them nonfinancial but none of them nonserious. We suggest what it means for business when there's a change in the spectrum of measurement and the form of returns being sought.

Capitalism, we believe, has succumbed to a runaway effect along the lines of the peacock's tail, because capitalists have been bred to focus on one proxy for value—financial returns to shareholders—rather than on value itself, in all its rich variety. By homing in on that single mark of achievement and pursuing it with little regard for other aims, capitalism compromises its power and surely makes itself vulnerable to its attackers.

Remember the scene in *The Wizard of Oz* where Dorothy is spun out of her grayscale Kansas farm and wakes up to Technicolor? It isn't that the colors in the first ten minutes of the movie weren't there to be filmed; it's that they weren't captured by the equipment. In the same way, today's capitalism takes a reductive view of value. The equipment we use to measure it decolorizes commercial life to the extent that it is presented in varying intensities of one drab shade.

Our suggestion is that no one who has the capability to look at something in all its rich dimensions should be satisfied with seeing it in only one.

Measuring What Matters

Is it really tenable for a corporation, an entity beholden to shareholders, to set its sights on goals beyond financial returns to its owners? That's what we tested for at Natura Cosméticos, a Brazilian company selling high-end cosmetics and skin care products. Natura went public in 2004, so it does focus on enriching its shareholders, but it doesn't seem to do so obsessively. What Natura is dedicated to instead is achievement on a *triple bottom line* (TBL), meaning net positive results not only in financial terms but also in social and environmental terms.

Natura comes across as a conscientious company. For instance, the body care products that make up its Ekos line are made from exotic nuts, fruits, and roots harvested responsibly in the Amazon rain forest, in other Brazilian forests, and on small, traditional plantations. But is its commitment to sustainability, we wondered, more than skin deep?

We spoke first with Marcos Vaz, who at the time was Natura's sustainability director. He described for us how Natura prepares external reporting documents to reflect its progress on social and environmental fronts, and how those nonfinancial goals translate to internal management discipline. In classic cascading fashion, objectives are set at the level of overall firm achievement and then translated into unit-level and individual objectives. For example, each year Natura sets a target for how much it will reduce its overall corporate carbon footprint, which it is able to gauge at an aggregate level. "Then we identify exactly what is the contribution of each process to the overall process emissions," Vaz said. "And then each process has its own target of reduction." This requires the company to perform a much more detailed audit of its processes but allows the goal to inform the daily decision making of individual managers. A manager in the firm's procurement function, for example, knows that once the carbon target has been set, it is his job to figure out how materials will be transported from suppliers to Natura's factories in some better way to meet that goal. Throughout the firm and at all levels, managers have their own targets and must make their own plans to achieve them. And if the favored supply chain choice is more costly but more effective, it may prevail; the three TBL components have equal status.

"Every month in the Executive Committee," Vaz told us, "we evaluate the results." And that evaluation has real repercussions for employees. Natura's compensation scheme makes heavy use of pay-for-performance incentives, and any manager who makes the numbers financially but falls short of established social or environmental targets feels the shortfall in her own wallet.

We should quickly note that the concept of a triple bottom line did not begin at Natura. It was first articulated by sustainability guru John Elkington in 1994, who favored the phrase "people, planet, and profits" to describe its three-part focus. Think of these as the three primary colors. His vision was that the same level of nuance and rigor that characterized firms' accounting for revenues, expenses, and profits should be brought to the measurement and reporting of other important goals. Since then, the idea has gained many adherents. (For a sense of this, spend some time browsing TriplePundit.com, a rich source of case examples.) It has also gained structure through, for example, the Global Reporting Initiative—a network creating a shared framework of principles and performance indicators for organizations to use in measuring and reporting economic, environmental, and social performance.

But for all that, our impression is that it is still greeted with some bemusement in the United States. We said as much to Natura's founder Antonio Luiz da Cunha Seabra, and complimented his achievement in overcoming skepticism among his peers and partners in Brazil. "To tell you the truth, it continues," he admitted. But he also noted a change in the push back: "It used to be more tough, it used to be more firm. As we are growing the company, we have our values and propositions and beliefs more and more accepted by the market."

We were particularly interested to talk to Luiz Seabra because he was trained as an economist and began his career as one. What's more, he began his career with an American firm, working in the Brazil office of Sperry Rand's Remington Electric Shavers division. When he founded Natura in 1969, he was certainly equipped to succeed in the existing model. Yet he chose a different path.

Why Settle for a Proxy Measure?

It may be that all senior managers know that their enterprises do and should create value of many kinds. That is hardly a controversial thought. The problem is that many of those forms of value (such as contributions to a community's vibrancy or individual employees' sense of pride) are very difficult to measure, as are many of the ways companies destroy value (such as pollution, negative impacts on workers' health, waste of customers' time). When some phenomena are measured and others are not, attention goes to the ones that are quantified.

But the science of measurement is an area in which the world can claim astounding progress in the past half-century. Much of this progress has been a story of growing granularity, whereby blunt measures have taken on more nuance. As a simple example, before the mid-1950s, a newborn baby was weighed and measured before being handed to its mother; now, the minute a baby is born it is assessed for its activity, pulse, grimace, appearance, and respiration, all combined into an APGAR score—and then five minutes later, assessed on all those points again. Likewise the day's weather, once a simple question of how cold it would be and how wet; tune in to today's forecasts, and answers make note of wind chill factor, barometric pressure, pollen counts, and smog levels—all of which are reported with reference to past averages and record highs and lows. Step on a doctor's scale these days and you're told not only your mortifying weight but also your mortifying body mass index.

And gauges like these of physical phenomena are only half the story at best. Just as dramatic has been the rise of social measurement, mostly a post–World War II phenomenon. Although public information gathering has been done in the United States since the 1790 national census was taken, it was the advent of marketing that pushed forward the science of surveying. Now, not a day goes by without new data being released on some group's preferences, prejudices, or habits. We hear that 64 percent of Brits prefer CDs to digital music; that 80 percent of Americans don't trust the government; that 86 percent of Croatian dog owners think that the oral hygiene of dogs is important. In the political sphere, the practice of polling the people began with democratic elections, but it now extends to an onslaught of issue tracking, phone surveys, exit polls, and approval ratings. When the same measures are taken at regular intervals of time, indices are created that track change over time. Since 1964, for example, the University of Michigan has compiled its

Consumer Sentiment index based on five hundred fresh interviews every month.

The explosion of measurements and rapid advance in measurement science serves society in two major ways. First, the ability to track more phenomena over time allows new correlations to be found among them, and provides a greater understanding of how they inter-relate. This gives us more insight into the key drivers of outcomes we care about. Second, many phenomena that used to be tracked by proxy (if at all) can now be measured directly. And when a more direct and reliable way of measuring becomes available, it means that old, inadequate proxies can be abandoned—no matter how attached we have become to them.

On that point, we should raise a special toast: as we write in 2011, it's the hundredth anniversary of the advent of perhaps the most famous proxy measure of all. It was in 1911 that canaries were first brought down into coal mines by British coal miners. The birds got the job thanks to their particular sensitivity to carbon monoxide and methane—and also thanks to their love of singing. Miners who noticed the singing had stopped would look to the bird. If it was ailing, that was a telltale clue that the air was filling with deadly but colorless and odorless gases and it was time to evacuate.

In 1987, however, the canaries, like so many coal miners before them, were made redundant. Miners were issued handheld electronic detectors instead, whose screens could tell them not only that gases were present but also their precise level of concentration in the air.

Everyone agreed that the new, more direct method of measurement was better. No matter how reassuring a live bird might be as a proxy, it could not be more reliable than direct atmospheric testing. But the BBC reported at the time that miners were saddened by the end of a practice "so ingrained in the culture miners report whistling to the birds and coaxing them as they worked, treating them as pets."

When it comes to monitoring well-being above ground, it may also be that people have become overly devoted to a canary—or more like a canard. It is common to fixate on financial income and the personal net worth it adds up to. Certainly these two metrics have the advantage of being very measurable, but income and financial worth aren't the point. Well-being is the real objective, and a financial metric is only a proxy for it. Moreover, it turns out not to be a very good one.

It's true that up to a point, financial well-being does correlate with happiness. It's hard to feel fine when you can't afford decent food, basic health care for yourself or your children, and a safe place to live. Once those basics are provided for, however, rising income stops correlating with rising happiness. This is the phenomenon Ruut Veenhoven described in his "livability theory." In fact, high-powered jobs that offer high salaries often take their toll. The researchers behind one study concluded that "people with above-average income . . . are barely happier than others in moment-to-moment experience, tend to be more tense, and do not spend more time in particularly enjoyable activities." Let us refer you to Carol Graham's book *Happiness Around the World* for an excellent survey of the evidence against the notion that income is a reliable indicator of subjective well-being.

So why don't people move on to better measures? Part of the problem is that they persist in believing that the proxy is better than it is, and that money can buy happiness. Studies show that, when asked about their own happiness and the happiness of others, people consistently overstate the impact of the varying incomes cited in the survey questions. In the case of personal income, Nobel laureate economist Daniel Kahneman and colleagues write, "Despite the weak relationship between income and global life satisfaction or experienced happiness, many people are highly motivated to increase their income." They attribute this to a *focusing illusion*—a tendency to assign too much importance to one factor because it has been made visible and top of mind. In other words, people default to thinking about their success in monetary terms because money is easily counted and wealth levels readily compared. "In some cases," they write, "this focusing illusion may lead to a misallocation of time, from accepting lengthy commutes (which are among the worst moments of the day) to sacrificing time spent socializing (which are among the best moments of the day)." They're unable to appreciate all the color in a life well lived, because they're viewing it through a black and white TV.

Certainly, it isn't easy to come up with alternative methods of measuring overall well-being, either for individuals or for society as a whole. Kahneman has been working on it for years. But the relative ease of calculating financial wealth shouldn't be an excuse for ignoring what really matters. We've all laughed at the old joke about the drunk looking for his keys under a lamppost even though he dropped them across the street. "I'm looking on this side," he explains to his friend, "because the light is better here." When we look for the keys to success, we routinely gravitate to the economic lampposts.

GDP as a Runaway Effect

The points we've been making are simple ones. First, the science of measurement has advanced enormously. This will continue, as mobile devices and the Internet of things relentlessly lower the cost and increase the coverage of observing and recording. And, second, as direct measurements of the phenomena we are interested in become more possible, it should become less acceptable to rely on proxy measurements, which are never quite adequate, rarely have explanatory power, and sometimes are misleading snares and delusions. This brings us to the topic of GDP.

Gross domestic product is a single number arrived at by measuring a nation's private consumption, government spending, gross investments, exports, and imports. Compiled in the United States by the Bureau of Economic Analysis, GDP is derived from what are known as the National Income and Product Accounts (NIPA), and they provide an objective view of the size of the economy and its growth or contraction over time. The historical data go back to 1929.

It may surprise you to learn that all the talk and obsessive comparison of GDP began only within the past century. Until the post-Depression years of the Franklin D. Roosevelt administration, there was no such system. Before the 1930s, the federal statistical program consisted of not much more than the Census Bureau. Herbert Hoover had earlier championed business statistics programs in the 1920s, as secretary of commerce and later as president, but it was only in the grip of the Great Depression that the need was widely felt. Congress and the public, not surprisingly, wanted insight into the causes and character of the economic disaster they were experiencing. Thus it was that New Deal statisticians devised the statistical series that is now familiar to Americans. GDP quickly became the measure by which to analyze the economic impact of changes in local and national policy. And the NIPA approach has radiated widely across the world's advanced economies.

We don't mean to imply that GDP is an "easy" measure to take. Compiling all the information required for an overall assessment of a nation's productive output is not a straightforward challenge. That's why, even today, it's hard to get good economic statistics for many countries of the world.

The dullest course Chris ever took—no contest—was a required course in the Penn PhD program called Economic Measurement. A semester was spent delving into, for example, the different ways to construct price indices. (Check Wikipedia if you're dying to learn why the Paasche formulation overstates, and the Laspeyres version under-states, inflation.) From this Chris took a few things. First, he gained a healthy respect for how much effort has gone into creating the feed-back loops the United States, more than any country so far, has created to measure and manage economic performance. Second, he learned that every economic report should be viewed with skepticism. There's an old expression that "liars figure." Economists, it turns out, figure more. Third, he recognized that further elaboration of the NIPA-based measurement apparatus would be more and more about less and less.

As sophisticated as GDP measurement has become, it misses the mark. As a proxy for social well-being it falls woefully short, because many pleasures and obviously beneficial activities don't enter into its equations. The parents of every preschooler in the nation could read bedtime stories nightly for a year and it wouldn't budge GDP. Indeed, none of the work done by stay-at-home moms and dads to raise those children is counted. Meanwhile, the fact that it does include expendi-tures on things like prisons and toxic chemical cleanups makes for a perverse logic: if a higher GDP indicates a better-off society, then crime and chemical dumping would appear to be boons. (The San Francisco–based organization Redefining Progress listed more such hollow ben-efits in a 1995 report, including divorces and natural disasters.) At the beginning of this chapter we mentioned the Facebook user who'd just discovered he did not have cancer—only a "plain ole ordinary tumor." How much better it would have been, from a GDP perspective, to get the bad news. By necessitating more expensive treatments, malignant tumor growth promotes marvelous economic growth.

Another anomaly of GDP as measured is that, because the output of the government sector is not priced—because, for example, defense against foreign enemies (the military, the intelligence services) and foreign substances (the Food and Drug Administration) are not traded in markets—the value to the society of government outputs is assumed to move with the cost of inputs. (This is a point stressed by France's commission on measurement, of which more later.) This undermeasurement of the value of the services performed by government has led, in the United States, to a conversation that must focus on costs (taxes) without an understanding of associated benefits, making it difficult to assess the economics of government and leaving the field open to virulent politicization.

Still another problem: some forms of progress that any of us would say add value to our lives don't show up that way in the National Income and Product Accounts. Remember the first time you realized you could buy a book online long past your local bookstore's closing hour and without changing out of your pajamas? And remember your additional delight when you found the online price even lower than in stores? In terms of contribution to GDP, a purchase delayed, made with effort, and transacted at full price would have come out more positive. It's a small example, but a major trend. We're living in a period when, thanks to the plummeting costs of information technology, many benefits are delivered at no additional charge. This unmeasured deflationary pressure is what led economist Robert Solow to quip, "You can see the computer age everywhere but in the productivity statistics." The book you bought online doesn't actually get less valuable; it gets more so, but in ways that are extremely hard to measure. Take that time savings you experienced by avoiding a trip to a store; your time is taken by NIPA to be a free good, so the trip avoidance doesn't increase GDP. In fact, the reduced consumption of fuel reduces it.

Such deflation has occurred before: in the Industrial Revolution. But the signs were easier to measure. The familiar facts are that (using 2010 prices) the Model T Ford, the iconic harbinger of mass production, was introduced in 1909 at about $20,500 at a time when most cars cost $50,000 and more; by 1915 the price had dropped to $9,400, and sales grew from 70,000 in 1911 to 501,000 in 1915. In 1914, an assembly line worker could buy a Model T with four months' pay. By the 1920s, the price had fallen to $3,300, just over a month's. Professor Solow would have had no trouble measuring the impact of assembly lines.

What happens in an economy already on the leading edge of productivity when innovation proceeds so rapidly? Conflict arises between those entities vested in the $50,000 car business and those delighted with the new affordability of useful goods. But in economies where no one can afford an expensive car, there's no resistance. Hence, as we've noted, the United States was able to fully embrace industrialization while Britain was struggling with the displacement of its prior production system. (The easy part was getting rid of imports. When in the 1770s two Brits invented the spinning mule, the resulting high-quality cloth was inexpensive enough to displace imports from India.)

So of course computers were slow to show up in the productivity statistics. They have been getting cheaper so fast that the explosive growth of the computer industry isn't enough to offset the implosion of pricing—and of productivity in other industries. Output as measured by NIPA reflects change through what are called *quality adjustments*; these figures add something to the value of the automobile because, say, the air conditioning is now thermostatically controlled, but they hide the underlying shift in value.

So GDP is rife with issues, as anyone with insight into its figuring would freely admit. That wouldn't be such a matter of concern if it had remained a statement of only the suggestive but incomplete measurement it was. It didn't. GDP pulled off the focusing illusion trick of the century and came to stand for something much greater—nothing less than the health of a nation.

It could be that was closer to the truth at the time the National Income and Product Accounts were established. The United States developed measurements centered on GDP at a moment, the Depression, when goosing economic output was central to improving overall well-being. Understanding what was happening to employment and growth was indeed an urgent and overriding need. But for citizens living under other conditions—for example, in a country whose annual growth is in the range of 15 percent—additional factors are at least equally relevant.

Once a measure has become well established, people tend to forget that it is a reductionist proxy for something more important, and they fixate on the performance of the proxy itself. A preferred measure then becomes self-reinforcing. Most managers have heard Peter Drucker's famous maxim that "what gets measured gets managed" and know it's true. In adaptive systems terms, Drucker was saying that where there's a feedback loop, there's evolution. One corollary of this is that if you change measurements, the system will take a new tack as the new feedback mechanism begins to operate. Another is that, if you want to aim a system in a new direction, a good start is to change what is being measured.

In the introduction to their book *The Politics of Numbers*, historians William Alonso and Paul Starr observe that official statistics affect society in subtle and not so subtle ways. "By the questions asked (and not asked), categories employed, statistical methods used, and tabulations published, the statistical systems change images, perceptions, aspirations," they write. The numbers reported by government "shape society as they measure it." For good reasons at the time, we shaped a measurement of societal wellness, the gross domestic product. But now we find ourselves guided—or driven—by the pursuit of it. Increasingly that means missing the real mark. If we were to aim more directly at value, how might that look?

Welcome to Bhutan

In 1972, the then king of Bhutan, Jigme Singye Wangchuck, made a startling announcement. Rather than measure the total economic output of Bhutan, he wanted to get a handle on its overall well-being. "Gross national happiness is more important than gross national product," he proclaimed to his subjects, and therefore "happiness takes precedence over economic prosperity in our national development process." By the time the king's son took the throne, in November 2008, the Royal Government of Bhutan had devised a formal GNH index.

In the spring of 2010, we had the opportunity to talk to a Bhutanese citizen, Sonam Laki Dorji, and hear her take on this. The first thing we found striking was that, although Dorji is not connected to the Centre for Bhutan Studies, the nonprofit research institution behind the index, she was thoroughly familiar with its work. She explained that most people in the country are quite informed about GNH and understand the rationale behind it. It's in the country's constitution.

"They struggled for a while, because GNH is a soft idea," Dorji told us. "It's very subjective. To come up with something generalized and applicable to the population as a whole was a big challenge." So why, we asked, should anyone try to pin it down with any precision? "It wasn't until recently that they tried to make it a concrete measurable index," she answered. "The reason was . . . to make the government accountable, and to make sure that these ideas were implemented." She offered an example of a specific development project's being undertaken, and how its leaders had to ensure in their planning and implementation that the ideals of gross national happiness were "taken into account in a way that's measurable."

The construction of Bhutan's index began with the identification of some core beliefs about the foundations of a happy society. Four pillars of gross national happiness were first articulated: good governance, sustainable development, cultural values, and conservation of the environment. Subsequently, the framework evolved to nine dimensions, all accorded equal importance. Here they are, along with a few notes we took on how each could be measured:

1. **Psychological well-being:** The thought of quantifying a nation's spiritual, emotional, or general psychological health might seem unlikely. But it is possible to count, for example, the number of people suffering from psychological problems. Likewise, spiritual well-being might be measured in part by how many people report that they meditate.

2. **Free time:** Potentially very simple to measure, this could be calculated as the amount of their time people spend doing things they are not paid for, whether those things benefit society (such as volunteering) or only themselves (such as sleeping). This rationale makes an assumption, not universally true, that a person's job itself is not a source of satisfaction and that something like "work–life balance" is required for well-being.

3. **Community vitality:** Here, the measures are envisioned to gauge levels of socializing within communities and levels of mutual trust.

4. **Preservation of culture:** Bhutan's government stresses this because it believes culture gives people a satisfying sense of identity. Measurements in this realm include participation rates in "living culture" as well as citizens' knowledge of the country's history.

5. **Health:** Key statistics to monitor in this realm include mortality rates and incidence of certain diseases, but also the awareness levels of, for example, HIV risks, and people's ability to take care of themselves. Access to health care is another measurable sign of the nation's health, especially in a country where, historically, many people have had to walk long distances to get to health facilities.

6. **Education:** Attainment statistics are the obvious metrics here, but Bhutan also wants to see growth in educational aspirations.

7. **Environmental diversity:** A specific policy is that Bhutan must have 70 percent of its land covered by forest, regardless of the opportunity to sell lumber.

8. **Living standard:** Here again, measurement focuses not only on attainment of objective standards of living but also on people's perceptions of their standard of living. Do they feel secure that they have enough food? If their house needs repair, are they able to fix it?

9. **Governance:** A happy population is one that is satisfied with its government's performance on various dimensions. Some of this can be measured objectively, but just as important are subjective assessments: do most people perceive their government as honest and effective? Is there high trust in its institutions?

The specific measures within each of these categories were developed in consultation with many people across the country, and the goal is to combine objectively measurable phenomena with opinion statistics on each dimension. Thus, community vitality, for example, includes five dimensions: giving and volunteering, social cohesion, safety, family, and duration of stay in the community. You could say that Bhutan has gone beyond the primary colors to the full set of Crayolas.

Are its metrics the "correct" ones? It's pretty early to be asking. Recall that, fifty years after the development of NIPA, economists were (and for all we know are today) still arguing about Paasche versus Laspeyres. Bhutan forged ahead with them and published initial benchmarks. It's establishing a process by which the measures it has settled on will be taken and the index published at regular intervals.

An Idea Spreads

By attaching measurable indicators to its nine dimensions of happiness, Bhutan is doing something quite deliberate and important: it is creating a set of priorities to guide its economic and developmental plans. For example, convinced of the centrality of health and education to happiness (number 5 and number 6 in its framework), its government reportedly spends nearly 18 percent of its national budget on those areas. Contrast this with, say, China, which spends more like 3 percent. By educating its population about GNH, it is also shaping its society.

Nevertheless, Bhutan's pursuit of gross national happiness was for years greeted with a mixture of bemusement and dismissal, a kind of global eye roll. The effort was regarded as more of a curiosity than a serious innovation.

Then the global financial crisis struck, followed promptly by the Great Recession, and the idea that there might be something problematic about purely economic measurement suddenly seemed less crazy. In September 2009, French president Nicolas Sarkozy addressed the French national statistics agency on the inadequacy of GDP in measuring national wealth. Soon after, he called on other world leaders to stop emphasizing GDP and replace it with a measure that quantifies well-being as well as economic strength. The idea of tracking GNH was on the map.

Sarkozy was not merely responding to the present crisis. In February 2008, when he recruited Joseph Stiglitz and Amartya Sen, both Nobel Prize winners, and Jean-Paul Fitoussi to assemble the Commission on the Measurement of Economic Performance and Social Progress, Sarkozy had three goals in mind: to consider the limitations of GDP; to suggest how to construct better measures of social progress; and to assess the feasibility of using alternative measurements.

Bhutan and the Sarkozy commission seem well aligned. In the worlds of Stiglitz, Sen, and Fitoussi, "Gross domestic product (GDP) is the most widely used measure of economic activity. There are international standards for its calculation, and much thought has gone into its statistical and conceptual bases. But GDP mainly measures market production, though it has often been treated as if it were a measure of economic well-being. Conflating the two can lead to misleading indications about how well-off people are and entail the wrong policy decisions."[2]

The efforts in Bhutan and France are only the beginning of what seems to be a major trend. U.K. prime minister David Cameron in late 2010 instructed Britain's Office of National Statistics to come up with the right measures to gauge well-being and implement them as soon as possible.

Other indices are sponsored by nongovernmental entities having an interest in influencing policy or producing greater knowledge of the global society. The Human Development Index, the Quality of Life Index, and the Genuine Progress Indicator rely on existing national data; the Happy Planet Index and the Legatum Center's Prosperity Index also include survey data.

Legatum's Prosperity Index may outdo the rest in the rigor of its research on quantitative methods for measuring happiness. Ninety variables feed into eight components that predict happiness as measured by surveys—economy, entrepreneurship, governance, education, health, safety and security, personal freedom, and social capital—and you can instantly compare any two countries on the eight. When Legatum's Jiehae Choi presented the index to a group we were part of, one listener objected that Hong Kong (ranked twentieth) could come out so close to France (ranked nineteenth). Choi clarified that it was true not because the countries were very similar (they are not) but because while France scored high on health and education measures, Hong Kong's were better in safety and security. Hong Kong also did well in social capital, she explained, pointing to a subindex showing the greater conviction on the part of its citizenry that hard work results in personal advancement. If Bhutan is playing with a full box of crayons, Legatum may have just introduced the first color TV of social measurement.

At the other end of the spectrum, perhaps the simplest index is one proposed by Ruut Veenhoven. He believes the best way to arrive at gross national happiness is just to ask every citizen a simple question—are you happy?—and then multiply their responses by their estimated life expectancies before rolling all those into one "happy life years" total.

Whatever their methodologies, happiness indices share a common theme: the "winners" and "losers" in comparative terms aren't the same ones declared by GDP-based scorecards. On the Quality of Life Index, published by *International Living* magazine, the United States ranks seventh—whereas France ranks first and tiny Malta cracks the top fifteen. The Happy Planet Index, calculated by the New Economics Foundation and measuring "how much of the Earth's resources nations use and how long and happy a life their citizens enjoy," shows the United States, China, and India all scoring lower than they did thirty years ago. Eco-rich Costa Rica comes in first.

We're not interested in playing favorites here, among indices or even less among nations. Each of these alternatives to GDP has something to recommend it, and perhaps none of them has quite got it right. Collectively, however, they raise the right question: what are we really trying to achieve, and how will we know when we've come closer to it?

The saying goes that the fish does not see the water he is swimming in. We've been swimming in National Income and Product Accounts data for so long that few people stop to question that state of affairs. But it's time get some perspective on the aquarium. Here's a thought from Nic Marks of the Happy Planet Index that strikes us as an elegant mashup of Drucker and complexity theory: "Systems change by becoming more aware of themselves."

"Beyond GDP" initiatives keep proliferating because GDP, the proxy measure we've been using, has gotten us into trouble. It has focused all eyes on one inadequate prize and has sent us too forcefully down one path of optimization. As the Centre for Bhutan Studies puts it, "Indicators determine policies. The almost universal use of GDP-based indicators to measure progress has helped justify policies around the world that are based on rapid material progress at the expense of environmental preservation, cultures, and community cohesion." Policies, in other words, only keep spurring a runaway effect. And although we're focusing on GDP here, in the United States, the increased importance of 401k accounts and, at work, "shareholder value" calculations, have also made the society more financially aware of itself—changing its priorities.

For some observers, the whole notion of measuring happiness still seems absurd, like carrying moonbeams home in a jar. But with all this monitoring of different possibilities, the measures will improve, begin to gain predictive power, and begin to build robust feedback loops. More than a decade ago, John Elkington said as much about the triple bottom line measures he was envisioning for firms. Coming up with them, he said, is "an extremely complex task, but one which will probably look much easier once we have worked our way through a decade or two of experimentation in sustainability accounting, auditing, and reporting."

As it becomes more possible to gauge the intangible benefits that are really the point of life, we can begin to move toward a system that will reliably deliver more of them.

The ROE Runaway Effect

So let's turn our attention back to firm-level metrics.

Imagine that some enterprising manager happens onto a reasonably successful business formula, and has a pretty good idea as to what makes the business work so well. He decides that his enterprise could do even better if he could zero in on that one key to its success and keep building on it. So he finds a way to measure it, sets a target representing the ideal, and goes about understanding why sometimes performance falls to the left or right of that number. Incentives then enter the picture to keep the members of his enterprise focused on hitting the target in that all-important dimension of performance. Before long, the enterprise is fixated on that metric and what it will take to nail it, to the point of ignoring other worthy objectives.

All the conditions exist for a runaway.

Alas, it is no figment of the imagination. Within the individual firms that make up economies, various behaviors have reached the preposterous extremes of peacock tails. Can we pin those tails on some key metric that puts too much emphasis on a certain dimension of performance?

Let's think about that. Is there a mother of all measurements in the typical for-profit company? Anyone? Yes, you in the back. That's right—ROE! Even the kid who hasn't been listening since chapter 1 knows it's return on equity, or the maximization of earnings derived from one's finite store of financial capital. And how did that come to be?

It certainly wasn't true in the eighteenth century. Back then, people were more interested in yield per acre than return on equity. But as industrial innovation arrived, it brought with it a need for financing on a new scale. If you were a blacksmith, you could likely finance a new anvil by saving under your mattress. But for Andrew Carnegie to build a steel mill, he needed don't-try-this-at-home financing. The opportunities to add value through capital investment—bringing down the price of a car tenfold and the like—were everywhere, and the demand for banking services grew like the demand for software engineers in the 1990s. Investors were willing to bet on a collectively implausible set of value propositions, leading to a nineteenth-century railroad bubble not unlike the dot-com bubble.

As the mania gave way to more considered investing, the cost of capital rose and debt to equity ratios became constrained. Financing depended heavily on a business's equity. And so equity became the resource that constrained growth. The leading management practitioners of the day—the Carnegies, Morgans, Rockefellers, et al.—adopted ROE as their primary control variable.

In 1918 the DuPont Corporation bought 23 percent of General Motors stock for $25 million (it was almost as big a mess then as it was in 2009) and dispatched its newly hired electrical engineer, F. Donaldson Brown, to sort out the finances of the automaker. To focus remedial efforts on the truly fundamental drivers of profitability, Brown developed a model that broke the goal—to increase return on equity—into its basic elements. DuPont's success with General Motors was impressive, and Brown's equation became known as the DuPont equation and was widely emulated.

The DuPont equation is a simple piece of arithmetic. Brown began with the definition of return on equity:

Return on Equity (ROE) = Net Profit / Average Equity

Then he parsed that a little further:

$$\text{ROE} = (\text{Return on Sales}) \times (\text{Sales to Assets Ratio}) \times \left(\frac{\text{Asset}}{\text{Equity Ratio}} \right)$$

And finally, he broke it down even further:

$$\text{ROE} = \left(\frac{\text{Net Profits}}{\text{Sales}} \right) \times \left(\frac{\text{Sales}}{\text{Average Assets}} \right) \times \left(\frac{\text{Average Assets}}{\text{Average Equity}} \right)$$

Once broken down to that level, an analysis of return on equity starts to reveal how efficiently a company is operated and also provides guidance for managerial interventions. It makes very clear the levers management has at its disposal to eke out the highest possible returns for shareholders.

Best of all, the DuPont equation provided the insight to decompose the assessment of a whole company into assessments of its most important organizational components. Increasing net-profits-to-sales (or return on sales) is the objective of the sales and marketing department; increasing sales-to-average-assets is the job of the manufacturing department; and upping assets-to-equity is up to the financial department. Brown provided new measurements to guide the management of the key tasks of the industrial enterprise—and in the process drew the blueprint for the silos that have been decried for the past thirty years.

Originally, this narrowed focus was powerfully positive. The sales and marketing department was given a strong incentive to build the brand and minimize the cost of its own operations. It also had an incentive to raise prices but, since this was held in check by competition, consumers were protected. Manufacturing strove for efficient use of plant and equipment. It was incented to reduce wages but anytime this went too far, unions effectively pushed back. And the finance group sought leverage based on other people's money. It was driven to reach risky asset-to-equity ratios but was constrained by risk-averse lenders. Right?

Sadly, no. Marketers understood that competition was the enemy of margin and sought to stifle it wherever they could. The strong offered unsustainable prices until the weaker firms could no longer survive and then bought the victims at distressed prices, consolidating their strength and moving on to the next territory. Without competition, prices rose, and the familiar ills of monopoly markets appeared.

Eventually, the society rebelled, and from the early days of mass production through the time of the Depression, Congress passed a series of laws we collectively label "antitrust," with the result that several major monopolies—including the sugar trust, John D. Rockefeller's Standard Oil, J. P. Morgan's U.S. Steel, and The Great Atlantic and Pacific Tea Company (A&P)—were broken up. Since then, monopoly has been held in check, sort of.

The operations story is similar. In the service of high sales-to-asset ratios, manufacturers created third shifts; because mass production techniques thrived on large numbers of unskilled laborers, factories treated workers like a commodity. Labor began to organize into unions, a movement fought furiously by owners. Famously, Andrew Carnegie's Pinkerton men fired on steelworkers at his Homestead, Pennsylvania, plant. Congress again reacted, eventually (in 1935) passing the National Labor Relations Act and allowing the formation of unions strong enough to fight for a rebalancing of the power of labor and capital.

In finance, the story followed a similar script—high risk, a financial crash, and a depression that got the attention of Congress, leading to a set of reforms of the financial markets, including the separation of banking services from trading activities within financial institutions through the 1933 Glass-Steagall Act. Later, suspecting that maybe that wasn't a good idea, we did an experiment: in 1999 the U.S. Congress repealed it. Turns out it was a good idea; repeal led to replay in the form of the banking crisis a decade later.

Each incentive spelled out by the DuPont equation, pursued single-mindedly, sets off a runaway that creates a burden for society. Marketers seek market power through monopolistic practices. Manufacturers seek capital efficiency at the expense of labor. Excessive financial leverage leads to unsustainable risk. As behavioral economist Dan Ariely points out, explaining why CEOs with more money than they can count compete on CEO compensation, if you give humans a scorecard and a reward system, they will compete. Score them on a proxy measure that doesn't quite align with the goal you want to reach, and they will run right past it, on an increasingly divergent path. Make that proxy highly measurable and reinforce the feedback mechanism with lavish rewards, and the runaway becomes almost unstoppable.

Reflecting on the global banking crises, it's tempting to claim that ROE stands for "root of evil." The DuPont equation was a breakthrough at the firm level, but sent us hurtling down a path toward economic suicide. Is it possible to check this runaway dynamic? In an environment where investors are trained to select for splendid ROEs and firms have evolved ways of producing splendid ROEs, can a firm aim for something better, something more complete, without going extinct?

The Happiness of Firms

Capitalism is a powerful force whether it's put in the service of financial or nonfinancial goals. Toward whatever end, it marshals resources and allocates them efficiently. But it can assume a very different character when it's aimed more squarely at maximizing well-being.

Business, sports, and media mogul Ted Leonsis claims in *The Business of Happiness* that he became a more successful person in every respect after he "learned that happiness could not be achieved by overindexing on work." He wrote the book to help other individuals frame their success in terms more satisfying to pursue, and he ended up concluding that the same basic rules apply to institutions: "An enterprise that actively seeks to create happiness for the customers it serves, as well as its employees, partners, and yes, of course, its shareholders—a business that in its multidimensional ambitions for fulfillment has an outlook similar to many of the happy people I have known and studied—is more likely to be successful than one that doesn't care about the happiness it creates or over-indexes entirely in favor of shareholders at the expense of everyone else."

Leonsis, for all his inarguable success, might not strike many observers as a management scholar. But it must be a good sign when the scales fall from the eyes of someone as renowned for his study of capitalism as Michael Porter. The Harvard University professor and author of *Competitive Strategy* published an article in *Harvard Business Review* in 2011 that, even as it stated ideas that had been in the air for years, managed to raise some eyebrows. Porter, of course, is the name synonymous with strategy formulation in a competitive environment. He taught a generation of managers to frame their market challenges in a certain way. Now he has proposed another way. In the article he urged managers to look beyond near-term returns for business owners to long-term benefits to communities—as he put it, beyond shareholder value to *shared* value.

It's fair to compare that about-face to the moment Alan Greenspan treated us to in October 2008 when he admitted, "Yes, I found a flaw" in the logic that had guided him for many years to resist greater regulation of financial markets. Greenspan told the U.S. House Committee on Oversight and Government Reform that he'd been shocked by the subprime mortgage crisis and what it implied about the fallibility of his mental model because "I'd been going for forty years or more with very considerable evidence that it was working exceptionally well."

Perhaps it is too much to claim that today's captains of industry believe our current version of capitalism is working exceptionally well, but it is probably fair to say that most have accepted it as the only system workable at all. But now they are beginning to understand that they have been seeing their world and their work in drab black and white terms. The Technicolor moment is upon us.

Standing on the Sun

In its time, the DuPont equation was a gift: it helped the economy create more growth given the most important constraint of the day. But by focusing on equity as the scarce resource, it set in motion a feedback loop that put the investors in the role of the peahens: they held the power to decide which companies had opportunities to grow and which dropped out of the economic gene pool. But those individual choices were made with long-term cost to the species.

Winston Churchill observed that "first we shape our buildings; thereafter they shape us." The same may be said of the economic measurements we shape. A good one first teaches people what's valuable, and then, as measurement drives feedback, it changes their behavior. The shaping doesn't end there, however. The new behavior becomes the norm, and the norm shapes the society. As people strive to perform well, and better than their neighbors, they gradually lose sight of what's valuable and focus more tightly on what's measured. Along the way, better and better measurement instruments are constructed, so that any alternative measurements look "soft" and "fuzzy" by comparison. Various forces of selection—not only of investments but also of employees, mates, or schools—reinforce the central role of the measurement.

Copernicus saw that taking Earth out of the center of the system helped clarify the behavior of the planets. In this chapter and the next, we're saying that removing financial profit maximization from the center of capitalism will achieve two important goals. First, the puzzling exceptions to that pursuit—corporate social responsibility, venture philanthropy, sustainability—will be recognized to have a logic consistent with capitalism. Consequently, society will be able to provide the feedback and constraints needed to pursue the goals of all stakeholders, rather than yield status of *primus inter pares* to financiers.

If you stand where the center of capitalism seemed to be in the 1930s, running the show by the DuPont equation makes all the sense in the world. By analogy, black and white television was a huge breakthrough. But today, from a Standing on the Sun perspective, Adam Kramer's question becomes the obvious one: why don't we measure the full spectrum of what matters to us? The development of individual and national measures of happiness, and even the idea of firms being happy, becomes an imperative.

We don't think a handful of converts, even leaders like Ted Leonsis and Michael Porter, will be sufficient to impel such a fundamental change. In the next chapter we describe the process by which capitalism's new environment will drive firms, in their own self-interest, to this position. Then in chapters 5 and 6 we take up another runaway effect in capitalism. We ask whether competition deserves the obsessive attention it receives from capitalists or, if it doesn't, what else might be more central to their concerns.

CHAPTER FOUR

Embracing Externalities

How corporations will adapt to new forms of feedback

The government can require warnings which are straightforward and essentially uncontroversial, but they can't require a cigarette pack to serve as a mini-billboard for the government's antismoking campaign.

—Floyd Abrams, a lawyer for Lorillard Tobacco Company, regarding a federal lawsuit challenging the constitutionality of tobacco regulations

It was just after dusk on a warm night in Bangkok when the first in a mile-long flotilla of resplendent, dragon-headed boats made its way down the Chao Phraya River and past a party of fifty-two guests. Then, conversations that had been animated fell still as an ethereal noise reached the shore and gradually resolved itself into the sound of chanting. It was the ancient boat song that kept two thousand oarsmen rowing in unison. This was October 20, 2003, the closing night of a week of high-level meetings, and even before the spectacle of the royal barge procession—followed by thousands of candles bobbing along the surface of the water, their tiny flames turning the river to glittering—this trip had exceeded everything Chris had experienced or heard previously about the Thai standard of hospitality.

Thailand's dramatic economic growth had made it a natural choice for that year's Asia Pacific Economic Cooperation (APEC) summit, a gathering of political and business leaders from every country with a Pacific coastline. But at the same time, there was much talk

---

To discuss these ideas on Twitter, use these hashtags:

#externality   #scale   #sensor   #sensibility

---

of the new environmental challenges its growing industrial base was creating. Not so far away, another river, the Nam Phong, had become a symbol of industrial pollution at least as potent as Cleveland's burning Cuyahoga, after dead fish by the hundreds of thousands littered its shores, the victims of a paper plant's chemical dumping. Only a month before the APEC meetings, Thailand had become the sixth Southeast Asian nation to ratify an agreement on transboundary haze pollution. At issue was the outrageously bad air quality suffered by some countries, thanks to common practices in others: farmers and land developers clearing land by fire that often spread uncontrolled through forests.

A half-dozen years later, two developing stories brought that 2003 trip to mind. The first was captured in the title of a *New York Times* article: "In Industrial Thailand, Health and Business Concerns Collide." It described a surprising crackdown on businesses in the industrial zone of Map Ta Phut—home to forty-five petrochemical plants, eight power plants, two oil refineries, and twelve chemical fertilizer factories—after a group of citizens brought suit against the government for not enforcing environmental regulations. The second story was a series of accounts of the growing medical tourism trade and Thailand's efforts to become a preferred destination for it. Each story in its own way showed the same thing: Thailand getting serious about externalities.

Externalities is the term economists use when they talk about industry's side effects or, more positively, spillover effects—the various changes that a business contributes to in its broader milieu that do not show up on its books. That pollution in Map Ta Phut is a classic example: Thailand's National Cancer Institute discovered in 2003 that eight different forms of cancer were more prevalent there than in any other province. Another study found that people living near the industrial zone had 65 percent higher levels of genetic damage to blood cells than people in neighboring rural areas. But as long as regulations against discharging carcinogens weren't enforced (or, in an earlier era, didn't exist), those public health effects could remain external to the decision making of the various plants' management. The effects were out of scope, and the companies causing the pollution were off the hook.

Negative externalities come in all shapes and sizes. The traffic jams at the end of a factory's shifts are a local bother that, to the company, lies beyond its gates. So are (in most countries) the landfills overflowing with products and packaging discarded by customers. And then there are the myriad impacts that don't have to do with the environment. If a new menu-driven phone system keeps callers on the line a bit longer and eats up their minutes (not their billed minutes, their *life* minutes), or if a subcontractor cuts costs by exploiting workers, or if homeowners near a facility see their property values decline, those are also impacts for which a business might not be called to account.

Meanwhile, however, businesses produce various *benefits* for societies that also don't show up on their books, because they are never monetized and turned into revenues. These are the positive externalities that are sometimes recognized by tax breaks but, for the most part, go uncompensated in financial terms. As the simplest example, if one company employs a security guard to keep watch over its building entrance, that uniformed presence wards off threats to its neighbors as well. More broadly, when Google traced the source of an information security breach in 2009, the beneficiaries of its prior investments in counter-hacking capabilities included at least thirty other U.S. firms. Wikipedia is an enterprise that is essentially all positive externalities.

Reflecting on that trip to Thailand, it's easy to see how millions of acts of hospitality by hoteliers, restaurateurs, and others have created a very large-scale positive externality: the country's global reputation as a gracious and welcoming land. This is the spillover effect that any entrepreneur choosing to capitalize on the growing medical tourism trade would tap in to. (Indeed, IBM's Smarter Cities initiative recently chose a Thai city, Chiang Mai, as one of twenty-four cities it will invest in, in this case to design the infrastructure to make it a medical hub.)

Both positive and negative externalities, we believe, will increasingly be accounted for and often internalized by enterprises in the evolving system of capitalism.

In chapter 3 we point out that prosperity is not the same thing as GDP (or, for the individual, income). Likewise, at the corporate level, value creation is not the same thing as financial performance. *Externalities* is the catch-all label for the differences. For societies to adapt to their full-color portraits, their business sectors must internalize their externalities.

In this chapter, we describe the three major forces driving businesses to embrace their externalities. For shorthand, we label them scale, sensors, and sensibilities. We also argue that most businesses will see a steady expansion of the scope of impact they *can* manage. Most helpfully, perhaps, we offer a framework that will help firms, their stakeholders, and even their antagonists get on the same page with regard to "responsibility"—something that should reduce the antagonism. We know that companies get the message through many channels that they must be good corporate citizens, and many of their leaders think so themselves, but often the result is an incoherent mishmash of charitable giving, pro bono work, and going-green initiatives. The next generation of capitalists will respond to the challenge in a far more disciplined and productive way.

Ubiquitous Feedback Forces the Issue

The first stake we put in the ground is that greater accountability for negative corporate impacts is unavoidable. Think about what's involved in an externality: it's a situation wherein one party takes action that has effects on others who did not have a choice in the matter and whose interests were not considered. How long can that persist before feedback starts impinging on the actor? Perhaps indefinitely, if the effect is too small to notice; or if the effect is noticeable but it's difficult for the affected party to trace it to a cause; or if the affected party doesn't make any objection known. But with every passing year, each of those "ifs" becomes more unlikely.

Scale

To begin with, for many types of externality, effects that were formerly small have grown too large to ignore. When the Eureka

Iron Works, the first Bessemer steel mill, opened in Wyandotte, Michigan, in 1854, it probably wasn't very clean or efficient. But however much soot it sent into the air, a single furnace wasn't going to have much effect on Earth's atmosphere as a whole. When global production levels reach something like a billion tons of steel per year, however, the impact becomes prominent. One recent analysis shows that before 1850, global fossil carbon emissions were negligible, and by 1925 the figure had reached a billion metric tons per year. By 1950 it had doubled to 2 billion. By 2005 it had doubled twice more, to 8 billion. Simply, industrial activity has now achieved planetary scale.

Scale has changed not only for industry collectively but also for companies individually. Given the size of many multinationals' operations, even their smallest decisions, or nondecisions, add up. UPS recently decided to stop printing paper labels and sticking them to packages; instead it designed a device to stamp shipping information directly on boxes. That sounds like no big deal—except that it saved 2.6 million pounds of paper per year. McDonald's buys more than 3.4 billion pounds of U.S. potatoes per year to turn into fries. Depending on which variety it decides to favor, farmers in the Midwest lay down significantly different levels of pesticides. Jeanne Debons, who directs something called the Potato Variety Management Institute, told an AP reporter in 2009, "It's a card game where McDonald's holds nine-tenths of the cards."

Larger corporate scale gives a company a greater proportion of the responsibility for a negative externality as well as more leverage to create a positive one. Hewlett-Packard is the world's largest tech company, for example, so it recognizes that its annual procurement budget of $50 billion gives it an undeniable ability to influence vendors. Rather than use its capital only to strong-arm them into price concessions, HP created a "Supplier Code of Conduct" in 2002 to ensure its partners were doing business in a socially and environmentally responsible manner. Similarly, what Walmart—the world's largest retailer—wants from suppliers, Walmart gets. And Walmart knows that at the volume its stores sell, a change to, say, recyclable packaging will be meaningful. It's now asking the consumer goods manufacturers clamoring for its shelf space to report on the sustainability of their products.

Sensors

The growing scale of business makes its impacts collectively more visible. Our increased ability to measure those impacts makes it easier to trace accountability. Thinking again of the Eureka Iron Works, it wasn't feasible a century ago to measure parts per billion of sulfur dioxide in the atmosphere. Now we can, and do, measure parts per trillion of many pollutants.

Sensing technology has advanced at an unbelievable rate, largely driven by the need to understand and predict natural phenomena. Following the devastation of the 2004 Indian Ocean earthquake, for example, a new tsunami warning system was created that relied on deep-ocean sensors as well as twenty-five seismographic stations on land. Now, when seismic activity suggests that trouble is brewing, twenty-six national tsunami information centers have their hands on the relevant data in almost real time. Such devices continue to become ever more tiny, dispersed, and networked. New wireless nanosensors, such as those recently tested on the Golden Gate Bridge to detect vibration that would signal wear and tear, are so small they are known as "smart dust."

And technical measurements are only half the story of today's sensing. Thanks to the "local favorites" feature maintained by film rental service Netflix, it's possible to see the top 25 movies that people in a given city are renting more than people elsewhere; Foursquare (foursquare.com) allows people to display their current and recent locations. A research team at Cambridge University has combined speech-recognition software and special sensors in a smartphone to create a technology called EmotionSense that can unobtrusively gauge the emotion of the person holding the phone. (Start working now to tone down your road rage. They're talking about embedding it next in cars.)

We're gaining the ability to "fuse" such diverse data to see patterns. Sitting in a Tel Aviv cafe, you are simultaneously "seen" by the GPS system on your phone, the credit card validation track of your purchase, the IP address of your computer, the record of your subway card swipe at the nearest station, and the shop's security camera. A friend at one of the global credit card verifiers tells us he can predict a couple's divorce six months before the couple know they're in trouble themselves.

Such insights are all the more amazing when we recall sociologist Theodore Caplow's observation that the twentieth century was "the first measured century" of social phenomena. Public opinion polling, for instance, didn't exist in any meaningful form until 1935, when George Gallup launched a syndicated newspaper column called "America Speaks."

But all this sensing and measurement are not done just for the sake of prediction, let alone simple awareness. The idea in most cases is to use the knowledge of how things are changing to make positive interventions. The power of a sensor, in other words, is to enable a feedback loop. It can be a very small loop, focused on one individual's concerns. Here in Boston, a start-up company called Zeo Inc. recently brought a "personal sleep coach" to market. People who buy it receive a special headband and alarm clock. Sensors sewn into the headband detect REM activity, calculate a ZQ score—a measure of sleep quality—and then transmit that information wirelessly to the clock. Not only does a problem sleeper get useful feedback on his night's sleep, but also he can set the alarm to ring only at a point in a REM cycle when it's easiest to wake up.

Feedback loops can also work on a very large scale. Consider, for example, the "bucket brigades" that nonprofit organization Global Community Monitor has set up in twenty-seven countries around the world. The buckets involved are the brainchild of the late Ed Masry, an environmental lawyer: low-cost, simple-to-use air sampling devices housed inside eighteen-liter plastic buckets. Using them, neighbors of industrial polluters can collect the valid scientific data they need to pressure businesses to clean up their act. The buckets test for more than seventy gases (VOCs, or volatile organic compounds) and twenty sulfur compounds. Since 2009, one of these bucket brigades has been active in Map Ta Phut.

In a data-gathering effort like this, assigning accountability is very much the goal. "There are many fixed air-quality monitoring stations in Map Ta Phut, but these fixed stations cannot tell us where the pollution is from," Global Community Monitoring's executive director Denny Larson told the *Bangkok Post*. "With this handy air monitoring machine, we can check whether the amount of toxic chemical emission is beyond the safety standard at the pollution source."

The bucket brigades—and along the same lines, the "Lab in a Can" developed by Monterey Bay [California] Aquarium Research Institute (MBARI) to perform the same task for ocean waters—underscore one last point we will make about sensors. Not only are they increasingly dispersed, but also they are increasingly democratic. This is true, first, because the information they yield is broadly available. Not long ago, political contributions by individuals were cloaked in obscurity; now they're published on the Web for all to ponder. In Brazil, citizens can go to a "check my school" Web site and see metrics about staffing levels, qualifications, and more. The U.S. AQS (Air Quality System) now stores data from more than five thousand active monitors on 188 pollutants publicly—and anyone can register to download this EPA data free.

But second, and just as important, the sensing is increasingly democratic in its *process*. Consider CitySense, an app that BlackBerry and iPhone users can use to find, in real time, the spots where the nightlife is liveliest. The app works by noting the locations of all those pub-crawling phone holders *themselves*, using GPS technology, and simply spitting back the collective results. Google Flu takes note of Google searches for information about the flu and assumes many of them are spurred by people's experiencing symptoms. Based on their addresses the application is able to spot an epidemic reliably, and two weeks ahead of the U.S. Centers for Disease Control and Prevention. And then of course there are the more deliberate acts of sensing that are enabled by ubiquitous digital cameras. When a newsworthy event happens—such as a plane landing on New York's Hudson River or a bomb exploding in London—we get waves of data not only from surveillance cameras but also from bystanders' snapshots.

As our friend Andreas Weigend, former chief scientist at Amazon .com, is fond of observing, "We have the privilege of living in that one time when the world got connected." First, he notes, computers were connected in networks that allowed them to communicate with each other. Then social networking sites such as Facebook did the same thing for the people sitting at their keyboards. The next frontier of Big Data is the Internet of things, projected to add a trillion sensors and devices to the Web, giving voice to the silent components of the economy.

Before we move on to our last driver of change—shifting sensibilities—this is the point we want to underscore about sensors: if someone is concerned about something—anything—the chances of her laying her hands on relevant information have gone way up.

Sensibilities

So suppose you were concerned about air quality in your neighborhood and wanted to find out who was polluting it. In 1950, how would you have done that? We'll leave that as a rhetorical question, but today, a good place to start in the United States is with Scorecard (scorecard .org). We tried it. It took us fifteen seconds to discover the twenty largest polluters in our area. We also checked how each ranked relative to its industry. The next step was right there for us, too: we clicked on Take Action and were presented with a roster of options, from sending a fax to the company's management to joining an online discussion.

Equipped with easy mechanisms like this, growing numbers of people are indeed taking action, seemingly inspired with a new level of sensitivity to problems in the world around them. We've seen this phenomenon in the response to natural disasters. When catastrophes happened in other nations in the past, they elicited sympathetic noises from a vaguely aware public, which was content to know its government was sending emergency aid. Today, a calamity like the earthquake in Haiti occurs, and the individual contributions to an organization like the American Red Cross—$4 million via mobile phone texting alone within the first twenty-four hours—overwhelm its ability to process them. Retailers have noticed the change in attitude. It is now commonplace for them to offer customers a chance to make a donation at checkout—$5 or $10 for food for the poor at Whole Foods Market, $4 to give a book to an urban child at Barnes & Noble, a dollar for the nonprofit of the day via eBay's PayPal—but ten years ago neither of us had experienced it. It's a sign of retailers responding to a change in the sensibilities of U.S. consumers.

It isn't just that people are opening their wallets for social change. They are opening their apertures, seeing themselves as parts of a large, interconnected world. More of them are eager to identify with movements, to campaign for justice, to rally for action. And those sensibilities are both raised and activated by the new level of connectedness people experience online.

Another sign: in 2005, the *New York Times* reported, "A year ago, a group of Swarthmore students decided to take on an unusual extracurricular activity: stopping genocide." That wasn't long ago, and the growth of the grassroots campaign started by student Mark Hanis seemed extraordinary. Five years later, it's still impressive but seems unexceptional. A sea change has happened by which, to use philanthropy consultant Tom Watson's term, we've all become "causewired." Individuals, emboldened by the proliferation of groups, are more likely than ever before to take on social problems, from local homelessness to global warming.

Avaaz (avaaz.org) takes causewiring, and ease of organizing, up a level. Avaaz is a group of 9.1 million members—a month ago it was 8.7 million—that calls itself the "global Web movement bringing people-powered politics to decision-making worldwide." Started by Australian Jeremy Heimans, Avaaz is a shared infrastructure easily mobilized in support of causes selected by the members through Web 2.0 techniques. "Each time an important issue arises—a disaster, an abuse, a bad law—a new movement has to form, donors have to be found, a Website has to be built, critical mass has to be reached" to create an international community that can make a difference, Heimans points out. As we write, the options include stopping Uganda's antigay bill and supporting Syrian rebels, and more than 600,000 signatures had been obtained in support of a strong anticorruption bill in India. The most recent three signers were from Brazil, France, and Sweden.

The Web site makes a ringing claim: "Avaaz's online community can act like a megaphone to call attention to new issues; a lightning rod to channel broad public concern into a specific, targeted campaign; a fire truck to rush an effective response to a sudden, urgent emergency; and a stem cell that grows into whatever form of advocacy or work is best suited to meet an urgent need."

So some of the apparent shift in sensibilities is a simple matter of lowered barriers to action. Impulse activism is as possible now as impulse shopping. But most of the change comes down to greater awareness of problems and understanding of their underlying causes. John Elkington, mentioned earlier in connection with the Triple Bottom Line, states that heightened sensibilities go hand in hand with more capable sensors. His example is the measurement by the British Antarctic Survey of the hole in the ozone layer, in the mid-1980s, and the impact that had on the public conscience. "Suddenly people felt that there was real scientific evidence that things they were doing every day, particularly using things like aerosol cans with CFC components, were actually tearing at the global fabric. And they didn't want to continue just sub-contracting their conscience to Friends of the Earth or Greenpeace or whoever it might be."

This brings us to an important point. As members of the public have become more personally aware of, concerned with, and involved in environmental and other challenges, their trust in corporations has plummeted.

Royal Dutch Shell was an early target of enormous dissatisfaction—activists railed against its environmental and human rights impacts in the 1990s—and by all accounts its management was blindsided by the change in mood. The company is widely credited with pioneering a process for engaging stakeholders, many of whom were on the attack, to gain an appreciation of their expectations. That kind of process simply hadn't been needed before.

Since then, firms of every kind have experienced the same growing pressures. Before the turn of the millennium, few coffee drinkers paused to think about the struggling farmers who had harvested the beans. Now, thousands of customers are sufficiently concerned to boycott a coffee seller that turns a blind eye (as Starbucks discovered), and millions more are willing to pay more for a cup with a Fair Trade seal of approval. Before 2010, how many spared a thought for the process of natural gas extraction and how well regulated it was? But let a group of journalism students write something called "The Fracking Song," and it gets more than 79,000 views on YouTube within a week of its posting.

Watchdog organizations do their part to raise awareness and heighten sensibilities. Whereas in the past a minerals company like UK-based Afrimex could quietly pay off an armed rebel group to leave its operations in the Democratic Republic of Congo alone, now such an action is noticed by an NGO like Global Witness and reported to a public appalled by the human rights abuses the company "directly contributes to." Increasingly, influential celebrities also heighten sensibilities through their choice of films (for example, Leonardo DiCaprio starring in *Blood Diamond* or Bollywood star Sunil Shetty in *Red Alert*) or ads they will appear in (as in Khloe Kardashian's "I'd rather go naked than wear fur" declaration for People for the Ethical Treatment of Animals or, Bollywood again, the stars of *The Merchants of Bollywood* teaching children to dance), or the opinions they express in interviews.

Some of the change in sensibilities even comes through formal shareholder channels. Although shareholder activism usually focuses on forcing management to optimize financial returns, sometimes the buyers of a company's stock bring other concerns to the annual meeting. Thus Coca-Cola saw a resolution brought in 2010, and again in 2011, requesting that it address consumers' concerns over bisphenol A, a substance used to line its beverage cans. More than a quarter of shareholders supported that resolution in the April 2007 vote—not enough to force the beverage giant's hand, but certainly enough to exert pressure. And it's a form of pressure that is growing. Leon Kaye reports on TriplePundit that in 2010 there were "165 or so" CSR-related shareholder resolutions, of which "two passed, 17 received over a 40% approval vote, and about half earned more than a 20% 'yes' vote." All of those numbers are trending upward.

The developments we are seeing in scale, sensors, and sensibilities all fuel each other. The average company feels the effects because as measurement improves, access to those measurements also becomes ubiquitous, thanks to heightened sensibilities. Anyone interested in a certain form of impact can obtain relevant data and at least begin to connect the dots. Formerly unseen and unremarked effects of doing business start getting measured, and the affected people, armed with data, seek recourse. We're at the point now that, whenever scale demands it, sensors detect it, and sensibilities drive it, a feedback loop will get closed. In fact, this process will contribute substantially to the trend to seeing in color described in chapter 3.

Those loops can only close faster as the term *shareholder* becomes more synonymous with *citizen*. The increasing participation of ordinary folk in the stock market has been a long-term trend; we're now at the point that, in the United States, 44 percent of households are invested in mutual funds, and about half of those assets are in equities. Participation in equity markets is rising in the emerging markets as well: in 2007, eighty million Chinese owned stocks. We suspect that people leading full lives of which investing is only a part are less likely to be single minded in their pursuit of value, and that more democratic participation in markets will mean businesses are less driven to externalize costs. Why drive a cost out of one area of your life only to incur it in another?

Here's how Srisuwan Janya, the lawyer who won the environmental case in Thailand, summed things up for the *New York Times*: "From now on, industries will not only care about making money," he said. "They have to care about the environment and the well-being of the people in the community." From his perspective, reported the *Times*, "the injunction signaled a new dawn in the country's development and the end of an era in which Thailand's paramount objective was bolstering gross domestic product." Seeing in color, indeed.

Business Squaring the Circle

In a rather lurid 2003 documentary called *The Corporation*, a corporate governance advisor named Robert Monks does a memorable turn describing public companies as "externalizing machines." He was repeating a sentiment he had published previously, in a 1991 book coauthored with shareholder activist Nell Minnow: "Despite attempts to provide balance and accountability, the corporation as an entity became so powerful that it quickly outstripped the limitations of accountability and became something of an externalizing machine, in the same way that a shark is a killing machine—no malevolence, no intentional harm, just something designed with sublime efficiency for self-preservation, which it accomplishes without any capacity to factor in the consequences to others."

We appreciate the analogy but are less pessimistic than Monks and Minnow on the prospects for change. Sharks have evolved very little in the past 150 million years, but the corporation can and will adapt to a new capitalistic environment.

Traditionally, when the costs of externalities become sufficiently clear and onerous, they do get internalized in one way or another. For many decades, if you bought a car battery in the United States, no provision was made to sequester its toxic materials upon disposal. The resulting heavy metal poisoning inflicted real costs on society, in the form of health care costs and harder-to-measure suffering, which were externalities because neither the battery's maker nor its user paid them. Now, in many states, that externality has been internalized. The customer purchases a $25 certificate licensing her to dispose of the battery, and she is buying with knowledge of the full cost of the product. The stores that sell the new battery cash the certificate when they properly recycle the old one.

Society has a range of mechanisms for making this happen and thereby bringing corporate actions into alignment with the public good. Typically, in the traditional "business versus regulator" frame, the story unfolds as follows:

1. **Feedback is generated by parties affected by a negative externality:** Customers complain, public hearings are held, people write their government representatives.

2. **Outrage grows as that feedback is ignored, and people organize to apply pressure:** In the case we noted in Thailand, twenty-seven villagers in industrial Map Ta Phut filed suit against the government, citing a high incidence of cancer.

3. **New regulations are enacted:** In 2009, for example, a series of egregious airport delays led the United States to forbid airlines from holding passengers more than three hours on tarmacs. The uproar forced politicians to honor public sentiment above financial concerns or just inertia.

4. **Corporate leadership includes the new factor in its decision making.**

But it's possible to arrive at that last point by other routes. Feedback from affected constituencies can, and occasionally does, directly provoke an enlightened response from corporate leadership. And those are the responses we anticipate here, for a business-minded reason.

When stakeholders perceive that a company is steadily internalizing what have been considered externalities—taking advantage, that is, of growing sensing capabilities to measure and manage impacts that touch on public sensibilities—they regard that company as responsible. Conversely, when the public perceives that industry is producing an externality that it could take greater responsibility for—but seems to be refusing to do so—that's when regulation and other mechanisms of compulsion are brought to bear.

This is an important point: if an impact can be measured, it can be brought into an operational equation—and it won't be possible to keep it external for long. Therefore, the scope of impact that companies are responsible for managing will continue to grow. Their main choice in the matter is whether to take charge of that change or have it thrust upon them. In terms of corporate reputation, that makes the choice easy, because the worst of all worlds is to be *made* responsible but still not be *considered* responsible.

A Rational Response

Firms have certainly noticed how the combination of scale, sensors, and sensibilities has turned up the heat. Pat Tiernan, Hewlett-Packard's vice president of corporate social and environmental responsibility, described the effect of all this on his company: "Nongovernmental organizations (NGOs), social responsibility investment (SRI) fund interests and the media continually demand responses from us." Lynette McIntire, who holds an equivalent role at UPS, told us her organization filled out more than 130 sustainability-focused surveys in 2009 alone.

Many firms are receiving these signals, but naturally feel they can't be the first to own their externalities; although they might increase their value creation when all stakeholders are considered, they could find themselves at the mercy of shareholders and financial analysts if profits decline as a result. One way out of this bind is to take coordinated action. The global electronics industry, for example, in 2004 created the Electronic Industry Citizenship Coalition (EICC); its membership includes almost every electronics company you can name around the world (Acer, Apple, IBM, Lenovo, LG Electronics, Samsung, Science and Technology Corp., Xerox, etc.) and many you likely can't. The EICC establishes standards for its members regarding various externalities—for example, the risk of electronics operations polluting the Chinese water table. In April 2011, rules banning the sale of conflict minerals in the Congo went into effect. The EICC lists among its objectives productivity improvement and risk reduction for producers; better working conditions for labor; and improved environmental quality for host countries. By banding together, the electronics giants have taken any competitive sting out of investing in these externalities.

But in many individual firms, the response to the pressure feels very disorganized and ad hoc. Managers find themselves involved in disconnected and sometimes inconsistent initiatives relating to corporate social responsibility, sustainability, "giving back" through pro bono work, cause branding, going green (or, more cynically, "greenwashing"), and philanthropy. The resulting decisions and actions, viewed from the outside, make for an incoherent response. From the inside, the demands appear endless; it seems impossible to do enough.

Business leaders need a way to sort all this out, and the best way is to translate it all into terms of externalities. By focusing on a company's own footprint—the problems of the world that really can be laid at its doorstep—an externalities-based approach allows it to set priorities, commit to measurable goals, and take actions that are defensible to all stakeholders as proper and coherent. Among these stakeholders are, of course, a company's own people, who long for a sense of confidence that their organization is wielding its considerable power for the good.

Ripples of Responsibility

We've pointed out that many corporations (and we're speaking mainly of the United States here) tie themselves in knots trying with corporate social responsibility programs that have little apparent rationale. We believe that businesses needn't be responsible for society— only for themselves, today's externalities included. The challenge is clarifying what corporations are reasonably accountable for.

We see a core surrounded by three concentric rings of responsibility, decreasing with distance from the center (see figure 4-1). The core of this conceptual diagram is a business as it exists today: the domain that is actively managed by its leaders, the key performance indicators that are tracked. Beyond this core, every impact made is something managers consider today to be an externality. The first ring, however, consists of externalities that could fairly readily be internalized. These are the impacts that managers know they make, and could measure if

FIGURE 4-1

Ripples of responsibility

A simple framework can help you come to terms with your company's externalities. Start by drawing four concentric circles: the core is the business you manage today; the rings beyond are impacts on the world for which you haven't had to account.

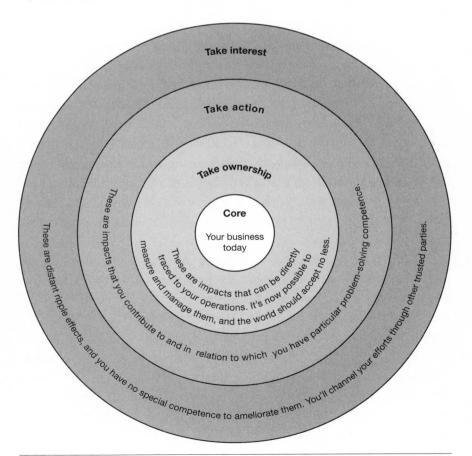

they wished, but that they have not yet seriously factored in to their decision making. Call it the regulatory battlefield; if they are actively holding these considerations at bay, there is probably at least one constituency trying to force them to do otherwise. And if the business counters by estimating the costs to customers of a given regulation, it has already measured the externality. Carbon taxes are a salient example of this second circle. We believe that the new feedback loops created by scale, sensors, and sensibilities will force businesses, sooner or later, to take ownership of these items.

The remaining two rings represent impacts that are less directly attributable to the business's decisions and actions but where at least some contribution to an overall outcome cannot be denied. These externalities are either secondary or shared, so it is not currently feasible to assign responsibility with any precision. Think of it this way: if the center of the diagram is the footprint of a business today, the rings are the ripples its footfall creates.

As a practical matter, this model implies that a business must understand the impacts its operations are having on the world, discover how they are being measured or could be measured, and find ways to make those measures improve. An organization's investments of resources and attention should be directly correlated with the immediacy of the impact. If a problem is directly attributable to a company (such as emissions levels), it falls within its first ring and the onus will be on it, and not someone else, to make up for it. If a problem is one it contributes to but to which its contribution can't be measured (whether a collective problem or a knock-on effect), it falls into one of the outer rings.

What's the difference between the outer rings? We see it as a difference of capabilities. If a company has a particular set of skills or resources that it can usefully bring to bear on a problem, it should take action even if not taking full ownership of it. That's the second ring. The third ring consists of the more distant ripple effects to which it contributes but has no particular competence to ameliorate. Here, a company should at least take an interest, and a visible one. Don't worry: we make this more clear in the subsections that follow. But the upshot is that this analysis can help a company become truly responsible for its impact.

Taking Ownership

The first priority, corresponding to the first ring of our model, is simply to bring into managerial scope all the side effects of a company's operations that should no longer be called externalities because they are known or knowable. Peter Drucker wrote, "One is responsible for one's impacts, whether they are intended or not. This is the first rule. There is no doubt regarding management's responsibility for the social impacts of its organization."

By those lights, it seems clear that Nobu, a London-based restaurant group famous for its sushi, has broken the first rule. Fully aware of the dangerous collapse of bluefin tuna populations, and even in the face of a celebrity-fueled campaign against it, it persists in serving the delicious catch daily. Its one concession has been to add a footnote to menus: "Bluefin tuna is an environmentally threatened species—please ask your server for an alternative." That's not taking responsibility; it's foisting it on others. Management is basically insisting that the blood is on the hands of its customers, and the restaurant (if not the bluefin) is off the hook. Another restaurateur, Tom Aikens, had this commonsense reaction when the *Independent* contacted him for comment: "That's insane . . . If you're serving it you shouldn't say don't order it. It's contradictory. They should take it off."

In contrast, consider the case of UPS. The parcel delivery giant is heeding Drucker's rule when it makes the effort to translate all its package truck miles (something it already measured) into data about emissions of CO_2 and NO_2—and then moves package volume onto rail routes to lessen the impact. Similarly, sportswear manufacturer Nike heeds the rule when it compels all its suppliers worldwide to adhere to a code of conduct forbidding, for example, the child labor that human rights watchdogs had discovered. In both cases, the impacts are obvious candidates, if not easy ones, for mitigation.

Sometimes, however, the opportunities are not so obvious to the world or the company. Coca-Cola, when it decided to think about its carbon footprint, discovered that the most greenhouse-ghastly aspect of its business system was its installed base of more than nine million coolers and vending machines. It's changing over to more fuel-efficient units. With the same cost of cooling in mind, Nestlé's

VP of innovation, Helmut Traitler, says his company is working to develop ice cream products that needn't be frozen until they reach the grocer.

Carpet manufacturer Interface may be the company that has taken Drucker's "first rule" most to heart. Its goal, as evangelized by long-time CEO, the late Ray Anderson, is to achieve zero impact on the environment (in a notoriously chemical spewing business) and in fact to become a closed-loop, *negative*-impact business by 2020.

Taking Action

It is probably most often the case that a company knows it is contributing to negative externalities, and the world knows it, but the contribution is not direct or precisely measurable. Coca-Cola, for example, might know precisely how much water its production process consumes, but it might not know, as global water supplies come under increasing pressure, how much that matters. In such cases, the wrong thing to do would be to deny the seriousness of the problem or one's role in it. If the world perceives, however vaguely, that you are part of the problem, you will only gain by being seen as part of the solution, as Coca-Cola has been.

A perfect example of a company taking action in an area where it had impact, but was under no pressure to take full ownership, is Walmart's green construction efforts in China. As it expanded into that market, the retailer wanted to uphold the same environment-friendly building standards it had established elsewhere, but it was thwarted by the fact that local contractors lacked the required skills and knowledge. The easy response would have been to say, "Oh well—we tried." But Walmart opted for the much harder response, taking it upon itself to train those local contractors to do the job. Meanwhile, in another realm of responsibility, Walmart took a similar level of action with its private-label jewelry line by choosing to label each piece with the origin of the precious metal it contains. No one could reasonably say that Walmart itself is the cause of social ills associated with gold and silver mining in many parts of the world. It does not need to take ownership of those externalities. Yet it can, by taking action, refuse to be complicit—and perhaps can contribute to a solution.

Sometimes, taking action is a step toward taking ownership. This is how we would characterize the campaign taken by John Browne of British Petroleum in the 1990s by inviting government regulation of emissions in his industry. Browne knew BP was part of a problem, but, as in the EICC example, he also knew that no company could survive a unilateral, principled stand. He also thought BP was more adaptable than its competitors, so it could be very competitive in a changed game.

Taking Interest

For impacts that are too remote to assign accountability but where it is possible to see a connection to a company's activities, it makes sense to contribute to amelioration efforts, often as they are undertaken by respected third parties. This action is not admitting any culpability; it is demonstrating a special concern for troubles that are closer to home, so to speak.

For the most part the actions taken in this outermost ring of responsibility are acts of philanthropy, and yet they imbue a company's philanthropic activity with relevance. Shell Foundation, for example, has decided to steer its contributions into areas associated with cleaner and more efficient energy consumption. Its partnership with a nonprofit organization called Envirofit falls into this scope; its mission is to create an affordable and much cleaner-burning alternative to the cookstoves used extensively in poorer regions of the world.

And remember: there is goodwill to be gained by producing positive externalities as well as in diminishing negative ones. When we spoke with Chris West, who directs Royal Dutch Shell's global philanthropic efforts through the Shell Foundation, we became convinced that this was the essence of his vision. "We deliberately took as a starting point the fact that we would focus only on issues aligned to the business footprint of our parent," he said. "So, for us, that means tackling energy poverty issues and energy environment issues." By choosing spots where Shell's resources and brand resonate most, Shell Foundation accomplishes more for the dollar for its beneficiaries, creating positive externalities.

And what becomes of every philanthropic opportunity that falls outside this framework? Breast cancer, for example, is a terrible disease but cannot be said to be, even remotely, an impact of most corporate activity. Yet a broad swath of companies have seemed to make curing it a priority. Some observers salute those pink-ribboned campaigns as evidence of growing corporate social responsibility. Others might say, "You're naïve—it's all cause branding." Given our externalities lens, that is not a debate that interests us. We would certainly not dissuade any company from donating to worthy causes. Who could argue with that? We recognize that marketing is a responsibility of management, and it might as well serve shareholders and society when it can. And some employees may see such engagement as a benefit. But we wouldn't call it an act of responsibility, because none of these companies is responsible for breast cancer.

Likewise, although ExxonMobil is one of the largest corporate donors in the global fight against malaria, we can't imagine anyone thinking that the disease was a ripple effect of its operations. Profitable companies can afford to be generous, and their acts of charity win them goodwill, but we doubt it buys them any "offsets" for all the negative externalities they are failing to address.

We know that it will never be possible for businesses to internalize all their externalities. But with every passing year, it will be possible to do more in each of the spheres we've described. Managers will take ownership of more impacts, they will take action to right more wrongs, and they will take an interest in increasingly relevant realms. We were putting the finishing touches on this chapter when Julia found herself at a graduation ceremony for a friend. The dean of the school delivered a brief message to the students about going out to make their impact on the world, a topic that struck her as equally relevant to the new generation of capitalists. The speaker quoted the great poet Rainer Maria Rilke:

> I live my life in widening rings
> which spread over earth and sky.
> I may not ever complete the last one,
> but that is what I will try.

Signs of Change

If you're unconvinced that capitalism can evolve to a point where for-profit businesses willingly embrace externalities, let us point to a neat study in contrasts, perhaps surprisingly coming from the United States. Compare the recent actions of the key players in the food industry to those of the tobacco industry two decades earlier.

In the 1980s executives at Philip Morris were still fighting energetically to hold back the tide of evidence that cigarettes cause lung cancer, claiming that customers were exercising freewill choices to smoke. A 1993 *Washington Post* article with the damning title "Scientists Testify Tobacco Company Suppressed Addiction Studies" tells the tale: publication of company-sponsored research had been spiked a decade earlier by senior executives. And as the epigraph at the top of this chapter shows, the tobacco companies to this day take the posture that they should oppose each attempt by the society to limit their negative externalities.

But if you fast-forward now to the turn of the millennium, you see a very different kind of behavior by companies in the packaged-food and restaurant industries. This time around, the alarms were being sounded about trans fats, not tobacco. But this time, managers in the most powerful firms took the health implications to heart and responded quickly, before the issue became a cause célèbre. We saw them changing recipes, funding public education campaigns, and pushing reduced-fat products. By 2005, a trade publication was already announcing, "Kraft completes trans fat reformulation," and every one of the company's competitors was following suit. Note that the first U.S. state law outlawing trans fats in restaurants went into effect only in 2010. These were voluntary changes taken well in advance of legal or regulatory compulsion—or public anger.

What transpired in the meantime to drive such different managerial responses? In the space of those twenty years, as business impacts got too big to ignore in many realms and as cheaper and easier ways to measure those impacts were devised, the rules of doing business shifted. Considerations that hadn't previously complicated the plans of corporate strategists started getting factored in. It became, in other words, no longer a viable strategy to ignore externalities.

When Kraft Foods, PepsiCo, and Nestlé decided to reformulate their recipes, and national restaurant chains like Wendy's and Burger King switched to less artery-choking fats in their Frialators, they were choosing to internalize an externality. They were taking ownership of a problem that they could, by law, have continued to say was not their problem. Yes, they did so under some activist pressure, and yes, they could do still more. But note the change under way. At the stage when tobacco companies were still denying the data, the food companies didn't wait for regulation or legal action. They acted.

Standing on the Sun

The shift in perspective we're describing here is a logical one and follows directly from the arguments we've made so far: capitalists will adapt to their environment, whether in Thailand or Tennessee. One change in that environment—due more to technology than the shift to the emerging economies—is the ease of sensing and acting on information about the nonfinancial impacts of business on stakeholders other than shareholders, that is, externalities. Standing on the sun, we see not a debate about social responsibility but an about-face in the practice of capitalism: if the old rule was to be an externalizing machine, then the new rule is to be an internalizing machine. Rather than work tirelessly to push costs on to others and thereby maximize profits for shareholders, managers in firms work to push the envelope of their ability to manage and gradually increase the scope of their purview. To the extent that they resist regulation, it will not be because they do not desire greater responsibility; rather, it will be because they know better than government bureaucrats how to integrate ever more sophisticated measurements of impact into feedback loops that help them manage better. This practice will lead to more EICCs in which industries figure that if they want it done right, they'd better do it themselves.

This trend suggests, however, that business and those who regulate it will become better aligned. True, business and government may weight the balance of stakeholder interests somewhat differently, but both will be increasingly subject to the same feedback, a common, multidimensional yardstick visible to all sectors—consumers, business managers, philanthropies, regulators, citizens. Many kinds of benefit engineering (viz financial engineering) will emerge: today you can pay to offset the carbon footprint of your flight; tomorrow, Brazilian villages will package their carbon fixation for sale to emitters, and who knows what the carbon default swap of the future will be? However an enterprise balances its externalities, it will be rewarded or penalized and become part of the workings of the invisible hand that allocates resources in a market economy. It will be the job of government to set the standards for measurement and to ensure that these measurements are properly carried out and made available. The markets, now in possession of full information, should be able to do the rest.

In chapter 7 we return to the idea that the sectors of societies will align better. But first, having attacked the unalloyed pursuit of positive financial feedback as a peahen's folly in the past two chapters, we need to take on a second runaway effect in today's capitalism: the fetish for competition.

CHAPTER FIVE

Pseudocompetition

Killing the sacred cow of capitalism

Winning isn't the most important thing—it's the only thing.

—Vince Lombardi, coach of the Green Bay Packers 1958–1967

Not every critic loved the 2009 film *Duplicity*, starring Julia Roberts and Clive Owen. The British newspaper the *Telegraph* complained of a lack of "any sexual charge" between the stars. *Slate* called it muddled and quibbled that a film should make "actual narrative sense."

But seemingly everyone who has seen *Duplicity* loves its opening sequence. The scene is a rain-slick tarmac, with two corporate jets facing each other at showdown distance. The two chief executives in command of the aircraft—Howard Tully (Tom Wilkinson) and Richard Garsik (Paul Giamatti)—emerge from their retinues and stride toward each other. Then, as the opening credits roll, they engage in a petulant, flailing, ineffectual shoving match, ending up on the wet ground. By presenting all this in silent slow motion, under ominously dusky lighting, the director, Tony Gilroy, mocks the whole idea that their struggle could be epic.

Even the *Telegraph* called it virtuoso.

> **To discuss these ideas on Twitter, use this hashtag:**
>
> *#PseudoComp*

Why does that sequence speak to people? Is it because the spectacle of head-to-head corporate competition has in reality become so ridiculous? We suspect that's it (although old guys in $5,000 suits slapping at each other is always good fun). Capping off the uselessness of the two executives' scuffle, we ultimately learn that the focus of it—an innovative product—doesn't even exist. Sadly, much of today's competitive energy is exerted in this kind of titanic and ultimately low-impact battle.

For us, this passionate pursuit of one-on-one advantage constitutes a second major runaway effect that G7 capitalism has fallen prey to. Businesspeople, politicians, and regulators have become focused on competition, and its pursuit and protection has sent us down a certain path. It is as if Adam Smith died and left Vince Lombardi in charge.

But competition in itself is not the desideratum. What the economy needs is *innovation*. And even though competition can do a lot to spur sellers to seek an edge with innovation, it can also spur them to seek an edge in other ways. Meanwhile, too much emphasis on competition can even impede innovation. Like the peacock's tail, in other words, competition is a very imperfect proxy for what we really want to cultivate and pass on to the next generation. But the pursuit of it is shaping business in the mature economies. In this chapter we show how competitiveness became a runaway and describe the pseudocompetition that prevails. Then in chapter 6 we discuss how capitalism will remedy the problem.

Ironically, the effect of the runaway devotion to the idea of competition is to produce a system that features less real competition with every passing year. More and more markets that used to feature many sellers have come to be dominated by only a few. And the dynamic that arises between those few behemoths is a lot of activity that seems like a pitched battle but ends up producing very little of what we've been told (since Adam Smith) that competition in free markets should yield. Instead of efficient resource allocation to meet society's needs, we see lavish resource expenditure on nonessentials—not only large retinues and private aircraft but also advertising and selling activities designed to drum up demand that does not naturally exist and may actually lead to unhappiness. Instead of innovation that makes life meaningfully easier and more enjoyable, we see a slew of superficial line extensions and product differentiations without a difference.

What we see is, to coin a term, pseudocompetition. It celebrates the idea of competition but actually pulls its punches. To define it more precisely: *pseudocompetition* refers to a market in which more than one firm is engaged in a battle for market share, so that competition technically exists and the competitors in the arena do exhibit some signs of pugnacity, but the really important benefits associated with energetic competition do not materialize. Those benefits, generally summed up as the best allocation of resources to fulfill desires, include not only minimal waste of resources in the face of society's needs and increasing affordability of goods already established in the marketplace, but also a continuous stream of innovations that solve consumers' problems better than the existing offerings do. (Whether the hair restoration product that turns out not to exist in *Duplicity* would be such an innovation we leave for you to decide.)

In a system of pseudocompetition, well-established and well-matched combatants fail to deliver these benefits because they collectively manage to hold real competition at bay. Indeed, under pseudocompetition, firms that would seem to be head-to-head competitors effectively collude to compete half-heartedly, and they expend only enough energy to go on doing so unmolested by antitrust lawyers and regulators.

These are serious charges, we know, and we present the facts to support them as this chapter unfolds. Our point is that, as fans of capitalism, we must admit that this is one of the things that capitalism, as it's currently practiced in mature economies, isn't getting right. It is one of the runaways that threaten its viability. If capitalism is capable of evolving, as we say it is, then entrenched inefficiency and institutional rigidity are traits it will leave behind.

We also argue that, in the shift of capitalism's main action to emerging economies, there may be a way out of this runaway effect. The assumption of "end of history" adherents is that the emerging economies will adopt the West's prevailing model of capitalism—and end up in the same place. This belief implies that, just as there is no uncharted wilderness left on the globe, in a matter of years there will be no remaining territories of unbounded innovation. From our perspective, though, the end of history is nowhere in sight. We think the world is ever new, and once a new generation and a new set of economies come to sit at the center of capitalism, it will evolve. There's no need to conform to a competition favored by players past their prime. If you had already seen how ridiculous Paul Giamatti looked ruining his suit on the tarmac, would *you* go and do that yourself?

Competition Isn't What It Used to Be

Competition among sellers is thought by nearly everyone to be one of the key pillars of a capitalist system. And it's true that, when it exists, for the most part free-market competition serves society well. Adam Smith, himself a pillar of economic theory, described why: it leads to efficient resource allocation and low, low prices. Allowed to respond rationally to market signals, he explained, unfettered players move swiftly into any area where there's an imbalance between supply and demand, signaled by higher-than-normal profits. Thus the economy's total capacity for production is allocated optimally to its areas of need. Meanwhile, because any demand that exceeds supply is quickly spotted, no company can exploit it for long. An influx of competition remedies the mismatch, and prices fall.

You might say, Yes, isn't it pretty to think so? And it's true, the reality has never quite matched the theory. But across modern history, the evidence broadly supports Adam Smith's logic. Economies, like that of the United States, in which resource allocations, prices, and other marketing decisions have been determined primarily by competitive market forces have tended to spin off increasing value for money. Economies wherein alternatives to market mechanisms were employed, like that of the former Soviet Union, have made the case in the negative.

At some point, however, reality started diverging seriously from theory. Stop for a moment and conjure up the image of the model competitors in the U.S. economy today. Companies like Coca-Cola and PepsiCo come to mind, locked in intense competition for share points in the beverage market. Hertz versus Avis Rent A Car is another classic, the latter famous for trying harder thanks to being number 2.

Detroit's Big Three automakers pounded on each other for many decades. Now consider: is it in these markets that we see optimal allocation of economic resources to fulfill society's needs?

When competition was first enshrined as an element of capitalism to be kept free from tampering, the world was simply different from what we have now. Adam Smith was writing long before industrial-scale organizations roamed the earth, when individual competitors were too small to change the market and the large size of the required investments didn't create barriers to entry. Smith's world was one of "atomistic competition." That's an economist's term, not his, so let's define it. *Atomistic competition* is a market in which all the following are true:

- There are many small firms competing.

- No player enjoys major economies of scale.

- Individual firms do not have the ability to set prices; they are "price takers."

- Profits are low for firms.

- Prices are low for buyers.

It was a world that existed in the eighteenth century, certainly, but if you fast-forward to the twenty-first century the vestiges of atomistic competition are hard to find.

The history of the beer industry is instructive in this regard. It started out extremely atomized; in the mid-1800s, there were several *hundred* small-scale local breweries in the United States alone. The top producer in 1860, according to beer historian Martin Stack, brewed only thirty thousand barrels of beer annually, in a nation drinking more than three million. In other words, the market leader held less than one percent of the market (though of course the relevant market was not national at the time—that's part of the point). By 2000, only three firms dominated the market, together accounting for 81 percent of U.S. sales. And today, despite the recent proliferation of independent craft breweries, beer distribution is dominated by two companies—Anheuser-Busch InBev (the Belgian company that bought Anheuser-Busch) and SABMiller—which between them serve about 50 percent of the global market. SABMiller, despite being the smaller of the two, operates in 75 countries with 150 market-leading brands. (Note, too, that domination of one business can confer advantages of scale and market power in other categories. SABMiller is also among the world's largest distributors of Coca-Cola products.)

The history of the automobile industry follows the same pattern. What began as literally a cottage industry, with hundreds of tinkerers creating motorized vehicles for sale, underwent an even faster consolidation to a small handful of firms. In the space of one decade, the 1920s, the number of automakers in the United States fell from 108 to 44. By 1929, three-quarters of the cars bought by Americans were made by Ford, GM, and Chrysler—and the next five companies (Hudson, Nash, Packard, Studebaker, and Willys-Overland) accounted for most of the remaining one-quarter. It would be only a matter of time until the Big Three were the only three. More recently, the process has continued, but on the global rather than national scale.

These are not isolated occurrences. The pattern is the same in every major sector of the economy, to the extent that *being a mature industry is synonymous with being a highly concentrated one*. So let's be clear on this: there is no possibility of turning back the clock and reintroducing atomistic competition, even if some apocalyptic horseman (say, the European Union) should choose to pursue antitrust actions in every industry. There is, on the other hand, the possibility of moving past a devotion to competition that took hold in an atomized context, made sense in that environment, but doesn't anymore.

We return to this theme presently. But first let's establish why vibrant competition in markets is hard to keep in place. The next few sections explore why consolidation is inevitable and why firms, however much they personify capitalism, can't be expected to be champions of competition.

The Inevitability of Scale

The truth is that, even though the hunger that drives firms to seek monopoly status may be unattractive, there are compelling benefits associated with concentrated industries. That's because the more concentrated the industry, the larger the scale of the players. And with scale comes efficiency of operations.

Since the dawn of their discipline, economists have observed that a producer's average cost per unit falls as its scale of output increases. Because it costs a fair bit to set up, say, a potato chip plant and distribution system, and because the setup and maintenance costs must be spread, diplike, over the chips, it follows that the more potato chips you make, the cheaper each chip is to ship. This economies-of-scale argument becomes a spur to greater investment in marketing: getting more orders allows a company to ratchet up the scale of its operations, and that leads to greater efficiency and lower unit costs. Actually, the economics of scale turns out to be a nuanced topic. Classically, economists have also asserted that there is a point of diminishing returns. "Nothing grows to the sky" is an economics cliché, intended to convey that at some point adding an extra unit of output will begin to *increase* unit costs, generally because the costs of coordinating the elements of the firm eventually overwhelm the benefits of adding yet more scale. So industrial economists speak of *minimum efficient scale* as the sweet spot where economies of scale have leveled off and before coordination costs have begun to rise steeply.

The theory got a boost from studies of production during World War II, studies that established quantitative laws for the relationship between costs and volume in aircraft production. Based on this foundation, in the 1960s, strategists at The Boston Consulting Group offered the then-surprising advice to firms that, even past that point where further scaling up would eat into profit margins, clients should keep investing in an aggressive pursuit of market share. This was one of the implications of BCG's famous Growth-Share Matrix model, and here is the reasoning: every market matures eventually, and the companies operating within it, unless they exit, end up facing declining growth rates. Whether the part of a company serving a mature market turns out to be a cash cow or a dog comes down to one thing: whether or not it attained the rank of market leader and thus low-cost producer during the earlier, high-growth phase of the industry. Scale, in other words, throws off not only efficiency but also annuity benefits. In this frame it is always a strategic imperative to achieve the largest market share.

This reasoning applied originally to manufacturing operations. But in the second half of the twentieth century, manufacturing diminished as the determinant of costs and of value added. Expenditures on supply chain, branding, and marketing began to rise, making consumer businesses more dip, less chip. And for information products— for example, Microsoft Office—direct costs of the marginal unit fall to zero. Today, it's a rare industry whose economics are determined by direct cost, so the imperative is to absorb the high cost of branding by selling lots of units. In the 1980s, AT&T could afford to drown everyone in messages because it had 97 percent of the market; imagine Sprint advertising enough to put a dent in your consciousness while servicing one-thirtieth of the leader's market. So peahens—oops, corporations—have had a hundred years of responding to the incentive to increase scale and market power.

And if costs really do decline with the size of the provider, isn't it to the economy's advantage to have larger providers? In G7 capitalism, it is presumed that (market) power corrupts and that those having the ability to raise prices unchallenged will do so. But in some cases, for reasons of both cost and benefit, certain services have long been thought to be best delivered by a single provider. In the United States, these businesses were deemed "natural monopolies," and a series of laws passed early in the twentieth century exempted them from antitrust constraints while containing their potential abuse of power through regulation. As the national telephone network grew, Theodore Vail, president of AT&T, argued that telephony should be a monopoly, both because costs were minimized by having a single telephone network (i.e., minimum efficient scale was the whole market) and, uniquely for the time, because the service was more valuable the more people subscribed to it. The Communications Act of 1934 made competition in the U.S. telephone industry illegal; in exchange, the monopolist agreed to regulation. (Many other countries concurred with this logic, but built state-owned utilities rather than authorizing regulated monopolies.) This arrangement endured until the consent decree of 1984 restored the industry to competition—or at least pseudocompetition. Similar laws traded competition for regulation in the rail, electric power, and natural gas industries.

Note that all these businesses are network-based enterprises. Highways, by the way, are a natural monopoly, too, but because they are provided by governments (as telephony is, or was, in many countries), they are not classified as utilities. Networks will always have a minimum efficient scale equal to the entire territory, both because they minimize redundant investment and because they offer suppliers (of gas as fuel or as conversation) a single interface to reach all their customers or friends. Networks do grow to the sky.

We find ourselves now in an era of networks; should all of them be declared beyond competition? In 1984, economist Brian Arthur articulated the idea of "network effects": the greater the number of players in the network, the more valuable it becomes to be part of it. Period. With no qualifications or limits. Arthur said that network-based businesses are characterized by "lock-in." His simplest case involved information products, where technology creates onerous switching costs for buyers: the VHS and Betamax formats could not coexist indefinitely, because studios, rental stores, and viewers did not want to make an extra investment to support two systems they perceived to do the same thing. The same struggle was replayed scene by scene in the more recent battle of Blu-ray versus HD-DVD, a corporate shoving match that resembled the *Duplicity* scene more than most.

Equally, for someone selling or buying goods on eBay, expansions of its scale can only be increasingly good, because each new addition means another potential customer or vendor of some coveted collectible. Organizations in these markets see not diminishing but increasing returns to scale. When a firm achieves lock-in, its customers perceive that switching vendors would be onerous given the investments they have already made in it, and thus the value of staying in a network is reinforced by the pain it would entail to leave it.

We have no prediction about the outcome of the looming battle between Facebook and its new rival Google+. But consider the history of competition for the social networker: MySpace was the first to enjoy a viral takeoff, only to be eclipsed by Facebook, famously a dorm-based start-up. Given Facebook's dominance today, we doubt even Google could mount this challenge if it didn't have millions of Gmail users to begin with, because for these subscribers, switching costs are lower than they would be for an entirely new competitor. Nothing deters us now like the need to remember a new password.

Arthur's great contribution was to show that as the proportion of economic value produced by network-based businesses rises in the digital economy, the nature of competition shifts from ongoing battles over market share to winner-take-all contests for market niches, and victory means owning a segment for a time—until an innovation comes along so compelling that buyers will pay the switching costs. Nowhere in the world are regulatory doctrines adapted to this model of competition.

Note that the battles for such supreme market power can be transparent, because lock-in often has broad support even when we know it reduces market competition and raises prices. In many ways it makes life easier and most of us happier. (Google searches work better, for example, because so many people search there.) Few of us consider our time so ample that we would welcome greater inconvenience in assembling solutions to save a few cents. Pause for a moment and gaze upon your iPhone, with its many apps.

OK, we need you back now.

We should quickly dispel any impression we might have created that this phenomenon is limited to electronics platforms. In fact it is pervasive in information-based businesses, which every year constitute a greater proportion of the economy. For example, think of an airline's frequent flyer program: it offers a proposition to customers by which each marginal purchase adds to the value of the relationship, and it gives customers a reason to pay a little extra. That's an increasing returns dynamic. And it is leading to the global concentration of airlines, despite their national alliances. Growing to the sky, indeed.

We make one last point on why it is inevitable that firms will scale up and broad fields of competitors will shake out. Even in the most atom-based businesses, returns just don't diminish like they used to. Given today's technologies of coordination, the transaction costs that used to make scale hard to support past a certain point are dramatically reduced. In some cases, we would argue, it is already true that the point at which returns begin to diminish is at some scale beyond the size of the total global market for a good. Is it true in the beer industry?

Could a single company, if it were lean, serve the global market for beer most efficiently? It's very possible that beverages are one of those industrial businesses that now, in practical terms, has unlimited increasing returns to scale. If market power didn't corrupt, a single firm would be the optimal solution because it could serve the world market at the lowest possible cost, without sacrificing product diversity. The argument, of course, is that without competition, these low-costs champions would not pass on these efficiencies in the form of lower prices; they'd keep the savings, just as BCG told them they should.

Increasing the scale of a business's operations, to sum all this up, yields all kinds of across-the-board benefits. Adam Smith's work imagined a sort of static equilibrium where competition did not lead to a sustained increase in the market power of any competitor. He wasn't thinking about feedback effects and the potential for runaways. But the Industrial Revolution was cruel to this beatific vision. For all the reasons we've cited, scale no longer sows the seeds of its own destruction. Is it any wonder, then, that industries reliably consolidate?

The Quest for Sustainable Competitive Advantage

With the deck stacked thoroughly against atomistic competition and in favor of the concentration of market power into fewer hands, it would take a determined force indeed to ensure a highly competitive marketplace. But if you think that today's leading capitalists represent such a force, think again. Individually, they are committed to creating the opposite.

That might sound like an outrageous statement, but it isn't at all. If you are a reader of business books, as evidently you are, you cannot have failed to encounter the phrase "sustainable competitive advantage." This is what all managers in all firms aspire to; it is the Holy Grail that lies at the end of Tom Peters' Search for Excellence, the promise of optimizing Michael Porter's Five Forces. The point is simple: that a firm does best when it finds some way not only to prevail in the current market with its current offering but also to ensure that its advantage is not purely temporary.

Sustainable competitive advantage, in other words, is the thwarting of Adam Smith–style competition. In his world, whenever a producer responded to a market opportunity with a uniquely valuable proposition to buyers, it had the ability to enjoy excess profits. But immediately, those excess profits would be spotted and coveted by other producers, which would rush in with rival offerings. Faced with multiple options, buyers would look for value differentials through lower pricing, and the profits would rapidly be competed away. This, to a firm, is a horror to be avoided, invoking specters of price wars and "cutthroat competition." The entire enterprise of management has been to find a way around it.

There's an interesting extra angle to the pursuit of sustainable competitive advantage, or what we are tempted to call from here on out the catbird seat. At the level of the firm, it's a matter of being the alpha competitor. The company in possession of such an advantage enjoys a high P/E ratio, continues to grow, endures. But it's also important to remember that firms are collections of individuals, and people have their own reasons for wanting to be above the fray. Life in the free market is an unending king of the hill game, with others constantly scrambling to dethrone you. Staying there is a relentless, exhausting battle. Isn't it much nicer, having scaled some peak of business success, to coast a bit and still remain in the lead?

This was the observation made by economist Harvey Leibenstein, who stands as the great unacknowledged father of behavioral economics. (His seminal text was *Beyond Economic Man.*) Given the mania for the subject today, it may be hard to believe, but in the 1970s Leibenstein was pilloried by his colleagues for his heterodoxy. One of his pet subjects was the ways the behavior of firm members differs when firms are sheltered from the rigors of competition. Firms with market power, Leibenstein observed, share the objective of, and have the ability to, reduce the elasticity of the demand from infinite (perfect competition, where buyers have zero brand loyalty) to a point where they can count on customers' habits. This relief from daily battle means that people are comfortable coming to work and being able to spend some part of their day standing around the watercooler. Living a life sheltered from the worst gales of creative destruction is so appealing that it can become preferable to put forth an "appearance of differentiation" in place of the real thing.

Leibenstein coined the term *x efficiency* to denote the gap between the efficiency level that would exist under perfect competition and the level that really existed in a fat and happy firm. And he described how that inert space is sustained by norms about acceptable levels of effort, hierarchical structures, and employment relations. Again, his ideas did not get the uptake they deserved; for the same reason that members of Congress don't want to tax frequent flier miles, no one in the corporate world wanted to hear Leibenstein's thesis; they liked their own benefits. But he was on to something fundamental.

Much more recently, Rob Axtell, formerly of the Brookings Institution, created a software simulation of the maturation of firms based on workers' desires to balance work and leisure. In the artificial work world Axtell created, individuals have the ability to choose where to work, and each is endowed with some level of preference for achievement versus comfort. This is therefore an agent-based model, and the overall industry patterns are emergent, being the result of their collective and interdependent choices. If you run the model, you see that it essentially captures Leibenstein's thesis (this is a connection we make, not Axtell, although we believe he would agree): as firms grow, they are increasingly populated by *free riders*, who expend less effort than their founding colleagues to enjoy similar gains, and the firms become less competitive. The founders depart to start anew without the deadweight of free riders. But the firm may continue to grow, as the benefits of scale subsidize the comfortable life of the big firm, for some time. The simulation mirrors reality in many respects. Most important, the system never reaches equilibrium. Firms arise and disintegrate continually, not because their superior performance attracts market competitors but because they attract parasites.

Perhaps we digress, so let's connect our next dot. Given that no firm individually relishes raw-knuckles street fighting, in a highly concentrated industry, where it is possible for a few major players to implicitly agree on how business will be done, the agreement that is arrived at looks nothing like constant, fierce competition. That's almost inevitable: it's in all the leaders' interests to maintain a stable market and profitable prices. Their small numbers permit mutual understanding to develop, and then, because that understanding supports premium profits, the players have an incentive to maintain the oligopoly. Fat cats don't fight like alley cats.

OK, perhaps we should retract that last sentence, because we can already feel the cats' backs getting up. The very phrase *fat cats* was a lightning rod for the business community when Barack Obama used it. "I did not run for office to be helping out a bunch of, you know, fat-cat bankers on Wall Street," he told CBS's *60 Minutes* in mid-December 2009. In the year following, his administration was broadly accused of being hostile to business, not only by Fox News but by thoughtful executives like GE's Jeff Immelt.

But we're leaving that sentence in, because it's important to recognize when a knee-jerk response is happening and when that reflex needs to be called out, challenged, and changed. Please think about this with a mind unclouded by what you think your politics are: it is not a necessity to be on board with business interests to be a defender of free markets. In fact, as we've described, the two are deeply at odds.

There is undeniably a common attitude in the United States that to be pro–free market is to be pro-business, and vice versa. Routinely we see defenders of American values reflexively taking the side of corporations in policy disputes. But it's important to understand that, although in the abstract corporate leaders are defenders of free markets, when it comes to their own competitive settings, they would much rather sit apart from the scrum, up in the catbird seat.

It's hard to understand what advocates of the free market believe in because they so often defend the rights of the company that already has market power to do whatever it can to strengthen its position. This is a point we feel strongly about: people tolerate huge market power in large corporations under the banner of free competition, when in fact what those firms are engaging in is not competition. It is pseudo-competition.

The Growth Imperative

Is it really fair to say that the beer and automotive sectors we've mentioned are typical of all industries? Have most of the West's markets become similarly concentrated? Steve Hannaford of Oligopolywatch. com would say yes. He makes it his business to look out for situations wherein a few sellers are taking the lion's share of sales of a product or service. When that is the case, and when the condition persists, it's an oligopoly, and oligopolies have the habit of changing the workings of free markets. It's not as dire as a monopoly situation, in which one firm is able to dictate the price and availability of what it sells. But oligopoly is not much better, because when only two or three firms dominate a market space, the competition turns friendly on some level.

Hannaford sees that everywhere. In the global health care industry, he notes, there were more than ten thousand mergers and acquisitions in a single recent ten-year span. On one hand, that bespeaks the vibrancy of the entrepreneurial space; clearly there are plenty of start-ups being spawned, if only to be eaten by bigger fish. More to the point, it inevitably means that the big fish are becoming humongous. And even that doesn't tell the whole story of their market domination, because, in the drug business, every therapeutic area—such as blood pressure relief or treatment of depression—is its own market. Within those areas competition almost always comes down to a very few players. With regard to statins, for example, which is the leading drug category in sales, it's a simple matter of Pfizer (whose Lipitor commanded 50 percent market share in 2004) against Merck (whose Zocor had 30 percent).

And lest you think such oligopolistic situations are only the realm of multinational titans, consider a local (for us) example. In many communities in New England, one car dealership owner, Herb Chambers, dominates—and to a degree that apparently even Chambers himself finds unseemly. After placing some forty dealerships under the same brand umbrella, ranging from BMW to Vespa, the company bought yet another BMW dealer but obscured the Herb Chambers ownership.

We could go on, but the point is made—and if you're not convinced, we suggest you spend some time with the economic census reports created by the U.S. Census Bureau. Julia does this occasionally in her editorial role at *Harvard Business Review*. Once recently, a management guru was claiming that industries were in flux, with many becoming more disaggregated and competitive as many others become more concentrated. No dice. After some hours poring over concentration ratios and Hirschmann-Herfindahl indexes (the HHI is the bureau's favored metric for reporting on how much market power is held by how few), she was hard pressed to find more than a couple of small-potatoes industries that had not become more concentrated.

Again, this concentration is not happening thanks to any diabolical intent. Even Steve Hannaford, who considers oligopolies a scourge, concedes that they aren't "sinister." He acknowledges that "most oligopolies are based on struggles for survival, not a result of innate evil. Like those proverbial sharks moving forward, businesses either grow or fail."

He's right. Any CEO is acutely aware of the growth imperative he or she faces and knows that there are two ways to pursue it: organically or by acquisition. Organic growth, many agree, is the preferable route if you can pull it off. But a company in a mature market where it sees little potential for new sales often sees a faster route in buying other companies. In any case, once a company reaches a substantial size, it is an enormous challenge to use what you can make from scratch to rack up the percentage growth gains investors desire. Jim Kelly, former CEO of UPS, once expressed the challenge to Julia in attention-getting terms. "Once you get to be a $30 billion company, you realize that if you're going to grow 15 percent next year, you essentially need to create a $4.5 billion business from scratch." That's like adding revenues the size of, say, biotech company Genzyme every year. Obviously, the easiest way to make sure this happens is just to buy a Genzyme (as Sanofi-Aventis did, albeit for $19 billion). In 2010, IBM CEO Sam Palmisano predicted his company would spend $20 billion on acquisitions between 2011 and 2015. We'd bet he's low.

So AT&T's bid to acquire T-Mobile, opposed by the U.S. Department of Justice as we write, is true to form—as is its effect on the mobile industry's HHI. DOJ guidelines state that any merger that would result in an HHI of 2,500, or would raise the index more than 200 points, is anticompetitive. Looking at the New York, Chicago, and Seattle markets, this merger would result in an average HHI of 3,523, an increase of 1,154 points.

Stopping Just Short of Monopoly

If a society believes in diffuse competition and yet all the forces in the economy conspire to concentrate it, then this is what happens: government stands by and watches the consolidation happen until the concentration of power is knocking at the door of monopoly, and then it steps in and cries halt. Certainly, at times when one competitor has become truly dominant, we have seen the guardians of the commonweal screw up their courage and bring an antitrust suit, as in the cases of Standard Oil and U.S. Steel and Microsoft (er, strike that last).

The statutory purpose of antitrust laws is not only to protect consumers but also to prohibit the use of power to control the marketplace. In the United States, Supreme Court Justice Douglas framed the argument along these lines, in a dissenting opinion on an early steel industry case:

> The Curse of Bigness shows how size can become a
> menace—both industrial and social . . . In the final analysis,
> size in steel is the measure of the power of a handful of
> men over our economy . . . Industrial power should be
> decentralized. It should be scattered into many hands so that
> the fortunes of the people will not be dependent on the whim
> or caprice, the political prejudices, the emotional stability of
> a few self-appointed men . . . That is the philosophy and the
> command of the Sherman Act. It is founded on a theory of
> hostility to the concentration in private hands of power so
> great that only a government of the people should have it.[1]

Let's pause to note that the very fact that antitrust laws had to be written, at the turn of the twentieth century, to limit the exercise of market power was ringing proof that perfect competition was not self-sustaining. It was self-defeating.

As noted, governments also conceded that there were such things as "natural" monopolies. In realms like electricity and telephony, they saw that a single firm really was the best solution. But also recognizing the potential abuse of such power, they invented regulation to keep these in check.

In both ways, the effect is to invoke a great deal of rhetoric about the preservation of competition while actually condoning a form of it so defanged as to defy the name. Determined to hold the line on competitiveness, governments stop the process of industry consolidation just before it reaches its ultimate destination: monopoly. But in doing so they preserve competition only nominally. In reality, the difference between one firm dominating a market and two or three firms doing so is not as meaningful as it is merely comforting.

Bridled Competition

We aren't the first to see that firm scale has grown to the point that the invisible hand has lost its grip. Historian Alfred Chandler wrote about the change in his book *The Visible Hand*. Writing in the 1970s, Chandler traced the expansion of industrial organizations in the early twentieth century. The emergence of very large firms, he observed, marked a major new era in capitalism, dividing its history into two phases. Before 1850 there was the market economy, in which many players, engaged in something close to perfect competition, collectively met demand without any grand plan to do so. After 1850, the markedly different system that he called *managerial capitalism* emerged.

Recall our stripped-down definition of an economy: it allocates resources to fulfill desires. The difference between Chandler's two eras was in the mechanism by which that allocation happened. Under managerial capitalism, overall production was no longer driven by market mechanisms; instead, it was decided on by skilled managers in large companies. The invisible hand was replaced by a visible one, belonging to John D. Rockefeller or Andrew Carnegie, operating deliberately and with sufficient power and intent to change the shape of markets.

The change began, actually, with the Industrial Revolution, because it basically invented market power. Before that time, no organization had achieved or could have achieved the kind of scale it enabled. In the beer industry we've been referring to, it created the capabilities to brew huge batches and ship beer over long distances, creating the so-called shipping breweries that ultimately dominated an industry that was once nothing but microbrew.

The shift Chandler described was given a major shove forward, however, at the end of the Second World War, when the troops came home, households were formed, and consumption was no longer discouraged. With populations suddenly able and eager to spend, demand exceeded supply and excess profits resulted, throwing market equilibrium decidedly off-center.

A stark incident showing how things had changed came during a United Auto Workers strike against the major farm equipment manufacturers. The knee-jerk response of the manufacturers, led by J.I. Case Company, was to argue that the union's demands could not be met because it would force the company to raise the prices of tractors and so forth. The American farmer, Case declared, could not, should not, and would not pay more. The company also reasoned that giving in to the union's demand would put it at a competitive disadvantage. But as Case's factories went idle, its competitor John Deere sized up the situation differently. Whereas Case was acting like an atomistic competitor serving a price-sensitive buyer, Deere recognized that a large-scale tractor maker didn't simply have to live with the invisible hand it had been dealt. It had pricing power. Deere also saw a chance to acquire market power. Recognizing that a farm equipment dealer without tractors to sell is not a happy camper, Deere settled with the strikers and dangled product availability in the faces of the strongest dealers allied with other brands, who jumped at the chance to reap all the trade of farmers eager to get their own operations in gear. The result was enhanced, enduring market power for Deere through superior distribution.

Today it is almost wholly the visible hand that rocks the economy. Massive firms do not respond to consumption dynamics so much as they shape them. They have the means to manufacture demand as well as to serve it. There are still limits, to be sure, on what a powerful firm can foist on an unsuspecting public—New Coke being the textbook example. But even on such occasions, the new reality is reinforced: commentators marvel at the fact that a richly endowed company couldn't pull it off, and observers tend to chalk it up to a failure to really get behind the effort. Surely, we seem all to agree, when a big company truly sets its mind to making something fly in the marketplace, nothing can stop it.

How to Pseudocompete

Woody Allen famously observed that "eighty percent of success is showing up." Once a market has reached the point of pseudocompetitiveness, that's pretty much true. And what makes up the other 20 percent? We suggest it comprises three sets of activity: drumming up demand for easy innovations that yield little value, suppressing important innovations that threaten current offerings, and co-opting regulatory bodies that might challenge the status quo so that instead they sustain it. The visible hands at the helm of today's large-scale companies have the means to do all this.

Manufacturing Demand

What happens under pseudocompetition is that excess profits that could be spent inventing important new offerings are instead spent to achieve two ends: to erect barriers to entry by smaller, more truly competitive players; and to create demand without having created value. Advertising has been the favorite means to these ends since at least the days of the soap opera and the world depicted in the TV series *Mad Men*. It is probably even more so now, especially as advertising-supported models are not yet properly calibrated on the Web. The moment may have passed when every new Web venture featured an advertising-supported model, but the channels for advertisers are still rich beyond reckoning.

When people talk about a marketer having control of the airwaves or control of the shelf space, they are really talking about suppression of entry by others. Think of the volume of messages hurled at you by Verizon Wireless, AT&T Wireless, and Comcast. Their share of voice makes it hard for any new competitor to be heard, especially those whose cut-rate pricing keeps their advertising budgets small. The duopoly we mentioned in the statins market, where Pfizer's and Merck's combined market share is 80 percent, is all the more astonishing given that there was a generic equivalent available. Says Steve Hannaford, "Pfizer and Merck have managed to dominate the market through an energetic marketing campaign and a nonstop sales effort directed at physicians." Just as the late Leibenstein lamented.

Think too of the routine slotting allowances paid by consumer goods marketers to put new SKUs on national retailers' shelves. One might wish that her local supermarket would "curate" its shelves according to some convictions about quality and customer interest. In fact, positioning in the shopper's line of sight is bought and paid for. (If you bought this book from the front table of an airport bookstore, though, it can only be because the staff loved it.) One entrepreneur we know told us his appeal to a regional grocery chain in the western United States to stock his bottled beverages was met with a take-it-or-leave-it proposition: $200,000. Although a Procter & Gamble has the resources to pay for space until its new product takes off, a small producer offering a limited line rarely does.

Another favorite tactic of pseudocompetitors is to use advertising to drum up demand for their offerings beyond any level that might naturally exist. Luxury goods marketers are most notorious for this. Although there is, no doubt, a segment of society that would seek out ostrich-skin luggage for its admirable durability regardless of its being a totem of status, we can safely say that is a smaller group than has been persuaded to buy it.

There's a social argument in defense of advertising, of course, based on its delivery of information to consumers. Let's say that a spray were invented that could safely and inexpensively rid homes of bedbugs. No question, that would be valuable—and how would all the people who could use it find out about it without advertising? We're not here to condemn all marketing communications.

But we do see yet another runaway. Advertising has become an arms race, and beyond some point the additional expenditure would have no utility if only both sides could agree to stop. Our issue is with Mutually Assured Consumption: the misallocation of resources into creating demand for goods that, even on full display to a willing customer, can't sell themselves. This is the fate of economies that are over supplied and insufficiently innovative.

On the most cynical level, it's been known forever that *new* and *free* are the two words that will stop consumers in their tracks. Given that free is rarely viable in the physical economy, new gets a lot of attention. Thus marketers launch variations upon variations, to the point that a hapless customer just looking for a tube of toothpaste is now confronted with the likes of extra whitening, nonabrasive, free-range, omega-3 formulations—in gel or paste, Wintergreen or Fresh Mint. This continual reworking of an essentially unchanged product consumes resources but creates next to no real utility for the economy.

In her delightful book *Different*, Harvard's Youngme Moon describes the numbing sameness of the resulting products, and the marketing training behind it. "Products are no longer competing against each other," she notes. Instead, "they are collapsing into each other in the minds of anyone who consumes them. The fact that Verizon and AT&T Wireless are locked in fierce competition is meaningless to anyone who can't discern any significant difference in their offerings. If Martians were to land in this country, they would think there was a conspiracy of brands colluding in almost every category."

Moon's warning is that consumers aren't inspired by such monotony. Our society isn't well served by capitalist habits that encourage the channeling of investment into ever smaller niches. Firm revenues may remain healthy as the market acts on its addiction to the "new," but the advent of yet another limited-edition color of wildly expensive nail polish, the scarcity of which is a triumph only of marketing, can scarcely be called the best allocation of resources.

You may argue that we're trying to tell consumers what they want—after all, if people enjoy and are willing to pay for bogus scarcity, who are we to call them peahens? But it turns out that consumers are worse off for having such unimportant variety presented to them. This is the finding Barry Schwartz lays out in his book *The Paradox of Choice*. By increasing options, he argues, marketers not only place an additional decision-making burden on consumers—which they resent—they also create the conditions for consumers to be less satisfied with the choices they make. One reason is that they become more aware of the opportunity costs of their choice, as they forgo so many other options. Another is that their expectations are overinflated (that, having risen above so many other choices, the winner must really be a transformative experience), setting them up for disappointment. Schwartz is quick to point out that this flies in the face of what he calls "the official dogma of all western industrialized societies": that the way to maximize the welfare of citizens is to maximize freedom, and the way to maximize freedom is to maximize choice.

Trivial innovation, then, justified by the assumption that more choice is always good, turns out to be a predictable and costly outcome of runaway competition. If we had to choose one symbol of the way competition would evolve after World War II, we would probably point to the tail fin of the 1959 Cadillac Eldorado. By that point the U.S. economy had caught up with the pent-up demand to replace things that had worn out during the war. (It is not always remembered that the postwar boom was followed by the recession of 1953.) Automakers resorted to showy, non–value-adding features to make it obvious to any customers' neighbors that they were in possession of the latest model. Not long after that we began to hear consumer advocates crying foul over "planned obsolescence"—a kind of pseudoinnovation that deliberately manages the need for repurchase of goods that are not fundamentally obsolete. And ever since, marketers have been unable to resist exploiting consumers' hunger for status, with the result that competition has been debased across the U.S. economy.

Think of that Cadillac's ostentatious design as a biomarker of a new evolutionary path—one that would take us to today's economic runaway effects. Think of it, if you wish, as the peacock's tail fin.

Suppressing Innovation

We've described how pseudocompetitors create bogus innovation—or, at least, marketing innovation rather than service or product innovation. This is our core message, and most of the problem. But to make matters worse, many pseudocompetitors also engage in the suppression of true innovation.

This happens in ways both aggressive and passive. On the aggressive side, we sometimes hear (and, presumably, usually don't hear) about the deliberate quashing of valuable breakthroughs. Back in the 1950s, Alec Guinness starred in a great movie about such activity. Called *The Man in the White Suit*, its premise was that a scientist (Guinness) working in a lab had serendipitously discovered a super textile. Clothes made of it would shed stains on their own and last forever. Most of the action depicted the multitude of forces arrayed against him and his obviously socially useful innovation, starting with existing fabric makers and extending to shop owners and dry cleaners, all of them threatened by what today we would term a disruptive technology.

Unfortunately, movie makers can't make this stuff up. This kind of thing really happens. Tim Wu, in his book *The Master Switch*, tells the story of how AT&T ordered its Bell Labs to "cease all research into magnetic storage" and deliberately concealed and suppressed the innovation of one of its engineers, Clarence Hickman, after he came up with the first telephone answering machine—in 1934! It wasn't until the 1990s, when a historian named Mark Clark found Hickman's lab notebook in the Bell archives, that this was discovered. Why did AT&T put the kibosh on such a breakthrough technology? Writes Wu, "In Bell's imagination, the very knowledge that it was possible to record a conversation would 'greatly restrict the use of the telephone,' with catastrophic consequences for its business." In Chris's own upbringing, it was family legend that his grandfather had invested in a company that in the 1940s had patents on automatic transmissions that were bought by a Big Three company and never used. Chris's father claimed that they were bought with the express purpose of keeping them off the market.

And the behavior persists. Suppose that scientists working in small start-ups are on the brink of offering wireless electricity, for example, that is reliable and cheap enough for home use. That would be a valuable innovation. But what would you do if you were a company heavily invested in the success of batteries? One strategy would be to pay for the rights to commercialize that technology . . . and then sit on it. The same would be true if laser hair removal were ready for its close-up in the consumer market. Any company in the razor business might well be tempted to take that breakthrough out back and slit its throat. Synthetic diamonds are yet another example as their makers move beyond industrial applications and start wooing jewelry makers. A monopolist like De Beers might be passionate about the "four C's" of gemstones—their cut, clarity, carat weight, and color—but it has no taste at all for a fifth C: competition. By the way, all these examples come from a veteran consumer-goods executive who now advises companies on how to respond to what he calls "destructive technologies."[2]

In its most passive form, suppression of innovation is indistinguishable from incompetence. Probably all of us know of companies that acquired start-ups based on their promising new ideas or formulations and then proceeded to starve them through sheer inertia or failure to have a clue. This is the back story of Foursquare, a social networking service that taps in to users' mobile devices to establish their geolocation. Its creators—Dennis Crowley and Naveen Selvadurai—sold the service to Google under the name Dodgeball, only to become frustrated when the search giant failed to invest in developing it further. In their case, the story ended happily enough because they were able to quit their posts and start afresh, launching essentially the same service as Foursquare. Most innovators lack the rights or the appetites for reprising their ideas once more with feeling.

Co-opting Regulators

It begins to become clear how a firm can thrive without being particularly competitive or even while being downright abusive. John Judis of the *New Republic* wrote a column about his abysmal experience with the two cable and Internet service providers he's been a customer of:

> I have to admit that I didn't think it was possible to have worse service than Comcast. It was like trying to imagine a more devastating hurricane than Katrina or a higher mountain than Everest. But I have found it with Verizon. We're not talking here about companies on the brink of insolvency that have to pinch every penny, but two of the most prosperous and powerful companies in America. According to the vaunted theory of the free market, competition is supposed to make these companies more responsive to the consumer. We have a nearly free market, courtesy of the Telecommunications Act of 1996, and as far as I am concerned, it is not working. The FCC, and if necessary, Congress, needs to get on this case.

Well, what about that? Don't regulators have the power to shake the pseudocompetitive markets we've been describing and make them more truly competitive? Unfortunately, that power tends to be slight, because by the time anyone recognizes an oligopoly as a problem, the oligopolists involved have gained the power to evade the antitrust mechanism.

Oligopolies arise when competition goes unregulated, but that doesn't always mean there are no regulators in place. Sometimes, the regulators are co-opted by the industry. We saw accusations of this—and they appear to be warranted—in the aftermath of the BP Deep Horizon oil spill disaster. The U.S. Department of the Interior's Minerals Management Service was responsible for ensuring that risks were being responsibly managed, but its inspectors were on a friendly basis with the industry managers and their oversight was lax. (Whenever a regulator feels it needs to change its name to be taken seriously, as this agency has done—from Minerals Management Service to Bureau of Ocean Energy Management—you know something's gone wrong.) The same coziness was undoubtedly instrumental to the financial crisis. When we spoke with economist Simon Johnson at the outset of our research for this book, he bemoaned the "revolving door" that exists between the Fed and Goldman Sachs. Banking regulators have been accused of being not so much watchdogs as lapdogs. When it came time for recriminations after the exposure of the Bernard Madoff Ponzi scheme, whistle-blower Harry Markopoulos went even further in blasting the Financial Industry Regulatory Authority (FINRA), which neglected for years to delve into the fund's suspiciously steady gains. FINRA, Markopoulos told PBS, is "a blind, deaf, and mute lapdog."

A runaway is marked by the resistance of the system to new models. Peahens will stamp out any discussion of a new, short-tailed peacock, even though it might be able to outrun all its predators, by pointing out that their children's tails will become shorter. End of story.

In the United States, in June 2011, the House Appropriations Committee cut the budget of the Securities and Exchange Commission, the watchdog agency for the financial industry. The agency's responsibilities were expanded this year as part of the legislation aimed at improving oversight. The cost of the SEC is borne by fees to the banks, so the $223 million (requested on top of a budget of $1.19 billion), falls to the bottom lines of those regulated, shrinking the capacity of the regulator.

In the Soviet era, Russian laborers used to joke about the dysfunctional system they were part of. "We pretend to work," they said, "and they pretend to pay us." In a similar way, corporations today could fairly comment, "We pretend to compete, and they pretend to regulate us."

End of Life Care

Our analysis suggests that the part of the life cycle of an industry that is underregulated is at the end, when the competitive life goes out of it, innovation is seen as the enemy, and free riders are in the driver's seat. It's when the market has effectively become an oligopoly, and incumbent players hold sufficient political and market power to keep innovative newcomers from becoming a threat. Indeed, at this point, political management can become a higher management priority than product or market management.

Anyone who has seen the film *Tucker*—admittedly a caricature of the can-do spirit of the entrepreneur in an atomized market, but essentially historically true—recognizes the problem that regulators should solve. At the end of a high-growth phase in any industry comes the beginning of its senescence, and the emergence of what will replace it. A productive society will limit the ability of oligopolists to suppress that emergence. Regulation, in other words, should not be designed to combat restraint of competition but rather to combat restraint of innovation.

On this point, we must nod to the wisdom of our friend Bob Litan at the Kauffman Foundation. As he thinks about the innovation government should try to cultivate, he notes that the most important advances are new "platform technologies." In using that term he is not referring only to the information technology businesses, where platforms like the Internet are common foundations. Well before Microsoft's operating system established a platform, or Intel's chips created their platforms, alternating current in people's homes was a platform. Even a common standard like the metric system constitutes a platform.

Given that, what would it mean to reorient legislators, regulators, and judges away from protecting static efficiency and toward the protection of growth and innovation? Litan told us, "What you want basically is a legal system that will permit new platforms to challenge the old without the existing platforms abusing their marketing dominance to keep the new platforms from arising." This is, we noted, what the Microsoft antitrust case was about—not Office, but the use of Windows to suppress Netscape's browser.

Litan immediately conceded that it was easier said than done. And the reorientation will go far beyond just antitrust law. We will require a whole set of legal changes to create a system that is flexible, promotes experimentation, adapts to new real-world technology, and doesn't get in the way. A Kauffman task force on law and economics has been working to identify the changes that make sense and the pathways by which they might be adopted. Litan underscores that all the tweaks his colleagues are suggesting are informed by a theme that is simple to state and hard to argue with: "You want to make it as easy as possible for new big platforms to displace old platforms without diminishing the incentives to invent the new platforms."

Standing on the Sun

It's time to take some perspective. Again, just as Copernicus saw the workings of the solar system when he mentally sprang himself from what everyone thought was the center of the universe, it's possible to lift ourselves above the pseudocompetitive markets we're familiar with and get a more clear-eyed view of how capitalism could work with innovation, not competition, at its core.

No doubt more could be done to increase competitiveness in markets that have become highly concentrated. But our suggestion is that the watchdogs should reorient themselves, along with capitalism in general, and declare that protecting competition is not the main point. Bill Gates, offering his view on whether his company should be subject to antitrust, pointed out that Windows' real competition didn't come from other PC operating systems. Far more threatening to him was the prospect of being rendered obsolete by the next new thing (operating systems for mobile devices, as it turned out). That kind of innovation—the kind that yields improvements in quality of life, and not incidentally keeps oligarchs tossing in their sleep—has become the center of economic progress for the advanced economies, and protecting it should be the central concern. This is not a subtle difference. Although the competition and innovation do not stand in opposition, they aren't strictly aligned either.

True competition is often a spur to innovation, but as a society we have come to mistake means for ends, to the point that we now have a cult of competitiveness. It's been a central tenet of capitalist dogma that unfettered markets lead to efficient allocation of resources. But standing on the sun, we see that the overwillingness to celebrate oligopolistic markets as competitive yields inefficient waste of resources and dynamics that conspire to preserve power for incumbents, with the exact opposite of the hoped-for result: higher than necessary prices, and slower innovation than the market would prefer.

In particular, from our new perspective we see that the whole model of competition for market share is wrongheaded. It treats competition as a zero-sum game, putting into the background the more important question of whether a market is growing. This, infamously, was the huge mistake made by U.S. automakers, which operated for decades on the assumption that Ford plus Chrysler plus GM equaled 100 percent of the auto market, seemingly oblivious to the fact that there were cars being made in other parts of the world. (We are not issuing some vague indictment here. This analysis was really, truly done in their marketing departments in the 1960s, even as Volkswagen and other "econoboxes" were beginning to be a threat.)

If in place of competition, we put innovation at the center of a capitalist system, that would not spell the end of competition by any means. It would mean only that rivals in a marketplace, instead of competing to beat each other, would compete to arrive first at what the world wants next.

It would also hold implications for the regulatory framework. We are not knee-jerk advocates of more regulation, just as we are not knee-jerk advocates of free-market competition. But no one in the modern world feels that regulation has no place in a well-functioning capitalist system. The logic is simple. The invisible hand is the enemy of sustainable competitive advantage; but in the world of the visible hand some other constraint is needed to constrain the tactics by which sustainable competitive advantage is sought, just as in the initial creation of the U.S. telecommunications monopoly. The question is what sort of regulation is suitable for a world of increasing returns.

Our belief, though, is that the change in the U.S. and other mature economies won't arise from changes in regulation. As we describe in chapter 9, the smartest multinationals are positioning themselves on the front lines of innovation—a strategy necessitated by the demands of emerging markets—and incorporating them, where appropriate, in their global businesses. As Japanese manufacturers taught complacent advanced economies about lean manufacturing and customer-centric quality, competitors arising in the emerging economies will require pseudocompetitors to adapt as capitalism evolves.

Here's a stark example. In the U.S., in 2009, Verizon spent $3.7 billion on advertising. AT&T, its chief rival, $3.1 billion. Meanwhile, in India, Bharti Airtel was figuring out how to serve new customers—they add about two and a half million every month—who spend only $15 per year on their mobile services. It developed business models in which it shares equipment with competitors, ending up requiring only one tenth the capital Verizon invests to support a customer (of course, Airtel offers a frankly lower level of service).

The U.S. competitors' expenditure on advertising alone works out to about $35 per customer per year—more than twice what the Airtel customer spends for service. Will these companies be ready to compete globally? If they can't, they'll be at a severe disadvantage as they encounter truly competitive companies from the emerging world.

Bharti is innovating its industry's business model and growing at awe-inspiring rates. Verizon and AT&T are spending billions making it difficult for others to enter their market.

The very impulses that Adam Smith counted on for efficiency in the world of the invisible hand led to both misallocation of resources and the strengthening of market power—the two things that competition was supposed to prevent—when the hand became visible. That shift was the result of a fundamental shift in economics, as artisanal production gave way to mass manufacturing. In the next chapter, you'll see how the even more fundamental shift to information economics will give birth to the next form of industrial structure.

CHAPTER SIX

The Invisible Handshake

Collaborative production as the world's business model

> *Perhaps the most remarkable aspect of evolution is its ability to generate cooperation in a competitive world. Thus, we might add "natural cooperation" as a third fundamental principle of evolution beside mutation and natural selection.*

—Martin A. Nowak, Professor of Biology and of Mathematics at Harvard University and Director of Harvard's Program for Evolutionary Dynamics

On January 24, 2010, a doctor sent this short SMS message to the U.S. Coast Guard (personal data omitted here): *Two persons are trapped under the rubble at the Caribbean Market. One of them, Regine [M-- -] here is using this number: (+1) 305 --- ---- to call for help. Coordinates: 18.522547, -72.283544.*

The doctor was on the ground in Haiti in the immediate aftermath of its devastating earthquake. His message was read by volunteers at Tufts University, who relayed it to Coast Guard responders equipped to do search and rescue. Members of the Tufts group also recorded the incident and, using the coordinates provided, placed it on a map they were continually updating online. Before long, thanks to the fact that one Tufts student was a U.S. Marine, the Marine Corps also became aware of the messages being relayed and incidents mapped. They began using the information to direct resources toward the most acute needs, such as to provide fresh water to a displaced persons camp and to police areas where the breakdown of order had turned dangerous.

> **To discuss this idea on Twitter, use this hashtag:**
>
> *#InvHandshake*

All this depended on a rather humble communications technology platform developed for another use on another continent. Ushahidi, named for the Swahili word for "testimony," was first assembled as a quick mashup solution by a core team of four people—Ory Okolloh, Erik Hersman, David Kobia, and Juliana Rotich—concerned about violence erupting in Kenya after its December 2007 election. The notion was simple: to enable people with cell phones (the favored term now is *citizen journalists*) to text what they were individually seeing on the streets to a Web site for the benefit of everyone. Based on their reports, the platform then queries other cell phones in the locale to request confirmation of an incident. Individually, these confirmed reports give people a heads-up to avoid the danger. Collectively, they produce a dynamic picture of shifting hotspots.

Since its brilliantly useful debut, the Ushahidi platform has been applied to so many problems that the *Atlantic* called it "the Zelig of 2010 disasters." As well as helping to mobilize aid to areas of need in the aftermath of the 2009 Haitian earthquake, it was used to track the spread of the oil spill after the BP Deepwater Horizon explosion and to alert Washingtonians to impassable streets after a rare snowstorm buried the city. Even where the information need is not so immediate, it has found uses. In a testimony to its value on Ushahidi's Web site, the founder of a nonprofit group called Survivors Connect wrote, "We wanted to create a platform that allowed geospatial visualization of where major groups/resources exist on [human] trafficking, as well as overlay information about latest cases, news on trafficking and risk areas. Ushahidi allows us to do just that." In every case, a light platform, created by a small effort, has enabled thousands of volunteers to create social benefits.

In a solution like this one, we are seeing something special and new. It's part of a class of solutions that also includes high school teachers in Singapore posting their lesson plans on a shared Web site so that their pedagogy can be developed as a joint enterprise, and MIT taking that impulse to the level of making its courseware accessible to anyone who wants to know what MIT students know. It's the same type of phenomenon we see when Yelp users all over the world weigh in on their experiences so that anyone can benefit from them, and when fans of Radiohead "pay as they want" to get the rock band's music and keep rewarding the musicians for making more. It's the basis of Wikipedia, Linux, and much of the information on the Web, placed there by people with no business model or explicit incentive to do so and yet sustained by the individual motivations of contributors.

All these have been cited as clever applications of Web and mobile technology, but they signify something bigger than that. We think the global economy is pioneering new terms of trade and an arrangement we call the *invisible handshake*.

In chapters 3 and 4, we describe a runaway—the fixation on a single shade of value—and its seeing-in-color remedy which will lead to internalizing externalities. In chapter 5, we describe a second runaway, competition valued for its own sake even at the expense of innovation. In this chapter, we show that the growing importance of information as a factor of production will remedy this runaway and will lead to a more innovative form of capitalism.

We expect that you get that the invisible handshake is a fresh allusion to Adam Smith's invisible hand metaphor (in chapter 5, we talk about another one, Alfred Chandler's "visible hand") and also get that we've given it a different twist. Recall that economists use the image of the invisible hand to refer to an emergent good effect for society produced when individual participants are allowed to compete vigorously in a free market. Each actor, to recall Smith's words, "neither intends to promote the public interest, nor knows how much he is promoting it . . . he intends only his own gain, and he is in this, as in many other cases, led by an invisible hand to promote an end which was not part of his intention." But what if an economically beneficial outcome were just as emergent and undesigned but instead arose out of individual actors' impulses to *collaborate*? And what if that collaboration were not made "visible" by a contract but instead were governed only by an assumption that each contributor would stand to benefit by the collective achievement? Then it would be the phenomenon we're calling an invisible handshake.

A Definition in Four Parts

As with the invisible and visible hands, "invisible handshake" is a metaphor for the way actors in an economy relate to each other. Four criteria define an invisible handshake, and all four must be present to win:

- **Low coordination and transaction costs:** As any user of Amazon.com, outsourcer of business processes, or reader of *The Long Tail* knows, information technology has lowered the amount of effort required to make commercial arrangements. When transacting business is as easy as tapping a few keys, there can be many more transactions, and much smaller transactions become economically attractive. This can even reach the extreme of Freecycle.org, an online format that any volunteer can choose to implement for a local area, which gives people a way to give away stuff they no longer need to willing takers in their neighborhood. In Chris's case, it was a marionette dragon being offloaded. Within a few hours, a local dragon fan had not only laid claim to it but had already collected it from the porch. Think of Freecycle as an eBay for goods that have too little value to justify shipping them or even bothering to collect funds. With transaction costs of zero, simply knowing they are putting one less thing into a landfill, and making someone out there incrementally happier, is enough reward for the freecycler.

- **Exchange of nonrival goods:** Economists call something a *rival good* when it can be consumed only by a single user, or at least one at a time A jet engine is a rival good: if I own it, you don't. So is a ride on a ferris wheel: there are only so many rides to be sold. If you have a cake, I can't eat it too. *Nonrival goods* are the opposite; if I enjoy the great outdoors, that doesn't leave less of it for others to enjoy. Nonrival goods can be consumed by many without being exhausted. As Lawrence Lessig has pointed out—and we return to this later in the chapter—information goods are inexhaustible. Someone who takes a hilarious picture on her cell phone doesn't need to be choosy about whom she will honor by sharing it. It isn't consumed by use or physically constrained to be in only one set of hands at a time. There's something apt about *viral* and *rival* being anagrams. It's tough for something to be viral if it's rival.

- **Nonfinancial incentives:** Here let's mention the Web site Couchsurfing.org, which allows people with a spare room, or at least an empty couch, to offer it free to wayfaring strangers who want to visit their locale on the cheap. Why would anyone do this? What's in it for them? Well, perhaps it presents an opportunity for an interesting conversation or a new friend, or at least a satisfying sense of having "paid" for one's own couch surfing in a system that counts on reciprocity. Such "colorful" rewards, in the sense that chapter 3 described measuring in color, drive invisible handshakes.

- **Creation of a collective product:** Before Linux proved it could be done, the idea that tens of thousands of independent contributors could create something as interdependent as a computer operating system seemed absurd. The startling thing about Wikipedia is that a self-organized, nonfinancially driven, crowd-sourced effort could drive the well-established Britannica and well-financed Microsoft Encarta from the field. Even more startling, think of Windows Server, running second to open source Apache.

When all these conditions are fulfilled, you have an invisible handshake, Ushahidi being a perfect example. Transaction and coordination costs are *de minimus* in a system that requires only that ordinary citizens holding cell phones make a quick note of what their eyes and ears are perceiving. The information being produced is valuable but not exhausted by anyone's use of it; in fact it becomes more valuable the more widely it's available. People's motivation to participate is not financial, and, in any case, a piece of information about a single observation is not marketable. And the output that does have value is the collective output: a whole picture of the situation, and the security or remediation it enables.

And here's some proof that, when we venture beyond the world of disaster relief and nonprofits, this isn't simply a theoretical construct. Not long ago, we learned that IBM had teamed up with the World Business Council for Sustainable Development (WBCSD) to create an "eco-patent commons" that would allow IBM and other companies (Nokia, Pitney Bowes, and Sony were the first to join it) to make freely available to others patented discoveries of eco-friendly technologies and approaches. The patents are important innovations, although they tend to be peripheral, not core, to their developers' businesses. For example, one of the patents Nokia placed into the commons enabled the recycling of cell phones into other devices such as remote controls, calculators, and clocks. Core or noncore, the breakthroughs are valuable, especially when many companies are scrambling to reduce their environmental impacts.

Making them freely available went against every intellectual property instinct of their owners (or at least their lawyers). Why give away something that required an investment and is valuable to others? Yet putting the patents into a commons makes absolute sense, given that the point of these initiatives in the first place was to spare the environment some harm. Clearly, the more they are used, the more that goal is achieved. At the same time, broader use of a technique makes it more likely that it will be built on and improved. This is why an IBM spokesperson was moved to say that "new models for sharing intellectual property are essential to spurring the innovation needed to solve environmental issues." So the idea that the realm of capitalism might be infected by collective, noncompetitive endeavors is not unthinkable.

Quite the contrary, in a sense it is the biggest management story of recent years. The many collaborative efforts that fall under the heading of *open source* (meaning that many separate parties contribute to the creation of something to which anyone then has access) fit the description perfectly. In a project like Linux, for example, or Wikipedia, neither profit nor competition is the animating force. Instead, thanks to greatly reduced costs of coordination, we are now seeing other human impulses unleashed, such as generosity and the desire to be part of projects bigger than oneself. Altruism isn't required; Linux code is created mostly by individuals to meet their own needs—in other words, the specific impulse to do the work is selfish. But with faith in the collective, these inventions are donated to the common good—because if everybody does it there's more value to go around, so you don't have to do the work yourself next time. Conversely, once you've done it for yourself, there's no cost to contributing it.

Invisible handshakes, we argue in this chapter, will become central to the practice of capitalism. We explore why they're happening, how they work, and why the explosion of commercial activity in emerging economies will accelerate the shift. But first, we spend a little more time explaining why this is the right term.

Changing Hands

Let's go back to our starting point in the era of market capitalism, when Adam Smith perceived the invisible hand. The metaphor referred to an overall effect that was *emergent*, and not planned. And it was an overall effect that arose from the interactions of competitors that were interested only in their selfish gain. By contrast, in describing the "visible hand" of managerial capitalism, Alfred Chandler noted that the overall effect of the competitive market was not emergent; it was *intended*, even designed. Industrial-sized firms had gained enough heft to move markets and not simply respond to their signals. The emergent result this time was not the common good, but the higher prices, reduced output, and retarded innovation that go along with powerful cartels, the impetus behind antitrust laws. It's the story we tell in chapter 3 about the DuPont equation.

If you have intuited that our term *invisible handshake* refers to a new era of capitalism after Chandler's managerial capitalism, you're right. We see a return to more positive emergent effects based on the small-scale participation of many players, and this time around, more of them will be interested in collaborating and fewer in competing.

But on the way to that point, we would argue we've lived through even another variation and era (see table 6-1).

TABLE 6-1

The evolving hand of capitalism

Element	Invisible hand	Visible hand	Visible handshake	Invisible handshake
Competitors	"Atomistic"	Oligopolistic	Oligopolistic, but competition among suppliers	Many kinds, including individuals
Pricing mechanism	Market	Fiat	Negotiation	Often not priced
Emergent property	Maximum consumer surplus, efficient resource allocation	Corporations turn consumer surplus into monopoly profits, inefficient production	Reduced costs retained as profits, greater resource efficiency	Greater consumer surplus, some of it nonfinancial
Implications for innovation and growth	Positive sum; competition impels innovation	Zero sum; competition restrained by desire for stability; innovation retarded	Zero sum, but innovation spurred by supplier competition	Accelerated innovation; faster growth of financial and nonfinancial value

Let's call that one, for symmetry, the era of the *visible handshake*. At some point after firms had acquired the market power that Chandler described, some of them began to discover they were *too* big, or at least too broad. In the 1980s, driven in part by Japanese competition, they increased their focus on efficient operations. Rather than perform every task demanded by their value chains, they worked to become excellent at high-value activities and turned to other firms for other parts of the process. Importantly, to limit the risk that batons would be dropped in the handoffs, they went beyond transactional arrangements to gain those services and forged deeper relationships. Supply chain partnerships became the management focus of the 1990s, and by the turn of the millennium the watchword had become *outsourcing*. Value chains that formerly had been under one roof were broken into constellations of firms focused on doing bits and pieces well.

What we were seeing was the proof of Ronald Coase's brilliant contribution to the theory of the firm. Writing in 1937, around the peak of vertical integration, and also during the dawn of modern financial theory, Coase asked why firms needed to exist at all when in principle all the inputs and value added could be purchased on competitive markets. He argued that companies brought inside their organizational walls all those activities that were too much of a nuisance (or in his terms, had transaction costs that were too high) to contract out to suppliers.

Coase's formulation explains why firms took new shapes as advancing communications and coordination technologies kept bringing down those transaction costs, allowing them to become more specialized and connected to more multitudinous suppliers (just as the Net made Zipcar economically feasible). Thus by 1997 the then-CEO of Sara Lee, John Bryan, was using the term *deverticalization* to announce that the seller of baked goods and other products would no longer be the maker of those things. Sara Lee was divesting itself of all manufacturing facilities—more than a hundred plants and distribution centers—and would concern itself simply with brand management.

It was a high-profile example but only one of hundreds of firms that shed assets tied up in low-margin activities that could now just as easily be done by others—often better. Better, that is, because in large, integrated corporations, functions tend to be insulated from market competition. When managers in a firm have no choice except to work with a certain department of their firm to get something they need—whether furniture, marketing brochures, or safety training—there is little incentive for the people in that department to knock themselves out attempting to be world class at what they do. As we quote Harvey Leibenstein arguing in chapter 5, some people are not above taking a bit of a free ride. That makes for higher costs at the level of the firm and at the level of the economy. Add the new pressure from Japanese competition in the 1980s and shake well, and all the reasons were in place to capture the benefits of lower coordination costs—and the outsourcing trend began.

The arrangements these companies forged with their suppliers were visible handshakes because they involved coordinated action—that's the handshake—and the terms and the goals of the partnership were spelled out in (mostly financial) terms clearly visible to both sides. Certainly, a Sara Lee could not simply buy its cheesecakes on a spot market. Commitments had to be made regarding prices, order volumes, production priorities, quality levels, and protection of intellectual property.

The visible handshake certainly isn't obsolete, and in emerging economies it is helping to organize effective value chains where they haven't previously existed. We offer India's TeamLease Services as a great example of how far the visible handshake can extend. The Indian staffing company provides temporary workers to more than a thousand organizations, which is another way of saying it allows those firms to outsource to suppliers as small as individual professionals. Founded in 2002, TeamLease by 2010 had seventy-five thousand employees in more than eight hundred locations, making it India's largest private employer. You might say that it is essentially the equivalent of ManpowerGroup in the United States, but there's an interesting twist. In India, it is not legal for companies to hire temps. Only 7 percent of the labor force holds formal jobs, and the unions in India have supported legislation to reduce competitiveness in the labor markets, so that temps won't take jobs away from union members. Yet TeamLease operates out in the open because India needs it to. "We're a mezzanine layer between the formal and informal sectors," says TeamLease founder Manish Sabharwal. "We pay social security, we pay health insurance—we provide everything but formal employment."

We could linger in the era of the visible handshake; it's an immense topic in itself and has been thoughtfully written about by many. (John Seely Brown and John Hagel, for example, make an excellent argument that only highly specialized—that is, completely "deverticalized"—and constantly innovating firms can survive.) It's more to our purposes, however, to acknowledge it as a stepping-stone and move on. It's the next era that it made possible that is putting serious pressure on the practice of capitalism: the age of the invisible handshake.

Collaboration Emerges

By now, transaction costs have fallen so low and the ability to connect with others is so pervasive and rich that collaboration and collective action bubble up unbidden and unmanaged. It no longer takes an entity the size of a firm to strike a partnership; individuals can join forces with firms and with one another. Handshakes happen left and right, but often no one pauses to spell out or argue over terms and conditions. The gains are largely intangible in any case, and the motivations of the collaborators hard to pin down.

Think, for example, about the thousands of people who have pitched in to build Wikipedia. In a wonderful essay for the *New York Review of Books*, novelist Nicholson Baker, himself a longtime Wikipedia contributor, tries to describe why folks work on it. "It was constructed, in less than eight years, by strangers who disagreed about all kinds of things but who were drawn to a shared, not-for-profit purpose," he writes, implying that it's the project's noncommercial nature that is the lure. But only a few lines later he suggests another motivator: that "when people did help they were given a flattering name. They weren't called 'Wikipedia's little helpers,' they were called 'editors.'" And still further down, he layers on more motivation:

> It worked and grew because it tapped into the heretofore unmarshaled energies of the uncredentialed. The thesis procrastinators, the history buffs, the passionate fans of the alternate universes of Garth Nix, Robotech, Half-Life, P.G. Wodehouse, *Battlestar Galactica, Buffy the Vampire Slayer*, Charles Dickens, or Ultraman—all those people who hoped that their years of collecting comics or reading novels or staring at TV screens hadn't been a waste of time—would pour the fruits of their brains into Wikipedia, because Wikipedia added up to something. This wasn't like writing reviews on Amazon, where you were just one of a million people urging a tiny opinion and a Listmania list onto the world—this was an effort to build something that made sense apart from one's own opinion, something that helped the whole human cause roll forward.

This amalgam of motivations, or of forms of compensation, for contributors' efforts is typical in what Yochai Benkler of Harvard Law School has called "commons-based peer production," where there is a tacit agreement to contribute to a common purpose with only a vague sense of what one will get in return, and certainly no contract to enforce that return.

So in an invisible handshake, the effects emerge from the separate decisions made by individuals, and the rewards are to a large extent intangible (two good reasons to use the word *invisible*); and the collaborative behaviors (handshakes) roll up to collective outcomes.

Why have we taken such pains to define and name this novel arrangement for exchange? Because we believe that in economies driven by innovation and growth, populated by digital natives, and not indoctrinated with regard to controlling intellectual property, such behavior will become the mainstream, not the fringe—and will confer an important advantage. Is it a dynamic that will come to characterize the entire economy? It's hard to tell. Surely much collaboration will continue to be done explicitly, with clearly delineated contributors joining forces to achieve carefully architected outcomes. But in an environment that favors collective action in general, we expect to see many more invisible handshakes. And once we get used to the idea that it's not *always* worth the cost of negotiating the financial benefit, we might find a lot of cases where it facilitates getting on with what we really care about.

Implausible? Here's one startling conversion: when Microsoft released its well-received Kinect add-on for the Xbox, Adafruit Industries posted a $1,000 prize for the first hacker to post in public an open software driver that would allow other applications to interface with the new toy outside the Xbox. Kinect captures 3-D images of what's going on in the Xbox user's room, so that, for example, your virtual opponent in Ping Pong sees the shot you just made. Kinect goes the Wii controller one better, because you don't have to hold anything; Kinect just watches you (and can understand certain things you say to it, as well).

When Adafruit posted the prize, Microsoft's legal squad rattled the kind of sword you'd expect, warning that the misuse of Microsoft technology could lead to severe repercussions. Adafruit raised the reward to $3,000, and in forty-eight hours a driver was posted. A week after that a new Web site, kinecthacks.com, appeared, showing videos posted by the hackers. These ranged from the beautiful (visualizing dancing in real time) to the cool (getting a 3-D image of your apartment by strapping a Kinect on top of a Roomba vacuum cleaner robot) to the truly useful (a new way for radiologists to manipulate X-ray images).

So far, it's only hackers at work. What's interesting is that Microsoft noticed that it might stand to benefit from this handshaking if a bunch of imaginative people wanted to generate new uses for a Microsoft product. After all, isn't that what a company would call product development? Within another week, Microsoft was on board. Its nifty new toy had become part of a system of invisible handshakes, which meant the value it created multiplied vastly for the economy—and for Microsoft. Next time maybe it'll be the one to post the prize.

Atoms as Well as Bits

A final reason these terms of trade may radiate is that, increasingly, they will not be confined to software. Earlier, you might have wondered what Adafruit Industries might be. It is a company that supplies components and kits to "makers," members of a rapidly growing, high-tech do-it-yourself movement who love to, well, make things. Adafruit's founder, Limor Fried, was recently on the cover of *Wired*.

Makers use a lot of off-the-shelf parts, but there is an important new capability that brings the invisible handshake out of the software realm and into the world of objects. For the past ten years, the technology of "3-D printing" has been emerging from university laboratories to reach a widening community. In case you're unfamiliar with it, imagine that your ink-jet printer squirted resin instead of ink. Now take the design for an object created in a kind of CAD-CAM software, slice it into thin layers, and print each layer on top of the last. Hey, presto! You wind up with a 3-D object.

The main use of 3-D printing today is in the production of prototypes. Why see your design only on a screen when the same file that generates that image can make you a tangible object to have and to hold? Another eager adopter is the military. Imagine the logistics unit of an invasion force carrying all the parts the fighters might need to deal with any equipment failures—and then imagine instead that all you have to carry is a 3-D printer along with the digital designs of all the things that might break. It sounds like pie in the sky—and indeed the tolerances aren't yet at the level needed for field use—but this vision is closer than you suspect to becoming reality. Remember your amazement, twenty years ago, when you could order a PC online by midnight and have it the next morning? Now, using ZoomRP.com, you can upload the design of a 3-D object purely from your own imagination, and it will produce it and deliver your object by noon the next working day.

At the MIT Center for Bits and Atoms, the 3-D printing mecca headed by Neil Gershenfeld, the preference is for "peer-to-peer project-based technical training." The center is devoted to providing "technological empowerment" to engineers everywhere focused on "local problem-solving." Gershenfeld's team envisions a day when people equipped with a network and a 3-D printer will have everything they need to start making useful objects, from small wind turbines to components of houses.

Like the Linux or SourceForge community, Gershenfeld's FabLabs are an open source community. But instead of swapping bits of code, FabLab members swap designs and techniques for the fabrication of goods. Creation begins with an individual who wants to create something, creates it, and then contributes it to the commons, expecting to benefit from like actions of others. After that, anyone on the network with access to a 3-D printer (there are forty-five FabLabs around the world, including in India, Kenya, Ghana, and Afghanistan) can produce a copy. The design becomes a nonrival good, and the object can be obtained for the cost of "printing." Picture yourself downloading a physical object from the Web in the way that you might today print a pdf.

How much impact could this capability have on the world? To be sure, just as only computer owners can be Linux programmers, only those in possession of a 3-D printer can produce open source objects. But that might not be a sticking point if a project called RepRap goes much further. Its product is a 3-D printer that is made of parts that can be 3-D printed. As the project's Web site says, this means that "if you've got a RepRap, you can print lots of useful stuff, and you can print another RepRap for a friend."

This leads us to some implications for emerging economies. It's a little fanciful, but think of a 3-D printer as a seed. Plant one in a village.

If it's a RepRap seed (and you have the raw materials to fertilize it with), it will yield more seeds. And if there's a network, the village can have access to all the designs in Neil Gershenfeld's open source libraries—and everyone else's. To sum it all up, if information can be free and if goods are just information plus resin, then goods can be pretty close to free.

Put another way, if the designs can be freely shared and inexpensively reproduced without limit, then it blurs the formerly clear distinction between rival and nonrival goods. This means that invisible handshakes can apply to the development of physical objects, and not just software.

We're not at the point where the answer to "Hey, Dad, can I borrow the car?" is "Hang on, I'll print you one." But you get the idea.[1]

Surplus Left as Surplus

Another way of thinking about the products of invisible handshakes is in terms of externalities. In chapter 4 we talked about negative externalities—all the environmental and other impacts that businesses cause but aren't required to pay for. But we mentioned, too, the possibility of positive externalities—all the good impacts produced by economic actors for which they don't get revenue. Back where Julia grew up (yes, and when), the more common term for this was *gravy*. If you plant a tree for shade and it turns out to yield good fruit, well, that's just gravy. If you buy a dog for a pet and it turns out it's a decent watchdog, that's gravy, too. The extra benefit didn't figure into your original calculus. The proposition was worthwhile even without it. But it's sure nice to have.

It's hard to have a successful business, actually, that doesn't produce some gravy. You build a business on things people want to buy, and the economy also benefits from the jobs. You pay workers for output, and they also gain experience and a professional network, not to mention a place to get away from the kids. You recruit high-skilled employees, and they tend to be the types who support schools and community-building efforts. All those positive externalities are what justify the tax breaks local governments offer to attract businesses (a practice that, in a way, puts a price tag on the positive externality and thereby internalizes it).

But now think about how it would be to have a positive externality that was even more valuable than the paid output of the business. What if the gravy were more substantial than the meat? To make it easier to think about this, another term for positive externalities is *consumer surplus*. That's the phrase economists use (since 1890, when Alfred Marshall coined the term in his *Principles of Economics*) to describe any situation wherein there is a difference between the value of a unit of a good to the buyer and what the buyer actually pays for it. For economists, it's an inefficiency in the market, because it represents the creation of value that no firm captures for itself. At the level of individual consumers, this happens all the time. If the price set for a product or service is the amount that a mass market of consumers will pay for it, this means an average is being taken and many in the buying pool would actually have been willing to pay more. If you love Hershey bars so much that you would gladly pay $1 for one but in fact must pay only 75 cents, that represents a consumer surplus to you of 25 cents. Businesses have expended billions of dollars on pricing systems designed to claw back consumer surplus; the archetype is yield management in the airline business. Now taxis have nighttime pricing as well. But for many companies, like The Hershey Company, it is not feasible to price its products for each individual consumer, so the surplus in your transaction remains with you.

Consumer surplus exists at the market level as well, when consumers in total benefit over and above what they collectively pay for. Twentieth-century telephony took advantage of the great difference between value and cost to painlessly transfer surplus from business customers to rural households, who otherwise would have faced prohibitive costs. The Internet repeated this trick: originally paid for by DARPA and set up by universities using it for their own purposes, it very quickly offered capacity far beyond their needs and the general public got the use of it gratis. No question, that capacity is valuable, but the price could be free because the marginal cost of adding a user was zero. That vast foundational source of consumer surplus in turn enables many "gift economy" possibilities (in which market players produce valuable output for which they demand no pay, with the expectation that the indirect returns will constitute sufficient compensation). So open source software like the Linux operating system is another exemplar of consumer surplus. It's free in the same way that the Web is free, in that it involves contributions to a commons by people who have visible support from their day jobs.

But historically, any such substantial surpluses haven't tended to last for long. Where they have endured, it's generally thanks to government regulation. (Again, no one in the era of Ma Bell paid anywhere near the value of having a telephone.) Failing that, where there is a positive externality or the possibility of one, it isn't long before a market player spots that juicy opportunity and builds a company to extract a profit from it. Sometimes, too, a company that has created a bit of consumer surplus later realizes it can charge for it. As a tiny but sorry example, we noted this year that the Santa Claus's village in the Burlington Mall outside Boston had become a gated community. What had been a free extra for shoppers—allowing any children willing to endure the line to whisper their wishes to Santa—now exists only as a for-profit photo business. At a larger scale, now that the local telephone and cable monopolies are providing Internet access, they are clawing back a substantial part of the surplus generated by the Internet.

In the bigger scheme, positive externalities get turned into either consumer surplus or profit. Even something as seemingly commercially inviolable as the human genome turned into a battleground of this kind. Is your life's essence patentable? During the race to sequence the human genome, there was a team that thought so—Craig Venter's new venture, Celera—pitted against a team that did not, the international scientific effort led by John Sulston.[2] The government's Human Genome Project was launched in 1990 and targeted 2005 as the year in which it would finish sequencing the genome. In May 1998, Venter—who had previously headed a nonprofit research institute—announced that Celera could do it by 2001. Immediately an issue arose: if he succeeded, would the human DNA sequence remain freely available to all? Celera couldn't have hoped to arrive at its results without building on the data already produced and made available to all by the public consortium. Would Venter be able to seize this treasure trove of consumer surplus and start profiting from it? That incident got many people thinking that more effort would be required to keep scientific discovery in the public realm.

But here's the thing about the new information economy. With every decade it is becoming less true that a consumer surplus is immediately spotted and captured by profit seekers.

Why would that be the case? It's not necessarily because people have become more altruistic. More likely, it's because the consumer surplus being generated is so abundant, positive externalities are spun off at such a rate, that no one has the time to capture the value for themselves. And, too, when the surplus arises from the collective effort of many people it's hard to see how to lay a claim. Are you, for example, a consumer of Zagat's restaurant ratings? If so, you no doubt find the guidance useful, but could you put a price on your enhanced ability to choose one restaurant over another? If you could, how would you pay it? Even if you could say which particular rating—food, décor, service, or cost—drove your decision to dine at La Campania rather than Deuxave, that will be an average rating to which hundreds of people contributed. How would Zagat compensate the reviewers? Would the ones who gave the same rating as the eventual average get more? And would they receive more as more people went to the restaurant—because their data was used more—or would they receive less, because the effort of their posting their rating was amortized over more users? Clearly, anyone trying to capture the value of a crowdsourced product for himself would be in for a lot of work—so much, in fact, that the game might not be worth the candle. We're back into Ronald Coase's territory. Given that the product is collective and the contributions atomic, to impose the coordination costs of contracting for the information would cause the whole value creation process to collapse.

Contrast this with buying a car but getting a lemon: you know exactly what you paid for it and who sold it to you. Big ticket, clear accountability, low coordination costs.

There's another possible reason for consumer surpluses to endure past the point where we would traditionally see a profit seeker capture the opportunity. It's that the collective work by multiple interested parties can keep pushing forward the frontier of discovery, making it unwise for any one player to put down stakes and settle into a business based on today's state of the art.

To make this point clearer, let us introduce you to some research by Peter Meyer of the U.S. Bureau of Labor Statistics on the early development of the airplane. Meyer's analysis of correspondence and legal documents from more than a hundred years ago shows that there was a large and avid community of scientists, engineers, and tinkerers interested in the problem of powered, manned flight. For at least two decades, as the principles and mechanics were being developed, this loose community of enthusiasts shared ideas and discoveries quite freely. They were, to use the modern term, engaged in an open source project. That changed, however, as the breakthroughs came that made the potential of flying machines very real. Although there had always been speculation as to how such a capability might serve not only recreational but also military purposes, the recognition that the goal was within reach made people perceive and begin to covet the business opportunities inherent in a future of flight. Rather suddenly, collaborators turned competitive, correspondence dried up, and patenting activity began. The Cambrian explosion phase was over, and the species collapse began. The Wright brothers, just a bit ahead of the field, laid claim to some key discoveries and quickly built a business on what had been an avocation.

An implication of Peter Meyer's work is that the open source activity we are seeing in software might be only a reflection of its being at a point in its life cycle analogous to the late eighteenth-century dabblings in aviation. Any major innovation might feature a window of time, but only a window, for the sharing of intellectual capital. This implies, of course, that the land grabs can't be avoided, only delayed, and that the dawning era of collaborative production will turn out to have been a sort of mirage, tantalizing but short lived.

However, here's a competing hypothesis. What if things have changed such that, at every point where the pieces fall into place to make a land grab tempting, it is now also true that the next, bigger prize is already becoming perceptible, along with the fact that getting to that next level will require ongoing collaboration? What if the horizon now recedes at a rate that is beyond individual grasp but just within the grasp of crowds?

That, we believe, is the case in the information economy today, and it's becoming more the case every year. If we're right, this means that an economic culture in which players have a reflexive impulse to plant a flag on any positive externality they happen upon is behind the times, disadvantaged, even pathetic in its petty scrabbling.

Finally, there is a class—and we think a growing class—of solutions that requires broad-based collaboration even to continue working as solutions. These also fend off land-grabbing by necessity and in doing so may create habits of mind and behavior that make it less reflexive in other settings, too.

Clearly, Ushahidi is a valuable tool. But beyond the fact that its founding developers have now turned their side project into day jobs, the platform remains an open source platform sustained by volunteers. As with Wikipedia, it would be wholly infeasible to employ its army of contributors, and its creators realize that the crew would mutiny if it perceived its labors being exploited for someone's economic gain. (After such a handshake they'd feel like washing their hands.) It's hard to imagine any such solution, as valuable as it is, remaining in operation if some party decided to extract much of that value for itself.

UNIX as Progenitor

We know, we know—you're tired of hearing about Linux. But the very fact that you are tired of hearing about it raises some interesting questions, so bear with us.

Arguably, Linux came about as a free, open source product only because of the environment it sprang from, which was UNIX. The latter got its start as a joint development effort launched in 1965 by MIT, Bell Labs, and GE, all of which saw the limitations of having separate operating systems unable to operate in an integrated way. Although the first stab at what they called Multics (for Multiplexed Information and Computing Service) failed and the joint effort disbanded, some of the Bell Labs participants carried on work toward creating a viable mainframe time-sharing system. When this group, which consisted of Ken Thompson, Dennis Ritchie, Doug McIlroy, and J. F. Ossanna, came up with UNIX it was released into the public domain. Had AT&T

not been a regulated company, perhaps this act of altruism would not have occurred. There surely would have been more pressure to commercialize the discovery for the profit of the team's employer. But the fact that UNIX was made common property made it more natural that Linux would also be a product of the commons.

Linux was an exciting development and immediately was hailed not only for itself but also as an instance of a new class of thing: an open source software product. But for a long time, it seemed to be the only open source thing people talked about. This is why you're tired of hearing about it. It was constantly hailed as exhibit A of a whole class of projects coming down the pike . . . No, really, they will be coming along any time now and this will be big . . . Wait, don't leave, something must have detained them, but meanwhile, let's talk about Linux . . .

So what happened there? Was it actually the case that Linux was only a freak occurrence arising from a unique circumstance? Was it unlikely that more invisible handshakes like it would naturally occur?

Our answers to those two questions are yes and no. Certainly, the conditions that gave rise to Linux were unique. They involved the coming together of a new capability in the connectivity of the Internet, a committed leader in Linus Torvalds, and a conducive mind-set. Given the free availability of UNIX, no one was seriously opposing the notion that its operating system would be an open and shared resource. It was born to the world that way, of similarly open parentage.

Another vital point to appreciate in the Linux story is that its open source roots did not preclude the subsequent development of profit-seeking businesses following on its success. Red Hat, the software company founded in 1993 to provide Linux maintenance and support services, is proof that an open source platform still presents business opportunities. It is always possible to build a mill on a river, and it doesn't mean that the river itself must have a proprietor.

But we're convinced that the mutation that resulted in Linux isn't an evolutionary one-off. It isn't like, for example, the monotremes—an order of animals that contains the marvelous platypus and a couple of other egg-laying mammals but has proven to be a genetic cul-de-sac. Rather, Linux is the kind of mutation that gives rise to a new kingdom.

Once it was shown to the world, it became the progenitor for many other efforts like it.

Linux spawned SourceForge, a platform on which people suggest open source software development projects, and others work on the ones they're interested in. Some 260,000 projects have been completed by 2.7 million developers, and on the *day* we checked the site there had been 2.2 million downloads. The community directory includes 47 million users.

Beyond software, consider SETI@home. SETI stands for the Search for Extraterrestrial Intelligence, and the notion is that, if E.T. really is out there, he may be trying to phone home. Or somewhere, anyway. In that case, we Earthlings could detect his presence in signals picked up by massive radio telescopes. Those radio telescopes do indeed exist. One problem, however, is that it is an enormous task to sift through all the data being produced by them to find any narrow-bandwidth signals (which would denote intelligent life, because they cannot occur naturally). And the second problem is that no one is commercially interested in investing the vast computing resources required to do that. The solution was to find a way to allocate the enormous task across computing resources volunteered by people who may have only the mildest scientific interest in the quest. SETI@home created essentially a screen saver that can be installed by anyone with a home computer that sometimes sits idle. When it detects that the computer is not being used, it bites off a chunk of telescope data, analyzes it, and sends the result to the SETI site. Again, the exchange is unmeasured. Unlike the contracted labor in a visible handshake, no one is put down for, say, a certain number of cycles per week.

Finally, as a bookend to our earlier example of the race to map the human genome, perhaps you have heard of the Structural Genomics Consortium. It's an initiative by pharmaceutical giants GlaxoSmith-Kline, Merck, and Novartis to carry out basic research on proteins relevant to drug discovery. If that sounds unlikely—drug discovery being, after all, the thing pharma companies are thought to compete on—then listen as it gets even better. The results from this research will not even be contained to the three organizations. Instead, results will be placed in the public domain with no restriction. The rationale is that, by collectively investing in building an industry commons, these companies benefit everyone by the acceleration of new knowledge creation. Let's not give these three firms too much credit for the idea: it's also the central notion behind entities like Science Commons, or more generally, Creative Commons, all of which foresee a world where property rights are weaker. But give them credit for seeing it through the haze of all the pseudocompetitive dust they've kicked up over the decades. This is the kind of arrangement that can be struck when fierce competitors stop believing that the point of their existence is a pseudocompetitive imbroglio and instead put the emphasis on innovating.

What About Intellectual Property?

Bruce Sterling, in his sci-fi book *Distraction*, imagined a future in which the U.S. economy had descended into Mad Max disrepair because China had released all intellectual property into the public domain. It's a terrific premise and scary enough to make most readers, upon the finishing the book, just happy it hasn't happened.

But of course, the future of IP can be altered, and if anyone is in a position to alter it, that would be China. Its leaders have, under pressure from the West, promised to do more to protect intellectual property rights, but the truth is that they are not working very hard at it.

Many people console themselves with a piece of conventional wisdom: once China's own economy begins to create intellectual property having global value—patents, drug formulations, movies for the world market—its government will surely, finally see more gain than pain in a stringent IP regime.

But is that assumption likely to be right?

Think about it: if the industrial economy died and made you God (or China), what kind of IP rights would you design for the new, clean slate information economy? The knee-jerk response, we understand, is to favor the same kind of regime we already have. "Because information is so valuable," you might say, "it must be protected with even more Draconian rules." But the industrial paradigm just isn't suited to the information economy. The crucial difference, utterly fundamental but only in the early stages of being worked out, is the zero cost of reproduction of information goods.

We've explained rival and nonrival goods, but let's look straight at them: if a farmer picks an apple off his tree, one buyer at the market or another eats it, but not both. A steel mill's I-beam goes into a ship or a skyscraper, but not both. So a price mechanism and market are needed to mediate the competition for these rival goods. But when a hacker produces a new Kinect driver, any number of people can use it without taking it away from anyone else, and all can be inspired by looking at Kinecthacks.com. We can all have our code and eat it, too.

As Lawrence Lessig wrote in *The Future of Ideas: The Fate of the Commons in a Connected World*, "I recognize that idea is jarring—that 'my property' would be free for the taking just because I was not using it. But do you recognize why the idea is jarring? The assumption that fuels the dissonance about property 'free for the taking' is that the taken property is exhaustible." That is true of many owned things, Lessig noted. And even an owner who was not using a good—such as his car—during some period could fairly say that no one else had the right to make use of it then, because that use would involve some wear and tear, contributing at least some to the depletion of the property.

But the question on Lessig's mind as he wrote these words was not the use of cars; it was the use of spectrum. Although cars are exhaustible resources, he argued, "spectrum is not. When I use a bit of spectrum at a particular moment in time, that spectrum is just as good after I'm finished as it was before . . . And more important, when spectrum is not used, its value as a resource is not saved. Unused spectrum, like an empty seat on an airplane, is a resource that is lost forever."

Let's look again at the world's drug companies, who have a trove of accumulated research. The successful research is disclosed as part of the licensing process. The research leading to dead ends, however, sits alongside the Ark of the Covenant in the warehouse from *Indiana Jones and the Raiders of the Lost Ark*. In your Godlike view, which would be better for the economy—keeping it there or disclosing it to the world of researchers? Certainly there would be cases in which one scientist's ceiling would become another's floor, and a recombination of knowledge would accelerate progress—once again at no marginal cost. And if you add noneconomic considerations such as the benefits of accelerated drug discovery, there's a huge welfare gain to the world's population. In a society truly based on information economics, the nonsharing of drug research—not the sharing of Metallica MP3s—might properly be prosecuted as stealing.

The often-cited reason to crack down on free taking of information is that limiting it is necessary to incent production. Yet the free sharing of music files has hardly stopped people from making music. In fact, music has never been a rational economic choice of profession. Paying iTunes, or bands, for music you could download for nothing isn't "rational" either. But in that corner of the economy, all the players now seem to be working out new and appropriate models. And at least we've learned enough that no one is trying to sue iPhone app developers who give their work away for free.

What about patents? Lessig has been the definitive voice arguing that the supposed need for patents to provide incentives is a rationale, not a fact. In their 2008 book *Patent Failure*, Boston University law professors Michael Meurer and Jim Besson, who are also economists, push the point further. They conclude that "on average, the patent system is *bad* for innovation" because the disincentive created by *other* people's patents "outweighs the incentives to build your own portfolio." Thus, they say, "on average, the patent system discourages innovation."[3]

When the competition is someone not copying you but obsolescing you, protection becomes less important, and the delay of waiting for the patent system becomes absurd. In *Regional Advantage*, AnnaLee Saxenian, dean of the School of Information at UC Berkeley, analyzed the differences between Silicon Valley and Massachusetts Route 128 as the two regions vied for leadership of the high-tech economy during the 1980s and 1990s. Saxenian concluded that greater openness, through both explicit contact and circulation of people, accounted for Silicon Valley's triumph.

This is not an argument for doing away with all patents and licenses, only that their availability should be mandatory on some reasonable terms. Creative Commons, for example, is an attempt to provide a set of terms suitable for nonfiction authors.

We are still in the horseless carriage stage of the information economy. We've learned how to use new devices that substitute for and add capability to what we had before, but we haven't reoriented our thinking to organize our economy around the characteristics of the new technology. Just as the functional organization, the DuPont equation, standard costing, and the methods of twentieth-century management arose first in the innovative industrial organizations like DuPont and GM, the appropriate rules are appearing first in information-based organizations like Linux or Facebook. They are also appearing where there is no financial incentive, as in Ushahidi. Reputation, acknowledgment, privacy, and accessibility are among the dimensions that matter here, as direct cost, scale, and productivity did in the past.

Executives have snorted just as derisively at the "gift economy" as economists sneer at gross national happiness. But these scornful attitudes are founded on a deep belief in scarcity as the problem economies must solve. And to be sure, the economy in which this belief is warranted isn't disappearing. We will still need satellites, fibers, and silicon foundries to move our free information. (How the two sectors—the information economy and its industrial infrastructure—will interact is a subject for chapter 8.) But the next decade, as foretold by the Benklers, Saxenians, Litans, and Lessigs, will see a shift from protecting the old IP regime to figuring out the new.

Knowledge is as perfect a positive externality as pollution is a negative one. It may be that the industries that rely on charging for it will prevail and IP sharing will remain illegal. But if China chooses to maximize the productivity of information rather than the profits from it—and remember, for China profits are a means to an end and not the end in themselves, as they have become for the United States—we can begin to take Bruce Sterling's scenario seriously: widespread bankruptcy and decay in the United States after China has published all of its IP on the Web.

But there's another, offsetting sci-fi scenario, this from Neal Stephenson's *Diamond Age*: in this world, every middle-class home has a matter compiler (the less well-off can access public ones). The matter compiler is fed matter, in the form of ions, along with a design for whatever good is desired, whether it's an apple or an Apple. The former design is free; it's fully depreciated and thus available through a Commons license, open source. The latter is proprietary and must be purchased. In both cases, once the design is unlocked, the distributed devices "compile" the objects from their code.

The book is classified as sci-fi because, in 1995, it was. Now it's not so much.

Give It Away Until You Charge for It

It's fair to ask how anyone—an inventor, an author, a manufacturer, in fact anyone but a pirate—can make a living if all the value is to be created by contributing efforts to the commons for the benefit of who knows whom. Seth Godin, a spectacularly prescient marketer, once answered Chris on this topic with a Delphic principle: "You give it away until you charge for it." But "until" doesn't refer to time; it refers to value. You give customers twenty stories a month (*New York Times*) but charge for more. You give users five gigabytes of storage and a minimum feature set (Evernote) and charge for more. You contribute patents and code to Linux (IBM) and charge to provide service to customers who use it. You gather a community by offering an advertising-free site (Google) and then make it an ad medium. You provide songs for free (every band in the world) and then charge for concerts.

Google didn't know how it would make its money when it began. And IBM may never have expected to make money supporting Linux; at first it seemed to be only a way to damage its competitor Microsoft. These stories capture a current phrase in the start-up world to describe the process of developing a profitable business model: "Start, and pivot." In dynamic systems, you never know what the world will look like after you make your move, so be prepared to adapt.

In the transition from an economy run by pseudocompetition to one in which invisible handshakes find their useful place—as in KinectHacks.com for Microsoft—the global economy has started, and it will be pivoting for some time. There will be a synthesis: value-creating invisible handshakes will present themselves; if they create enough value, the society will agree to pay enough to keep them going, even if we don't always foresee how. Who knew ninety-nine cents a song would be—seen in color—cheaper than free?

Emerging Economies as a Catalyst for Change

Silicon Valley and Route 128 will not be the last places to prove that growth comes faster to those whose behaviors around sharing ideas are looser. In the emerging economies of the world we will see richer cultures of information sharing further accelerating their growth. We'll also see fresh evidence of how damaging it is to create rules that restrict sharing knowledge. The conventional wisdom that when China becomes a producer of intellectual property it will enforce IP laws will come to be seen as based on flawed assumptions. More likely, as China becomes powerful, it will use its leverage to eliminate IP laws—and from a standing on the sun perspective, that's a good thing.

The rise of the invisible handshake will be a story of the emerging economies at least because of their leapfrog opportunity—in this case, to skip over the step where things in the economic realm snap to a zero-sum mentality. More deeply, it may be that formerly socialist economies will engage in invisible handshakes more readily than the most private-property-oriented economies, because the whole notion of sharing will strike a more familiar chord. Environments of rapid growth also tend to make people ready to share and move on. By contrast, when people worry about shrinking opportunity, they tend to hoard.

In the mature economies, companies are the boundaries within which one assumes a positive-sum relationship; if you help your colleague, you don't expect to be specifically compensated for that because the added value aids a common cause: shareholder wealth. But charity ends at home. Outside that boundary, transactions—with customers and suppliers—have been viewed as zero sum.

This model is eroding precisely because of the zero-marginal-cost nature of information. The invisible handshake will come to be an important driver of growth because (1) it meets the desires of individuals both to consume inexpensively and to contribute voluntarily and (2) because the emergent properties of their doing so is an economy of innovation. The emerging economies will include a substantial and growing sector in which value is freely traded and no one thinks counting is worth the trouble.

Standing on the Sun

Since 1999, when Napster was released, there has been a battle raging in the media industry between copyright holders and file sharers. It has spread from music, to videos, to games. In different guises, the same issue affects the manufacture of proprietary drugs and high-fashion accessories.

These conflicts are like a rash that signals an underlying infection. They signal a shift from one kind of economy to the other, as the U.S. Civil War was in part a symptom of the shift from agriculture to industrial wealth creation. This time, it is a conflict between the visible hand and the invisible handshake.

If knowledge is the most productive of resources and if it can be shared at effectively zero cost, then from a standing on the sun perspective, one sees how central that is to growth. It should be obvious by now that the ability to share and build on knowledge at low cost is too valuable to turn back and, equally, that those who have invested heavily in sustainable advantage will have a tough time figuring out their new models. But just as agriculture in the United States used industrial technology to mechanize, the smart pseudocompetitors will see the power of invisible handshakes and incorporate them into their businesses, as in the case of the Microsoft Kinect, IBM's embrace of Linux, and the Eco-Patent Commons.

Invisible handshakes are not an entirely new regime; science has been done this way for centuries. Runaway competition led to an environment in which businesses tried to claw back the positive externalities generated by open approaches. Digital natives, whether in developing, emerging, or advanced economies, are committed to liberating that surplus.

Consequently, capitalists will search for new models for pricing nonrival goods and rewarding their creators. The search for those models is about to get easier, as we discuss in the next chapter.

CHAPTER SEVEN

The Fourth Sector

The social sector as capitalism's R&D lab

I'm deeply convinced that [humanity's] future relies on our ability to explore and invent new business models and new types of business corporations.

—Muhammad Yunus, in a speech to the Global Alliance for
Improved Nutrition

Imagine you're a venture capitalist. An entrepreneur is passionately pitching you a start-up: "Today, the World Bank says it's a $1 trillion market. And no one is offering a service to capitalize on it. It's an absolute virgin market!"

"Maybe," you counter, "but no one's ever figured out how to serve this market at scale. It's all individual practitioners."

"Exactly! That's the beauty here. By investing in a process model, we can totally roll this up! We've done dozens of pilot tests. Today, people are paying three thousand rupees. It only costs us two hundred to serve them."

"Wow!" you say, your attention roused. "Gotta love that margin! I like it!"

So far, the conversation is an almost verbatim transcript of the exchange between Shaffi Mather (one of the entrepreneurs behind Dial 1298 for Ambulance) and Chris Anderson on the stage of TED India in November 2009. Mather had just spent half of the precious twelve minutes allotted to him describing a business that indeed doesn't exist: a service that someone being asked to pay a bribe could hire to get her business transacted without paying it. People would flock to such

To discuss these ideas on Twitter, use these hashtags:

#fourthsector   *#CapitalismsR&D*

a business, Mather noted, provided the cost of the service was a much smaller price to pay than the bribe requested, which it easily could be. This is how Mather explained his thinking:

> The common man does not wake up every day and say, "Hmm, let me see who I can pay a bribe to today," or "Let me see who I can corrupt today." Often it is the constraining or the back-to-the-wall situation that the hapless common man finds himself or herself in that leads him to pay a bribe. In the modern-day world, where time is at a premium, and the battle for subsistence is unimaginably tough, the common man simply gives in and pays the bribe just to get on with life.
>
> One image that has haunted me from my early business days is of a grandmother, seventy-plus years, being harassed by the bureaucrats in the town planning office. All she needed was permission to build three steps to her house, from ground level, making it easier for her to enter and exit her house. Yet the officer in charge would not simply give her the permit for want of a bribe.
>
> Now, imagine you are being asked to pay a bribe in your day-to-day life to get something done. What do you do? Of course you can call the police. But what is the use if the police department is in itself steeped in corruption? Most definitely you don't want to pay the bribe. But you also don't have the time, resources, expertise, or wherewithal to fight this.
>
> Yet the market forces around the world have not yet thrown up a service where you can call in, pay a fee, and fight the demand for a bribe. Like a BribeBuster service, or 1-800-FIGHT BRIBES. Such services simply do not exist.

A group of us have been working on a pilot basis to address individual instances of demands for bribes for common services or entitlement. And in all forty-two cases where we have pushed back such demands using existing and legitimate tools like the Right to Information Act, video, audio, or peer pressure, we have successfully obtained whatever our clients set out to achieve without actually paying a bribe. And the cost of these tools has been substantially lower than the bribe demanded. I believe that the tools that worked in these forty-two pilot cases can be consolidated in standard processes in a BPO kind of environment, and made available on Web, call-center, and franchise physical offices, for a fee, to serve anyone confronted with a demand for a bribe. The target market is as tempting as it can get.

Chris was in the room at the time and reports the audience actually gasped before applauding when Mather got to "1-800-FIGHT BRIBES."

What caused the gasp? Mainly it was the shock of the new—the novel thought being that a problem long seen as a social issue, properly addressed by police forces, courts, the World Bank, education reform, and other policy apparatus, could be a business opportunity (and a straightforward one, responding to market demand, rather than a chance to subcontract to a government agency and do its work more efficiently). It's such a good idea that it causes one of those "how come nobody ever thought of that before?" moments.

But there's more to gasp about. To understand what we mean, put yourself back in the VC mind-set. You know the key question to raise about a business plan isn't "Does the market want it?" but "What's the exit?" In other words, how will value be built for the investors in BribeBusters? The short-term buyer behavior is predictable enough. Of course customers would pay, say, three hundred rupees to avoid paying three thousand if the service were good enough and marketed properly. Sales would go like gangbusters, and gross margins would be generous. But where does the business go from there? Well, let's think about that. If BribeBusters caught on, it would promptly establish a new feedback loop for corrupt officials: ask for a bribe, endure a hassle, and fail to get cash. As the return on extortion declined, the practice would die out (at least at this petty scale). Eventually there would be no reason for the permit seekers to hire an outside party, and the market would disappear.

Oops—no exit. Now will you fund this start-up? Maybe not. And yet Shaffi Mather is eager to do so.

It isn't that he hasn't thought things through to this point. To the contrary, this is the point he starts from. From his perspective, it's a bonus that the business could make him and his partners some money in the short term, but the larger objective is to stamp out corruption in the Indian bureaucracy. And what if competitors rushed into the space and grabbed market share from BribeBusters—and they all collectively put themselves out of business even faster? That would be the grandest success imaginable.

Mather envisions an enterprise that achieves decent financial profits in the course of producing immense positive externalities. Imagine putting in place a force that over time eliminates a kind of corruption in the Indian economy (and then elsewhere, because it's an idea easily spread) and in turn makes the economy more productive. To invoke our metaphor of seeing value in color, this would be a business that thrives forever in Technicolor, but only briefly in black and white. Strikingly—and this is something we believe will become increasingly common—it would blur the boundaries between what we think of today as the private and public sectors. A for-profit venture might succeed at solving a social problem.

This sector-blurring is what this chapter is all about. We'll explore why separate sectors have emerged and how they differ. We argue that the high walls that have been erected between them are eroding as capitalist enterprises begin to measure in color and take greater ownership of their nonfinancial impacts. The ultimate blending of the sectors that we envision will take time, to be sure, and patient capital will be required, because, in following the short-term profit signal, managers are actually led away from value creation. To follow the broader value gradient takes a different business model.

Where should we search for enterprises that see in color and engage in invisible handshakes? We foresee many new models being discovered by the social sector, because it values nonfinancial value more than financial. In contrast with the private sector, it cares more about spreading successful models and less about building bigger institutions (or should). Ideas developed there often challenge the traditional boundaries of business, government, and NGOs.

That makes the social sector, we suggest, the hotbed of disruptive innovation for business models in the global economy—by analogy, capitalism's R&D lab. Among the changes being incubated there are the next-generation solutions that will capitalize fully on new conditions and render today's narrow form of capitalism obsolete.

Why Separate the Sectors in the First Place?

The separation of the economy into for-profit, nonprofit, and public sectors is so familiar to today's Western capitalist as to go unquestioned. But why did these distinct sectors arise?

Often when economists talk about public goods, they speak in terms of market failures: these are broadly desired goods, such as a capable national defense, that don't emerge automatically from people's trading activities because they are nonrival and nonexcludable. If you're an Israeli, for example, the fact that your country's military defends you doesn't mean that it defends some other citizen any less; you two are not rivals for a scarce good. And there would be no practical way to exclude you from that defense if you chose not to avail yourself of it. So Israel provides for that public good by compelling all citizens to donate their share—of taxes and time served—to the Israeli Defense Forces.

More plainly, when society's wants and needs aren't met through market means, that constitutes a market failure. But it doesn't follow that every time resources are allocated through nonmarket means, it is because markets are unequal to the challenge. (This is a point made by those who argue for privatizing the U.S. Social Security system, for example.) Sometimes it's only through lack of human imagination and innovation that a market-based solution has not been devised. Our friend Michael Schrage, an MIT lecturer with whom we have valuable and enjoyably combative discussions, made this point at a recent symposium on the future of capitalism. Having heard the term *market failure* used one too many times to explain the persistence of some social problem, he decided to call the group on it. "Was it a market failure," he asked, "that for hundreds of years we had luggage without wheels?"

Schrage holds what we might call a Panglossian view of markets—essentially that markets will always do the most effective job of resource allocation. (Hearing the term *market failure* one too many times that day might have meant he heard it once.) But in at least some cases, Shaffi Mather (and his notional VC) would agree. One doesn't have to deny the possibility of market failure to concur that market-based solutions can be devised to meet most human needs, including many that have in some countries been provided by the state.

In some cases both solutions have been tried, and the nonmarket approach found better; for example, the Red Cross finds that paying for donated blood tends to attract tainted contributions to the pool. But probably in many spots where effective market solutions have not emerged—the yet-to-be-invented luggage wheels of the world—it's because the solutions are complicated. In economist-speak there may be conditions of *information asymmetry* and *bounded rationality*. (It's handy how these terms assign the fault to people for not knowing everything, allowing the free market concept to survive unscathed.) Alternatively, the apparent complexity may be the result of untested assumptions, or a simple lack of sufficient imagination to combine wheels and suitcases. For example, microfinancing turned a social problem—poverty—into a profitable business by inventing a business model that had not occurred to traditional lenders, demonstrating a market-based solution that startled the world.

It is the point of view of the Monitor Inclusive Markets (MIM) team, a unit of strategy-focused management consulting firm Monitor Group, that many more market solutions remain to be discovered.[1] Founded in 2006 by Ashish Karamchandani, who had previously led the firm's Mumbai office, MIM focuses on "using market-based solutions to create social change by improving the lives of lower-income Indians . . . by identifying, developing, and catalyzing business models that engage the poor in socially beneficial markets."

In May 2009, MIM held a conference called "Emerging Markets, Emerging Models" in Delhi. We are indebted to Karamchandani and his colleagues, among them Nikhil Ojha and Prashant Lalwani, for gathering an unmatched concentration of innovators in one place. The conversations that started there ramify throughout this book.

For example, MIM worked with Jaithirth (Jerry) Rao to help develop a business model for low-income housing in India. Here, to many eyes, was an instance of market failure. MIM's analysis showed that there was plenty of demand for small, well-constructed, no-frills housing; hundreds of millions of people—about one-third of Indian families—had sufficient income and savings to buy a home with perhaps 350 square feet of living space costing 3–4 lakh (on the order of $7,500). But there was no inventory of such homes being built by construction companies. Hence a family earning 5,000–11,000 rupees per month (about $450) might be stuck spending the same cash flow on a 200-square-foot rental flat instead.

Rao, born in Bangalore and educated in India before getting an MBA at the University of Chicago, had spent twenty years at Citicorp before turning his attention to this problem in 2005. A career that featured posts in various parts of the world culminated in his becoming country head for consumer banking in India. So perhaps it's not surprising that he would be the one to find a new market-based solution relying on a change in financing arrangements.

The solution the Value and Budget Housing Corporation (VBHC), of which Rao and Ojha are both board members, successfully piloted three years later makes for a dramatic story. The team recognized that the biggest sticking point in the system was the price of home loans. Banks demanded interest rates of almost 20 percent to provide mortgages. Rao, the former banker, knew that if the banks could be more confident that payments would be made regularly, those rates would come down—and he also saw a way to provide that confidence. If homebuyers' employers would only get involved, the banks could be paid directly and reliably through paycheck withholding. That payment assurance would lower rates to 12 percent or so, radically improving the affordability of the debt. It wasn't an idea that would have occurred to the employers themselves, especially given that it entails some administrative cost, but when it was presented to them as a key to labor productivity (through greater retention and more manageable commutes), it made economic sense.

Meanwhile the team made the case to construction companies that, by building dwellings at reasonable commuting distances from employers willing to set up such arrangements, they could get advance commitments to buy from workers, dramatically lowering the cost of marketing the homes. However, VBHC's support of the construction companies went further. It realized that by developing standard plans for homes across several developments it could create scale efficiencies not only in the design work itself but through the scale-efficient sourcing and construction acceleration such standardization enabled. This practice proved essential to the developers' ability to build housing at costs consistent with the market's ability to pay.

As market solutions go, this is a complex one. With so many moving parts, it's fair to say that it would not have arisen naturally; certainly it hadn't so far. Like BribeBusters, it required a nonfinancial motivation to catalyze a solution to a particular problem rather than look for an easier business to invest in. But once engineered, this business can sustain itself. VBHC expects to build one million homes in the next ten years, a whole lot more than its founders could hope to accomplish through philanthropy. At the same time, it still leaves plenty of opportunity for others to enjoy because that's less than 5 percent of the twenty-two million such homes India is expected to need.

And there's more than one way to skin a low-income housing market. We also met an Indian real estate developer named Joe Silva who delivered the first eight hundred flats of his plan in 2010. In his case, the insight was that low-income workers would buy farther from cities, where housing could be made affordable, if they could buy in to a vibrant community with schools, shopping, and medical facilities. Silva set out to assemble such communities. First came the challenge of making the homes as inexpensive as possible; he scoured the world for low-cost construction techniques and ultimately acquired a firm in the Philippines whose methods impressed him. Owning the builder in turn produced another benefit; Silva's model brings in cash up front, and he channels the profits into a mortgage company that makes affordable loans to buyers. Finally, to help subsidize all of the above, he collects rents from stores that move into his complexes. These rents are higher than elsewhere in the region but a fair price to pay for privileged access to a whole community of new homeowners.

Michael Schrage would be proud. Although Rao, Silva, and Karamchandani have assuredly been motivated by the desire to bring better lives to their customers, there has been no philanthropy or subsidy involved, only the experimentation with business models that hadn't been previously discovered.

Patient Capital, Mixed Returns

The implication of these stories for us is that market solutions can probably be devised to provide for many public goods so that provision for them need not be left to the public sector. But it's important to be clear that for these commercial arrangements to work, we need more than clever innovation. There also must be some relaxing of a few requirements that capitalists have traditionally insisted on. Capital must be patient; "mixed value" (or in our parlance, colorful) returns must be seriously pursued; and ways of gauging success on those non-financial fronts must be in place. This is bending the rules of capitalism in no small way. In fact, it is the lack of these conditions that has kept the sectors separate all this time. Is there any reason to think they could materialize on a large scale?

We think it's not only possible but also inevitable, thanks to the trends we've described in this book: the growing ability to measure what matters, the steady internalization of externalities, and the pursuit of innovation eclipsing the focus on zero-sum competition.

This seems like the right moment to introduce the name Varun Sahni to our narrative. Sahni was, until 2011, the director of Acumen Fund's operations in India. Acumen Fund, founded in 2001, is now probably the most renowned practitioner of what is known as venture philanthropy. Using charitable donations, Acumen funds the development of solutions in health, water, housing, and energy that will be self-sustaining, thereby producing an ongoing return (sometimes financial but at least social) on those philanthropic investments. Investors do not always require the return of their seed capital but will not commit to ongoing financial support. At the same time, similar to the venture capitalists who incubate businesses, Acumen provides management support to social entrepreneurs to help them thrive, rather than simply underwrite them at arm's length.

In its words, Acumen's mission is "to invest patient capital to strengthen and scale business models that effectively serve the poor . . . . [W]e champion this approach as a complement to both charity and pure market approaches." Sahni describes it as "a third way" to achieve socially desirable ends because it does not rely purely on either market-based approaches or philanthropy.

The importance of patient capital can't be overstated, because it removes some of the constraints of the purely financial world. As the word *patient* suggests, these investments assume a long time horizon for their payoff, in real contrast with the short-termism that infects many investors. As Acumen defines it, however, patient capital also involves a healthy tolerance for risk. And even though it aims for financial returns eventually, those will never be the returns it seeks to maximize; rather, it looks for the highest possible social return on its investment and sees the financial return mainly as a key ingredient required to sustain it. As a result, models that didn't work before can take shape. That's because even though a traditional VC wouldn't fund BribeBusters, you can bet Acumen would. By contrast, picture the typical team of MBAs preparing for a business model competition. A compromise on return or defensibility would kill their chances; the winning team's return on financial investment will be fast and sure. Unencumbered by those constraints, the social sector naturally runs a lot more experiments.

Patient capital is the core reason that fundamental, business-model–level change can be incubated in the social sector. In the private sector, the short-term profit signal drowns out all other incentives. Short-tailed peacocks need not apply. But profits can also be gained by following a long-term value signal if one is willing to be patient. We can envision the day when institutional boundaries and habits of mind don't prevent the typical business manager from seeing and seizing those long-term opportunities. But it won't happen until the infrastructure for measuring ROI in color becomes as well established as financial reporting is today. That day isn't here yet. Today the social sector still has a near monopoly on patience.

Sahni himself focuses most on experiments that involve "hybrid business models," in which affiliated for-profit and not-for-profit entities function together as a cohesive business unit and interact with each other on an arm's-length basis while leveraging their respective synergies.

If this sounds familiar, give yourself credit for being alert: Dial 1298 for Ambulance, a business we've mentioned, is just such an entity. Recall that this ambulance company in Mumbai, founded by a group of Indian entrepreneurs (one of whose mothers had suffered from the lack of such service), is for-profit. But its fleet of ambulances is the property of a nonprofit entity, Ziqitska Healthcare Limited, affiliated with it. The nonprofit is able to take donations of ambulances and funds to buy them, something the for-profit service cannot do. And the dispatching service is able to charge customers a market-determined rate, something a charity could not do. Pair them up and you have all you need for a viable system of emergency medical transportation.

We've discovered effective hybrids in other parts of the world. Shekulo Tov (outside Tel Aviv) sells decorative objects made by hand. It's a successful, growing business, but it might not have been if it had to pay for all those hands. As it happens, much of its labor is paid for by the Israeli government, because the manufacturing process involved is an ideal form of occupational therapy for some mentally handicapped citizens. We can almost feel our Western readers' suspicions rising. Is this just a form of exploitation? The equivalent of Victorian orphanages sending children to work in mills and keeping their wages?

But that's not the reality of the situation. Instead, Shekulo Tov exists because the need for occupational therapy services exceeded the government's ability to provide them. In 2001, Israel passed a Mental Health Rehabilitation Law enabling nongovernmental organizations to provide such services. Irad Eichler, who founded Shekulo Tov, worked with the mentally handicapped as a hostel coordinator and saw the limitations of the services available. In a business built on what they were capable of doing he saw a path to greater self-respect and self-sufficiency for many. Shekulo Tov doesn't only take its workers' efforts and pay them a wage; it also hosts many cultural and recreational activities for them and hundreds of rehabilitants who don't produce its products, taking them on bicycling tours, for example, and other social outings.

The fact that Shekulo Tov exists means that many more mentally challenged individuals have access to services. By the end of 2009, when its founders were recognized by the World Economic Forum as its Social Entrepreneurs of the Year, Shekulo Tov was providing employment and rehabilitation services to more than fourteen hundred individuals through nine separate creative enterprises and eighty shop sites across Israel. It's worth noting that the backgrounds of Shekulo Tov's leadership team make it as much a hybrid as the business itself. Eichler, its young, energetic, and passionate founder, had worked only in the social sector previously. His chief executive, Offer Cohen, brought the business skills to the table having been a chief operating officer in the food industry.

Varun Sahni anticipates that it will take this kind of hybrid arrangement to create self-sustaining solutions to many socially important problems. Sahni trod the path in reverse; he was a private equity investor before he came to Acumen. But he doesn't see any loss of opportunity in that transition. "There is no bigger opportunity in the world," he says, "than providing basic services—food, shelter, health, and education—to the next three billion." He's referring to the coming growth of world population, which will occur overwhelmingly outside the mature economies of the West. What many people foresee as a crushing social challenge he casts as the market opportunity to dwarf all others. Sahni told us his next plan is to raise a fund to invest only in hybrid organizations with this focus.

One of Acumen's signature investments in a hybrid enterprise has been the LifeSpring Hospitals network, which provides basic but high-quality health care to expectant mothers and their infants from low-income families in India. It sounds like a typical worthy cause in a part of the world where infant mortality is still very high by world standards. But LifeSpring's services are not provided free of charge; the hospitals are in fact a for-profit business, and LifeSpring has grown to be the largest provider of maternity care in South India.

The network operates as a joint venture between Hindustan Latex, a huge Government of India enterprise (public corporation), and a group of social entrepreneurs backed by Acumen. Note that the structure is a for-profit hospital chain, half-owned by the world's largest condom company—Hindustan Latex makes a billion of them per year—which is a public corporation, and half-owned by the Acumen fund. And the whole affair makes a contribution to two public policy goals: reining in the birth rate and reducing infant mortality.

All that sounds very weird to a Western capitalist's ears. Certainly it's an innovation harder to grasp than wheeled luggage. But at the end of the day, it works. Charging a tiny fee, a LifeSpring hospital can still manage to sustain itself once it is up and running if it maintains a very tight focus—and because it is operated as a business, it does keep its offering focused and its processes disciplined. Since its founding in 2005, LifeSpring has delivered seven thousand babies and cared for more than seventy thousand patients. By the time you read this, LifeSpring will comprise thirty hospitals in South India and will have launched a franchising model to spread its model even further. As a charity it simply could not have achieved the scale of the impact it is having.

The Social Sector as Capitalism's Silicon Valley

The realm of venture philanthropy, as we've been describing, is one place where we've seen the rules of capitalism relaxed and reformed to produce something new and important. The focus isn't so relentlessly placed on optimizing ROI in the short run. The returns being sought are grander—one might say more strategic. If you think about it, it sounds a lot like the R&D function in a business, doesn't it? Any business that hopes to endure makes investments in next-generation innovations and knows it must bend the rules for them in their early stages. Few ideas can hatch into new businesses unless they are sheltered for a while from the cruel world, so new-product development projects usually get to measure their progress in different terms (such as market response versus profitability) and enjoy the support of more patient capital.

By analogy, this is what we see in the development of next-generation capitalism. Cultivated in somewhat protected coves, new models like Varun Sahni's hybrids are being allowed to reach the point of viability. And among them will be the disruptive innovations that will ultimately supplant the incumbent model. As businesses increasingly aim to create returns not limited to financial (and therefore are willing to accept relatively low financial returns if the social returns are good), and as they relax the requirement of a defensible advantage (and, to the contrary, seek to spread any model that proves effective), this is what capitalism will turn out to be. But the early experiments and successes with such models are happening in the social realm. That's why the title of this chapter calls the social sector "capitalism's R&D lab."

The R&D analogy also implies that substantial experimentation is taking place without certainty that the results will prove useful—another given in the basic research undertaken by companies. (As Rick Rashid, head of Microsoft research, told *Forbes India*, "We're doing things that when we start, we don't know if they are going to be successful. For us it's more about ideas and taking risks.") Along these lines, we are struck by the new funding mechanism recently piloted in Great Britain called social-impact bonds. Essentially, this represents a new way of providing the funds necessary to take a chance on a promising but far from proven idea for accomplishing some social goal.

The best way to describe how social-impact bonds work is by reference to the first such effort. In this case, the social problem being targeted was recidivism by prison parolees. The idea, cooked up by a criminal justice think tank, was that relapses into criminality could be substantially reduced if offenders were subjected to a specific set of interventions both before and after they left prison. Most people who heard about the interventions proposed by the think tank believed they sounded reasonable. The problem was that there was no hard evidence that they would yield results, or that the costs of those extra activities would be justified by a sufficient drop in crime. For a government under pressure not to waste taxpayers' money, it was too risky to fund the program. Patient capital is not much in evidence in the government sector at the moment.

But the committed advocates of the new idea saw another way to get to the proof points it needed. They proposed that a pilot go ahead wholly financed by nongovernmental investments but with a commitment by the government that if the new approach proved efficacious it would be adopted. In that case, furthermore, they proposed that the funders of the pilot be repaid and even allowed to become financial beneficiaries of the cost savings realized, up to a return of 13 percent on their initial investment. U.K. justice secretary Jack Straw agreed, and the pilot was designed. It would focus on a group of three thousand inmates at Peterborough Prison who were serving sentences of less than twelve months. The services they received would not draw on government resources but would be delivered by social sector entities having experience working with offenders. To cover the costs, private investors would put up £5 million. A 7.5 percent reduction of recidivism was targeted based on the costs of the new program. If the outcome of the pilot wasn't at least that good, the investors would receive no recompense.

Pause for a moment to appreciate the beauty of this solution. It relieves a risk-averse government institution of the need to take a gamble on an unproven approach; if the new way doesn't work and recidivism remains too high to justify its increased costs, then the government is not out a penny and gets credit for engaging in a constructive experiment. But if the idea turns out to have been a good one, it finds its way to implementation at scale, and society benefits. If you squint a little, it's not unlike the ambulance hybrid: socially minded investors invest patient capital, accepting high risks for less than market returns; if the risk pays off, society improves and investors come out whole—or perhaps better.

Where did this piece of financial-cum-social engineering come from? The architect is Sir Ronald Cohen, founder of Apax Partners, often called "the father of private equity," who aspires to connect the capital markets to the social sector. "I think it is going to be . . . powerful," he says, "because the impact of the recent crisis on people's consciousness has emphasized the importance of dealing with the social consequences of the [capitalist] system." According to a June 2010 profile in the Telegraph, Sir Ronald is fervent in his belief that this is more than just the latest business fad, but a crunch-point moment for the entire Western market-based system: "It is not enough to increase the standard of living at the high end. I think societies everywhere will come to the conclusion that an important part of the capitalist system is having a powerful social sector to address social issues, because government doesn't have the resources."

Cohen continued, "Part of the problem in terms of the scale of social issues is financing, so we applied our expertise in the financial world as well as our expertise in the social sector with the same intensity as David [Hutchison, chief executive of Social Finance] did at Kleinwort Benson and I did at Apax. From that process came the social-impact bond."

Social-impact bonds (which are not technically bonds, but never mind) have so quickly been recognized as a brilliant means by which to incubate new models that the United Kingdom is now using them to fund other forms of early intervention that might fend off big social problems. And the idea has now traveled to the United States, as the organization administering the financing, Social Finance, announced in early 2011 that it is establishing a sister organization in Boston.

We'd say the same, by the way, about microfinance, perhaps the progenitor of the inclusive business models. Microfinance, according to analysts at Microfinance Information Exchange, by now comprises institutions operating in more than a hundred countries, serving more than 75 million clients. For something called "micro" it has become very big indeed. What's more, it has in turn enabled other micro-models to take hold. Famously, it gave rise to the "phone ladies" of Bangladesh. Starting in 2001, Grameen Foundation's Village Phone program allowed women in desperately poor areas to invest in a key piece of capital equipment—a telephone—that would produce steady returns as many people in the village paid tiny sums for the use of it. At one point, before the declining price of phones made them more accessible to even the poor in Bangladesh, it was estimated that each of the country's 250,000 phone ladies served a customer base of more than four hundred people.

More recently, there is the example of what could be called the "water men." Drawing on the same model, Iqbal Quadir, who founded Grameenphone, has launched the Clean Water Initiative. It provides microcredit to enable local entrepreneurs to buy small-scale water purification systems and then sell the clean, affordable, arsenic-free water to their neighbors.

Ironically, microfinance is becoming embattled because . . . it's profitable. Financial institutions with no particular concern for inclusiveness or other social goals stood aside while socially moti-vated businesspeople proved the value of the new business model. Then they jumped in. This makes those who see microfinance as all about inclusiveness suspicious. Our point of view is, "Who cares?" Loan-sharking and other forms of exploitation can and must be made unattractive through penalties. But adding profit to positive externalities sweetens the incentive and attracts more capital to an institution that is both financially and socially useful. In the end, low-income societies get more growth, and the luggage keeps on rolling.

Suppose you were an inclusive-minded businessperson who'd successfully pioneered an innovative business model and someone entered the same business for the sheer profit of it. How would you feel? If inclusiveness were your primary goal, you'd applaud: you'd have engaged in a valuable invisible handshake, doing what was necessary to make your socially valuable enterprise viral.

Microfinance is an icon of this: a sustainable business model innovation motivated by social goals that proved so valuable that profit-oriented businesses have adopted it. Inclusive housing will follow. And perhaps BribeBusters will turn its business into a platform that lasts a long time and operates around the world. The more recognition we give to nonfinancial motivations, the more the social sector will prove to be an R&D lab for business models.

To be sure, it will still be a long way from drawing board to common practice. Change is hard for incumbents even when it is in their interest (let alone when it isn't). When we heard the story about the new model Jerry Rao and MIM had piloted for low-income housing, we were struck by something that Monitor's Smarinita Shetty said about the construction companies involved in it. You might assume that, of all the players faced with the challenge of a new way of operating, builders would have the easiest time embracing it. With the financing issue resolved, marketing made easy, and enormous pent-up demand to serve, they needed only do the thing they already knew how to do: build houses. But according to Shetty, it wasn't as simple as that. Because the new arrangement involved up-front commitments from buyers, houses had to be built on schedule and on budget. In the past, builders could simply incur whatever costs they incurred and cover them with cost-plus pricing at the end, but now profitability depended on careful management of expenses. Delays had even generated positive returns for developers by causing them to hold on to land longer in a booming land market. Another painful adjustment was the necessary shift from a high-margin to a high-volume business model: instead of focusing on high-end offerings to ensure high profits, they had to count on many more homes sold at slimmer margins to generate the same profits. Therefore, the real drivers of the change were not the established builders Shetty and others on the team approached first. Instead, she said, the change came "from people starting this as a new business."

The Fourth Sector

The whole point of having an economy is to make people better off. If VC or corporate investments are required to develop new social networking apps, and government grants are needed to create the Internet, but venture philanthropist investments are the means of jump-starting new housing markets, is there a difference? Our friend Heerad Sabeti doesn't believe there is one. (We owe acknowledgement to Sabeti for creating the "fourth sector" label and developing a lot of this point of view.)

While we're watching much of the incubation of capitalism's next form take place in the social sector, Sabeti has been working hard to make it happen more within businesses. He points out that a legal innovation—the establishment of "for benefit" enterprises—would be a catalyst for companies to devote more patient capital to the pursuit of blended value.

Under U.S.-style capitalism, he reminds us, there is a bright line drawn between the sectors, not only in people's minds but also in matters of law. Whether an enterprise is for-profit or not-for-profit has hard and clear implications not only for taxation but also for the kinds of activities it engages in and where. The rigidity of those sector definitions is a constraint on organizations' being socially responsible.

To understand his thinking, picture the two ends of the spectrum of organizations that deliver value to society: public and private. *Public* means government, which by necessity and long tradition addresses those social needs that private enterprise passes over. But government is not the only source of service that does not seek profit. It has always been true that government is not capable of doing all society desires, and that some citizens are willing to devote more energy to social betterment than others, so a third sector emerged between public and private. This is the realm of the nongovernmental organization that works to cure social ills but is not part of the bureaucracy of the state.

If you picture this spectrum in your mind, then, with the public sector on the left-hand side and the private sector on the right, this third sector would sit between them but much closer to the left. Sabeti points out, first, that in the G7 economies the distinctions among these three sectors are solidified by laws, tax rules, reporting requirements, certification protocols, and ultimately habits of mind that have typecast people and organizations.

But as measurement and accountability are increasingly applied to NGOs and governments and as transparency and responsibility for externalities to businesses, it would seem the sectors are approaching one another. Sabeti's question is, Why isn't there a fourth sector, as well, situated in a spot where the existing three converge?

What would it mean to be situated there, just shy of the private extreme? These would be entities that earned a financial profit—that's why they're over there toward the right—but that operated by rules whereby pursuit of profit was one of several goals, such as avoiding social costs and producing social benefits. Sabeti uses the term *for benefit*. It emphasizes that for-benefit businesses are designed to pursue benefits that include but are not limited to financial profits for their owners. In addition, these fourth sector organizations could be funded by commercial customers, philanthropists, taxes, or individuals, depending, as with any business, on whom their product appealed to. These mixtures already happen when national parks accept donations, user fees, and tax money, or businesses donate goods to auctions for nonprofit entities, or a company pays to brand a municipally owned stadium, or, of course, when individuals make tax-deductible contributions.

On the for-profit side, Sabeti's fourth sector is not a purely theoretical one; we all know of many companies that color outside the lines in this way, and many managers who would be inclined to do more of it. But, as Will Patten, executive director of Vermont Businesses for Social Responsibility, has observed, "There's a problem: corporate law in the United States compels any publicly traded corporation to put the financial interests of shareholders above all other interests—and shareholders have come to expect immediate and sizable returns on their investments."

So Sabeti's focus has been on creating legal status for companies that choose to operate as fourth sector businesses, and simultaneously on building up the kind of armature that supports the other three sectors. The latter will consist of such practical supports as networks of like-minded managers, and specialized fourth sector practices within law, accounting, and other professional services firms. One potentially important element—investment funds with a social mission like green investment, or in times past shunning of South African investments—has been established for decades.

We're fans of Sabeti's work because it offers a way to alter the rules of capitalism and heal a rift that should never have opened. It would oblige and empower at least some management teams to embrace their externalities rather than be compelled by the threat of share-holder lawsuits to externalize as much as possible. Although Sabeti's theory of change is different from ours, the goal is consistent. Both envision social entrepreneurs and innovators discovering new kinds of value-creating business models by using patient capital and measuring value broadly.

But based on what we've said about externalities, you know where we're going: we would blur the sector boundaries even more thoroughly. Consider a simple example. We told you about Shekulo Tov, the home goods manufacturer that keeps mental health patients beneficially employed. Now think about one of the emerging models that Monitor's Inclusive Markets team likes to tout: the "paraskilling" model. You are familiar with, for example, what a paralegal is: a person who lacks the education and credentials of a full-fledged attorney but who is perfectly capable of mastering some elements of the service a law firm provides to clients. Now picture how that could translate to a medical or educational setting. Aravind Eye Care System has become renowned for performing cataract surgery that is high quality, fast, and cheap using a paraskilling model. Surgeons are supported by teams of workers who do prep and follow-up tasks expertly despite being otherwise surprisingly uneducated. Another enterprise, Gyan Shala, is doing the same in elementary schools by supplying software that equips paraskilled instructors to impart specialized bands of knowledge, under the supervision of an experienced teacher. One blog called it "the McDonald's of education." Paraskilling is the equivalent of industrialization for knowledge work—the dividing up of artisanal work into discrete tasks performed by lower-skilled workers. And by the way, just as the assembly line enabled the division of labor to reduce costs of the industrial product during the twentieth century, networks now allow the thousands of parateachers of a given subject to share their experiences and improve the impact of their work. It's assembly line 2.0.

But here's our question, then: is Gyan Shala the same kind of enterprise as Shekulo Tov? Do they belong in different sectors, or the same one? The question is either very hard or very easy to answer. If four sectors exist, it's hard to place them in their proper spot. But if every enterprise is a mixed-value enterprise and can support its mission with contributions from customers for each kind of value, then they are just variations on the same theme. Remember Whole Foods, offering a checkout counter impulse purchase of $5 for a food philanthropy? Same again.

The original three sectors have always had more in common than the U.S. tax code would lead one to think. Even the most share-price-obsessed business, for example, has provided a whole range of benefits to its employees. (Milton Friedman was right when he claimed that for-profit businesses produce plenty of social benefit even if they never offer a penny to charity, by creating jobs and products that make people's lives easier.) And likewise, even the most altruistic social sector entity has had the responsibility to maximize the productivity of its resources.

What Sabeti calls the fourth sector, then, we would say is becoming the whole ball of wax. Rather than separate the first three sectors and then add a fourth, we anticipate its ethos spanning the whole spectrum, as all entities pursue value defined more broadly. The distinctions among sectors not only have been raised too high but also are wholly artificial. Ideally we would have a system that allowed each enterprise to adjust its value mixture in the way its stakeholders liked it.

In effect, it will become true that all stakeholders are customers of the enterprise. Think of Shekulo Tov's employees; most of them are customers for occupational therapy. Others value the opportunity to provide it. Patient capital investors are customers for improving ambulance services in Mumbai. And some battery customers might buy at Walmart if the retailer pushed Duracell to abandon blister packs. At close range, this might look like "just marketing." Standing on the sun, it's the development of a mixed-value economy that puts nonfinancial benefit on equal legal, institutional, and cultural footing with profit. With the help of measurement systems like the Prosperity Index, the four sectors merge into a continuous spectrum.

As Varun Sahni has observed, the needs of the next three billion people are economic, but in the rich world we tend to label them "social," perhaps betraying a belief that only through philanthropy can the poor escape poverty. But as social entrepreneurs and innovators discover new kinds of value-creating business models, by using patient capital and measuring value broadly, they discover not only the social but also the business opportunities inherent in serving a world with growing needs.

Once businesses learn—from their customers and other stakeholders—that mixed value is part of their output they start to own an agenda that used to belong to regulators. P&G, for example, has published long-term sustainability goals, including reducing the amount of "postconsumer waste" from their products to . . . zero. In many parts of the world, pursuing this goal has led P&G to catalyze the development of sophisticated recycling capabilities. In the Philippines, for example, metals, high-density plastics, and paper could be recycled, but not the residual stream of plastic bags and organics. P&G has brought together Italian and U.S.-based companies to create that capability, but taken no stake in the business. Is it uncompetitive to devote management time to these goals? Not in the Fourth Sector, where feedback comes in color.

These labels—*fourth sector, for benefit, mixed value, in color*—matter. In a lovely piece of research, Stanford psychologist Lee Ross teamed with Israeli researcher Varda Liberman and U.S. Air Force Academy faculty member Steven Samuels on an experiment that asked subjects to play an iterated prisoners' dilemma game—one of those games you play in business school that teaches you that the temptation to sell out your buddy to avoid his winning at your expense is very, very strong. The twist was that some groups were told they were playing the "Wall Street game" and others the "community game." In the former case,

70 percent of players assumed the worst and accordingly betrayed their colleagues. In the latter, 70 percent collaborated, betting on reciprocal good behavior. In other words, 40 percent of the players' behavior was determined by the name of the game.

You might notice that this also means 30 percent of the people like to compete, community game or not, and 30 percent will collaborate and be cleaned out by their Wall Street colleagues. But additional research shows that to a high degree, people dropped into a system with established norms are likely to adopt them.

The emerging economies are a critical part of capitalism's evolution not only because they are where the growth is but also because they haven't labeled their societies the Wall Street game.

Crossbreeding

When two populations of a species, from *echidnas* to *Echinacea* to E. coli, come into contact, the mingling of diverse gene pools creates innovations. (It was a new strain of E. coli that produced the toxins of two previously known variants that killed twenty-four and sickened thousands in Germany in 2011.) While the social sector is providing the economy with broader measurements and noncompetitive scaling, the commercial sector still has the resources and muscle to implement ideas at scale. So the innovations being hatched in the R&D labs of the social sector are likely to be taken to scale in the business world. It helps that ideas and people are moving more fluidly between them, further eroding the boundaries and constantly creating new hybrids.

As we were writing this chapter, for example, California-based industrial design firm IDEO (recently acquired by Steelcase) announced it would launch a unit called IDEO.org. Starting in the fall of 2011, it would apply its "design thinking" methodology to opportunities for social change. The ".org" designation reflects the fact that these will be pro bono engagements. Essentially IDEO is making charitable donations in kind by devoting industrial design talent to social problems—the kind of work it has taken on in the past at the behest of other philanthropists like the Bill & Melinda Gates Foundation.

For traditional businesspeople, this might sound altruistic, but most would probably agree that the corporate sector has a thing or two to teach the social sector. Indeed, it has become commonplace for articles to be published and consultants engaged on the question of how philanthropic organizations can operate more like businesses. Over forty years ago, Roderick MacLeod began a *Harvard Business Review* article called "Program Budgeting Works in Nonprofit Institutions" with these words: "Professionals in nonprofit service organizations have long resisted the inauguration of cost accounting concepts (in many instances with good reason), but their resistance is breaking down in the face of supporters' demands for better controls over expenditure of the money, materials, and manpower they contribute."

In the intervening decades, many nonprofits have adopted practices pioneered by business to market themselves, manage their projects, and improve measurement of and accountability for outcomes. But one upshot of the infection of the social sector with business sector thinking and practices has been that the two realms, formerly thought to be miles apart, are increasingly recognized as having some things in common. As a result, increasingly, the door has been left open for some thinking to flow in the other direction. Thus we saw, as two convenient examples from recent months, Jennifer Aaker and Andy Smith writing in the *McKinsey Quarterly* about "What Nonprofits Can Teach the Private Sector about Social Media" and Nancy Lublin, in a book called *Zilch: The Power of Zero in Business*, offering lessons for motivating workers, branding, and more from the cash-strapped social sector outfits she's worked with.

The cross-pollination has reached a point where it is possible to believe Jeff Raikes, who migrated from president of Microsoft's Business Division to leadership of the Bill & Melinda Gates Foundation, when he claims that it was not a drastic change. Gideon Rachman of the *Financial Times*, who interviewed Raikes about the transition, had this to report:

> He remembers that when he moved over from Microsoft, everybody warned him he was entering a very different world. The foundation would be full of touchy-feely types and there would be no market forces with which to gauge

success or failure. But the basic job, as he sees it, is rather similar—managing a large organization that is growing rapidly, setting priorities, demanding evidence and numbers to back up hunches, developing new ideas that will change the world. "Microsoft is all about intellectual property," he says, "and so is the Gates Foundation." At the foundation, the staff is working away on everything from finding a vaccine for HIV to discovering drought-resistant strains of rice.

So will IDEO be a conduit for more innovations to cross from the private to the social sector? Without a doubt. But equally, we think, it will bring innovations back from that sector to its engagements with for-profit clients. Its work in the social space will grant it the design freedom to find wholly new ways of solving problems and to try them out in real-world settings. Increasingly, despite all the efforts of a capitalist system seemingly determined to keep a wedge between them, the sectors are interacting—and the distinctions between them are being blurred.

Advantage: Emerging Economies

BribeBusters, Shekulo Tov, LifeSpring and Hindustan Latex, Joe's and Jerry's housing businesses, all elicit that classic head-slapping response to innovation. It's an admiring incredulity, as in "no one's thought of this before?"—the same feeling you get when you discover you can now call your lost iPhone and it will tell you where it is (or, we suppose, that people got when the first luggage maker added those wheels).

But many mixed-value innovations that feel natural in the societies that spawned them seem out of place in the advanced economies. Why?

First, these emerging societies have not been trained by generations of DuPont equation acolytes to see in black and white and to dismiss those who don't. We'll theorize that where incomes are low and much of the economic activity is by barter, financial constructs do not provide the structure for thinking about so much of life. Second, the need for "social" action is in many ways strongest in emerging economies, given the proportions of their populations struggling for decent subsistence. And third, there seem to be weaker barriers to interaction among sectors, and fewer of the institutional distinctions that Sabeti points to. Because the lines between the sectors are brightest in the most mature economies (though drawn in different places, contrasting the U.S., the EU, and Singapore, as examples) it has been easy to draw the conclusion that compartmentalizing affairs in this way is one of the steps toward maturity.

Turn this around, though, and it means that the emerging economies don't have the West's artificial separations to overcome. In formerly socialist countries like India, Israel, and of course China, the role of the state is intermingled with the roles of business and NGOs. As only one example of this, we recall reading about a fledgling business in China called Sinovac Biotech, which was just beginning to make money on its production of vaccines when the avian flu scare erupted in 2005. Its founder, a physician-turned-entrepreneur named Yin Weidong, halted all work on Sinovac's own research and instead threw its resources into the quest for a SARS vaccine even though he had no hope of cornering the market on a breakthrough. To do otherwise in the face of such a clear social need would have been unthinkable. And the fact that he collaborated with the public sector so generously did not hurt his business. Today, Sinovac Biotech is one of China's leading researchers and producers of vaccines. In the West, we'd struggle with labeling this as philanthropy, as an assault on shareholders, or as cause marketing. In the fourth sector, we'd call it good business.

You may have wondered why we've offered fewer examples from China than its future importance to the global economy warrants. The answer is that we don't feel that the label "R&D lab for business models" applies there to the same degree. True, China is mixing free enterprise, state-led economic development, and "call it Communism and move on" politics to create something never seen at such daunting scale. Chinese capitalism, by whatever name, is a system of rules, and some of them will surely spread globally. But we have not discovered much in the way of business model innovations at the scale of the enterprise.

As for the strong role of the Chinese state, this constitutes a model that certainly won't be adopted everywhere. But state capitalism has worked well in Singapore for thirty years, seems to be showing promise in the United Arab Emirates, and is lifting hundreds of millions of Chinese out of poverty. China in fact illustrates the fundamental point of the fourth sector: that social and economic objectives can be pursued by mixed-value organizations without violating some rule of physics. Government organizations, too, are mixed-value enterprises—but until we measure them in color, we can't see their profits. In black and white, government is a cost center.

And China's unchallenged, centralized economic power may create business innovations to support the world's social goals that even Michael Schrage couldn't bring about through markets alone. A society growing 10 percent annually has a pressing need to minimize its consumption of energy and materials and its expulsion of waste, and the Chinese government has begun strong efforts to steer the nation's development down a more sustainable path.

This was in evidence at Shanghai Expo 2010, which attracted 73 million visitors—95 percent of them Chinese—over six months. China had announced that the expo would be the largest such event ever. In the end, it eclipsed the record of 64 million attendees set by Japan in 1970. On only one day, October 16, 2010, more than a million visitors entered the park. The *New York Times* wrote about the efforts made to ensure that success: workers at state-run factories were requested to take the eight-hour bus ride to attend and threatened with wage cuts if they declined. This was not much of a holiday; as Chris can testify, a visitor without some form of special access might easily have spent four hours sitting in the blinding sun waiting for half an hour's experience. The *Times* placed the effort in the context of the importance China places generally on breaking world records. But perhaps the goal here was deeper: to maximize the nation's exposure to a strong message about China's future economic direction.

The story forcefully told at the China pavilion was that the path of growth for China will be wiser than it has been, and more harmonious than the West's. Without ringing the alarm bells of *An Inconvenient Truth*, China's leaders were announcing that rising incomes would be spent in ways that consumed less energy and fewer materials. The event came to be called Green Expo because of its emphasis on sustainable cities.

Beyond jawboning the population at the China pavilion, the SAIC pavilion (SAIC-GM-Wuling is the Chinese company formed around GM's investment in China) displayed a vision of mass-customized public transportation that was part Jetsons, part green good sense. Need a lift for a quick solo trip to the store? Family of five going out to the park? Need wheels for a date? Ask (via smart device) and you shall promptly receive: a robotic, electric-powered pod of requisite carrying capacity rolls up to your door to take you where you need to go. Fully equipped with connections, sensors, and intelligence, it will let you drive—safely—or take care of the chauffeuring on its own if you're not in the mood, prefer to watch a video, or are suffering an episode of high blood alcohol.

Although there's nothing amazing about the technology—the apparatus involved seems a lot closer to reality than the Apollo program did in 1961—the idea of coordinating the investments and destructions (e.g., of car companies' markets, of existing rights of way) would make this a fantasy anywhere in the developed world. In Germany recently, Chris was part of a discussion that covered the small trials of electric vehicles, the scarcity of investment available for the smart grids needed for charging them, the uncertainty about carbon pricing needed to convince investors to underwrite development, as well as the mixed reception of shared vehicle programs in Paris, Copenhagen, and elsewhere. It's not that this mixture might not eventually cook up into electrified vehicles. It's that, whether or not EVs are an important part of a green transportation system, if China decides to develop and deploy SAIC's vision, the odds are good that it will achieve the goals it sets—as it did with Expo.

Is there a difference between the U.S. Apollo program and the (notional) deployment of green transportation in China? We think they are both great fourth sector examples. Government sets the goals (on behalf of the people it represents), the commercial sector profits, technological development advances, and national political, financial, and social goals are achieved.

The difference is that in the United States, the government had to go to the moon to find a green field. (We reject the pun on green technology but accept one on green cheese.) Although there was plenty of revolving-door pseudocompetition to build components for the

Apollo program (and the SAIC sourcing process would likely be more, not less, corrupt), no one owned the right of way through space, and the moon was the backyard of no voters. The SAIC model could well displace citizens and competitors—eight-hour bus rides writ large.

China's form of fourth sector economy will be influential in the global economy, without a doubt, because others will do what it takes to get a share of the funds it spends—our primary model of how old capitalists learn new tricks. But again, so far we have not seen China developing mixed-value business models that will invade the global capitalist ecology. Although it affirms the fourth sector argument, it makes little contribution to the contention that the social sector will produce the new business models of capitalism. You haven't heard accounts from us because we haven't found them.

"Bem Estar Bem": The Beauty of Mixed Value

Before we got to know Brazilian firm Natura, the firm we mentioned in chapter 3 for its rigorous use of triple-bottom-line accounting, it hadn't occurred to us that the cosmetics business might offer a model of mixed-value pursuit. It's an industry, after all, that is easy to see as representing the ugly excesses of the old capitalism. Dominated by a few large pseudocompetitors, it channels billions into the creation of brands designed to delude us with illusions of eternal youth. As a percentage of sales, its branding budgets dwarf the advertising of the mobile carriers we disparaged earlier.

Then we had the experience of talking with Luiz Seabra, Natura's founder. His company is a success story on many levels. It is fast growing (2009 sales grew more than 18 percent to top $2.3 billion, and net income grew 32 percent) and yields healthy returns not only for its shareholders but also for the million-plus independent beauty consultants who distribute its offerings throughout Latin America. Customers swear by its products, which aim to enhance their well-being through natural ingredients and innovative formulations, although that doesn't quite catch the nuances of the company tagline "bem estar bem"—"well being well." Natura also aims at making its customers more confident that they are well. The company is a darling of social responsibility advocates for its commitment to ethical and sustainable sourcing.

But if that sounds like the kind of success every company aspires to, Seabra himself seems to have no interest in being the typical corporate leader. He underscored that by quoting Joseph Campbell's observation that "the privilege of a lifetime is being who you are"—a celebration of individualism Seabra says applies to companies as well. How many corporate executives do you know who make offhand references to comparative mythologists in their interviews? But more important, how many really believe in forging a unique path rather than borrowing best practices and fast following?

Natura started becoming what it is when Seabra was a young man and connected an intriguing idea from his studies with the customer insights he was gaining in his fledging business. He told us that, spending time personally in consultation with clients, he began to appreciate better the meaning of cosmetics and fragrances in their lives. At the same time, he was turning over in his mind a lesson from Plotinus, a neoplatonic philosopher who intrigued him. One particular phrase, "The one is in the whole, the whole is in the one," was "hard to understand with my rationality," he admits, but it spoke to his heart.

Over the years that followed, that seed of insight turned into a conviction that what he was building should not simply be profitable in itself but should profit by being integral to a healthy system. That had all kinds of implications.

In going to market, it meant investing heavily in training its independent, Avon rep–style associates, for many of whom Natura is a first experience of paid work. The company accepts that every year one-third of them will move on, having learned how to do a job well. Natura's reaction is not to figure out how to reduce the cost of training or even to offer incentives not to leave so soon. Rather, it is to take satisfaction in contributing to the skills of the Brazilian (or other host country's) workforce.

In communications with customers, it meant stressing overall well-being and refusing to exploit women's horror of aging. Society's distaste for growing old, Seabra says, is (here he turned to Doris Lessing) "one of the prisons we choose to live inside." So although the rest of the industry scoffed—"They said we were completely crazy because you must create the impression that you can stop time"—he launched a skin care line called Chronos that celebrated the beauty and vitality of mature women.

Procuring the natural ingredients for its formulations meant pursuing sustainability. Working with local growers in the Amazon, for example, Natura created a system that provided for their livelihoods and the healthy propagation of plants. And, as we discuss in chapter 3, in the measurement of performance, it meant redefining success. The company became an early adopter of triple-bottom-line accounting, and it rewards its managers in the same way for social and environmental performance as for financial achievement.

Perhaps most important, in the heat of competition, it meant remembering purpose. On a trip to New York, Seabra later saw huge billboards by a multinational company promoting beauty beyond youth. He was momentarily irritated at the obvious rip-off of his concept. But he quickly reconsidered: "I thought, if this spreads in the world, then this is good for humanity." Why, in that case, consider it one company's property? He came to see it not as a failure of sustainable competitive advantage (that Holy Grail of pseudocompetitors) but as a good idea implemented at scale—the ne plus ultra of venture philanthropists.

The list of Natura's differences could go on and on, and its quest continues. Three times in our conversation, Seabra used the phrase "step by step" to describe the company's progress toward becoming a one that reflects and honors the whole.

A skeptic might mistake Luiz Seabra's philosophizing—his tendency, as he admits, to be "a little bit abstract and a little bit of a dreamer"—for a lack of practical discipline. But he expresses it otherwise: "We should all, all the entrepreneurs of the world, be applying principles of philosophy. We should think of our companies not just as concrete operations, but as projects of the soul."

Abstract it may be, but Seabra's characterization is not just cosmetic. The leadership team recently considered the company mission statement, which declared the intent to grow the number of customers served while maintaining the commitment to sustainability and "bem estar bem." The CFO demurred: "Not 'while maintaining,'" he corrected. "It should be '*through* maintaining.'"

Natura may be the most evolved example we've seen thus far of a company managing its world in full color and maximizing value added to its ecology.

The Surprise Twist

Chris first met Luiz Seabra in Santa Catarina, Brazil, where they were both on the platform of a conference called Expogestaio, which was not staged by an events company for profit but organized bottom-up by some of the city's leading entrepreneurs. They believe that to be a strong business community they need to bring expertise from all over the world to their attention. Annually, more than fifteen hundred people gather at this event.

Seabra's first words were, "Business is an elegant system of thinking and feeling." At the time, it wasn't all that clear what he was talking about. But upon reflection, we've come to see that Natura embodies a sophisticated understanding of this system that reflects all that we have written in part II of this book.

In chapter 3, we argue that the relationship between business and society has been distorted by runaway financial selection. By organizing around profit as the only source of value, business put itself in the position to destroy other kinds. Yochai Benkler has written, "Assuming that we were more-or-less uniformly rational and interested in advancing our own material interests gave us good enough predictions on human behavior, or so we thought, that we were best off designing our systems as though we were indeed creatures of such a character." First we shaped our systems, and thereafter they shaped us.

But society—globally, but particularly in the emerging markets where social issues come to the fore—is pushing back. As you saw in chapter 4, it's become a lot easier to organize this resistance, as connected sensors make visible the total impact of any institution, whether it's a polluting business or a brutal police force, and the generation accustomed to such transparency is motivated to hold organizations accountable. In the future, there will be no rug to sweep things under; externalities will all but disappear. Businesses will take ownership of their external impacts—whether because they believe it's the right thing to do or because they find that it's the profit-maximizing thing to do—because the costs of failing to do so will keep rising.

And this is the elegant surprise: that the ability of technology to empower the members of society ends up aligning the desires of the society with the incentives of the businesses.

It's a scenario that seems at once unlikely and inevitable. When we reach a time when everyone's incentives and economics are transparent, when artificial barriers are removed, and when invisible handshakes are a norm, today's sectors will be no more different than elements of a business value chain. Different societies will favor different solutions depending on attitudes toward individuality, government, income redistribution, and the like. But wheels will find their way onto luggage faster; growth and innovation will be enhanced, unimpeded by artificial barriers. And the benefits of growth will be better distributed; the next three billion will fare better than their predecessors. If the purpose of an economy, stated most basically, is to use resources to fulfill desires, the next version of capitalism will do a better job.

Standing on the Sun

Getting to Yes, first published in 1981 by Harvard's Roger Fisher and William Ury, has had one of the longest runs ever on the best-seller list maintained by *BusinessWeek* magazine. To save you some time, let us provide a three-word capsule: "Interests, not positions." This apothegm encodes a very big idea: that if we know what motivates our partners—business partners, life partners, dinner partners—and ourselves we can more often reach agreements that satisfy everyone, thereby achieving the by now hopelessly clichéd "win-win."

The lesson is sometimes taught through the parable of two sisters fighting over a single orange. The position of each is "That orange is mine!" In the world of rival goods, the positions are irreconcilable. Enter Mom, who in her wisdom (perhaps she attended Harvard's Program on Negotiation the previous week) asks each child what she wants the orange for. One is thirsty for the juice; the other wants the peel to make a cake. Turns out it was a nonrival orange. Win-win.

Standing on the sun, we can see that information technology, taking root in the emerging economies, has the potential to turn much of the global economy into a nonrival economy.

Lots of caveats apply, and we get to them. But let us first review how part II has built the case for this conclusion by viewing each chapter from the sun.

Chapters 3 and 4 are about measurement and its consequences. We argue that under Washington Consensus capitalism, runaway selection for ROE has given financial metrics so much power that the economy no longer allocates resources to their highest and best use. Awareness of this problem has been growing for perhaps fifty years (as evidenced by discussions of triple bottom line, corporate social responsibility, and gross national happiness), and now various factors have come together to make "seeing in color" a timely issue: the loss of confidence that the old way is the only way, the appearance of respected metrics like the Legatum Prosperity Index to extend NIPA, and the accessibility of nonfinancial data. Broader measurements of national economic performance have reached a tipping point; the eye rolling is mostly over. The emerging economies, where economic priorities favor real growth over financial wealth creation, will be first to adopt this point of view and these measurement systems.

Endowed with full-color images of their economies, societies will begin to account for all the costs and benefits of their institutions. Sensing and network technologies make the economy transparent, so there is nowhere to hide externalities. The combination of transparency and activism—each fed by technology—means that society will make its wishes felt and that prices will move toward true costs. In effect, if you drink the juice from an orange and throw the rest away, you'll have to pay for the peel as well. This means you'll be incented to find a nonrival partner, such as a recycler who'll pay you for your used mobile phone.

Chapters 4 and 5 deal with a second runaway and its cure: pseudocompetition and the invisible handshake. True competition is a phenomenon built around scarcity, and in Smith's world of atomistic competition and slow information transmission, well built to manage it, as the twentieth century mostly demonstrated. Pseudocompetition poisoned this beneficial system and entrenched itself very deeply in the rich economies. Without a major shift in the environment, it's hard to imagine how the world's oligopolies could be dislodged.

But things changed: innovation accelerated, and buying power moved into the hands of the young, low-income, emerging-economy buyer. Equally important: for an ever-increasing proportion of the economy, the explosion of digitally transmitted value changed the role of scarcity. The growth of nonrival goods will prove to be more profound a change in the economy than was mass production.

Both shifts are happening gradually, but in chapter 7 we see one of the results. To find organizations whose feedback is broader than financial, of course you'd look in the social sector. And to find entrepreneurs who want their business models to spread more than they want their organizations to grow, again, you'd look in the social sector. So it's natural to find that the social sector has become what we call the "R&D lab for business models" of capitalism.

The caveats: by putting social values of all kinds on a par with economic value, we leave ourselves open (living in the United States) to the dreaded charge of socialism. In fact our views are the height of market capitalism. The ability to measure value of all kinds means that arbitrage can take place across the social and economic worlds; BribeBusters, hardly a nanny-state solution, is a case in point. And the fact that artificial restriction of information sharing will disappear except when it facilitates a market—as in the ninety-nine-cent song download—is an exercise in free marketeerism. In passing, we note that the establishment of federal deposit insurance in the United States—a shift in the risk of putting one's assets in banks that restored confidence and caused funds to flow back to the sector—was attacked in the 1930s as socialism.

Caveat 2: we've told you capitalism is an evolving system of rules. And now we've told you about two major changes and have described the environment that will cause the new form of capitalism to flourish. But if we told you that fish were crawling out of the sea and lungs would give way to gills, and cold blood to warm, we hardly would have predicted the echidnas we mentioned a few pages ago.

The English landowners might have anticipated mechanized harvesters, but skyscrapers would have been beyond their ken because no one had yet thought of the elevator. The actual shape of the new organizations and entities that will arise in a new era of capitalism cannot be predicted.

We also know that the picture of shared value and collaborative trade will strike many as somewhere between naïve and beatific. Every productive system has parasites and free riders, and that won't change. And beachfront property will still be a scarce resource. But with respect to our core premises, (1) information is a nonrival good; as the global economy becomes an information economy it will need new economic rules; (2) information economics will create a new society in the emerging economies; and (3) this society will revolve not around finance and competitiveness but around seeing in color and invisible handshakes, we are confident.

And to return to part I, why will society, through some set of processes impossible to forecast, end up making these choices? Because society, equipped with robust feedback and selection forces, will ultimately choose innovation as the energy source that, like sunlight, leads to all growth. From the sun, it's plain as day.

Moving On

PART III

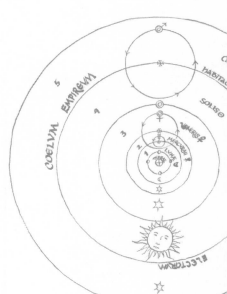

I n part III, we imagine the shape of the economy that will emerge when the rules of capitalism described in part II are in place. Chapter 8 offers a macroeconomic perspective, describing five insights into economic change and presenting a sample of the range of national business models. Chapter 9 focuses on firms and describes the operating rules that will be appropriate in such an economy.

Americans, in particular, may find some features counter to capitalist dogma. They should be as pragmatic as the Chinese.

CHAPTER EIGHT

Call It Capitalism . . .

Global monopolies and national business models

My travels, my discussions with people in Scandinavia, tell me that that
society has learned to combine the power of capitalism with the concern that
comes out of socialism.

—Narayana Murthy (in conversation with authors)

The voice on the line was Indian accented and unhesitating: "I do think that we will move towards a normative form of capitalism across the entire globe, thanks to the financial crisis in the U.S." The speaker was Narayana Murthy, founder of the Indian IT services firm Infosys, and it was late 2009. We'd been talking about the thesis of this book, that capitalism was evolving based on changes in the global economy, and had asked him whether he thought the future would bring convergence on some model. He went on to say which of today's competing models he thought deserved to win in the end: "I would rate Sweden and Norway at number one. It is a wonderful amalgamation of capitalism and socialism."

Murthy wasn't alone in his opinion; we heard similar predictions from other thoughtful leaders. The idea had been in the air for many months that the U.S. style of capitalism would encounter real push back. Narcis Serra and Joseph Stiglitz had recently convened a discussion among a prestigious group of developmental economists, for example, and in June 2008 packaged the proceedings in a volume called *The Washington Consensus Reconsidered: Towards a New Global Governance.* In anticipation of the void it would leave, the phrase *Beijing*

> **To discuss these ideas on Twitter, use these hashtags:**
>
> *#UtilitySector*   *#InnovSector*

Consensus was on many lips, reflecting the many headlines trumpeting the coming Chinese hegemony. After the United States dealt with its banking system woes with some moves smacking of nationalization, a friend, Milken Institute fellow Joel Kurtzman, remarked ruefully that "the French have won." (He was only half–joking).

We noted that even as people began to doubt that the world would converge on the U.S. model, there was yet faith in the idea of convergence. The various economic models around the world were seen to be jostling for leadership in a winner-takes-all contest. Did we believe it, too?

We do not. Although we agree that an amalgam of economic power and social concern will characterize the next era of capitalism, no single set of capitalist rules will fit every society. Global capitalism is an ecology, and we will continue to see cross-pollination among economic models yielding a perpetually diverse and continually adapting set of arrangements. Recalling Romer, we will never be done developing new technologies and new rules, and each will thrive better in some niches than others. Yet we anticipate that certain new features will arise and take root across many economies. In part I we described our "theory of change"; in part II we explained how new kinds of feedback would interrupt two runaways that afflict capitalism, and three positive outcomes that would result. With the repeated caveat that predicting all the outcomes of these changes and their interactions is impossible, the following sections explain the thinking behind five intuitions.

First, in the realm of production, *we'll see the rise of a new class of global "utilities."* Economies of scale are not going away, but they are shifting. The most important ones have to do with the scope and speed of learning, not physical asset utilization, and network effects apply. These global-scale networks of capabilities will become the infrastructure of the world's economy.

Second, to complete the production part of the economy, *a "failure sector" will thrive on the backs of those utility platforms.* More risk-tolerant and nimble firms will tap in to the utilities' infrastructure to take chances on innovative new businesses. Thus we will see a bifurcation of the supply side of the economy.

Third, in the realm of consumption, it's possible that *the famously receding bliss point will stop receding*. With broader measures of value, happiness will be less perceived to be a function of income and consumption, and marketers' urgings to keep up with the Patels, Hwangs, Botelhos, and perhaps even Joneses will fall on deafer ears.

Fourth, in the finance sectors of economies, *financial services firms will increasingly be called out for treating risk as an externality*. There will be an ongoing struggle to prevent the industry's practice of assuming risk but leaving others holding the bag. In addition, there will be a recognition that increased uncertainty "pollutes" the lives of those who don't benefit from it—meaning almost everyone. Reforms will focus on internalizing these nonfinancial costs. (Whether they can succeed is another matter.)

Fifth, in government, *policy makers will strategize about the "model" they should construct for their nation*, much as business leaders now periodically rethink their business models. And again, just as any number of business models can prove viable in a market, it will become clear that national economic models are more likely to coexist than to converge.

Before moving on to the implications for firms (in chapter 9), we'll consider how the explosive growth of emerging economies is implicated in these developments. First, though, let's make the case for each of them.

The New Utilities and the Global Sharing of IP

Did you ever see a movie (it would have to have been in black and white) where a character had several telephones on his desk (it would have to have been "his") to show he was a powerful executive?[1] When phone service first started, there were competing companies signing people up, and a customer of one company couldn't reach a customer of another. It was kind of like the old days of Windows versus Mac. If you needed to call a lot of people, you needed a lot of phones.

As we note in our chapter 5 discussion of competition, it didn't take long for people to realize that certain goods were most economically purveyed through geographic monopolies because of the investment required to set them up. Whether it was telephone wires, gas pipes, railroad tracks, or electrical conduits, the idea of duplicating all the apparatus of a capital-intensive business in the same territory made no economic sense. The competition among multiple players would not result in lower prices for consumers, but only push prices higher. Meanwhile, for some things—perhaps not natural gas but definitely telephone service—it was not only cheaper but also more beneficial to consumers to join a system that everyone else was using. (Recall Brian Arthur's observation of network effects and increasing returns.)

Here's a prediction: just as we now regard it as ridiculous that a desk ever held multiple phones, we will soon regard many additional businesses as natural monopolies—as utilities of a sort. Connectivity and the reduced emphasis on competition will encourage the rise of shared platforms for all kinds of businesses, from medical diagnosis to supply chain logistics.

The very different economics of the information economy, however, will give these new platforms a different character than their monopolist predecessors. It's hard to gain much of an advantage based on economies of scale now that manufacturing and distribution have become largely fungible commodities because of automation, outsourcing, and mass customization. (For example, mobile operators all over the world source their branded phones from the same Taiwan-based company: HTC.) Everyone's unit costs for a given product or service are pretty much equalized. Of course, we don't mean to ignore tactical strokes like Apple's mopping up much of the flash memory supply for a couple of years, but such an advantage is hard to sustain. Instead, competitiveness now hinges on innovation.

And because innovation is the result of firms' learning and adapting, the "economies" to focus on are not of production scale or distribution scope but of learning about and adapting to customers' needs.

The firms that compete best on the economics of learning and adapting will be those having the greatest access to customer experience, i.e., the greatest diversity of customers offering clues to what will be needed next. And these firms will have the most relentless drive and best capability to incorporate what they learn in their operations. Rather than focusing on economies of scale, then, it is more accurate to think in terms of *economies of adaptation*.

Pundits have been touting nimbleness for decades but only loosely tying that attribute to the required information access and learning capabilities. To understand what's needed as a practical matter, consider a well-publicized application of enterprise software in health care from a few years ago. As described by Tom Davenport in *Harvard Business Review*, the Partners HealthCare physician order entry system (POES) combined the patient records, knowledge base, and key operational system of the several Partners HealthCare hospitals in the Boston area. The beauty of this comprehensive database is that it quickly turned into an integrated *learning* system that supported the evolution of knowledge about health care.

As with any data aggregation system, the primary challenge is to get people to enter the data. POES achieves this by making it the only way for physicians to get anything done. When a doctor wants to write a prescription, order a test, or record an outcome, she accomplishes that by entering it into the system, so the data collection about the action happens as a matter of course. When any entry is made, the system performs a check against the patient's record and its accumulated knowledge base, and alerts the doctor to any information relevant to the proposed action. (It also applies algorithmic tests to flag what might be a needless procedure.)

At the back end, the various boards of the hospital—cardiologists, endocrinologists, and so on—periodically review the hospital's outcomes. Based on this fundamental feedback on the quality of decision making, they decide whether the knowledge housed in POES should be altered in any way. Changes, of course, are also made based on other sources of practice guidance the board respects, such as peer-reviewed studies. The result is that the knowledge embedded in POES continually evolves in response to outcomes and new learning elsewhere; this knowledge is then transmitted to practicing physicians in the course of their daily work.

It's hard to imagine how economies of this kind could ever turn south, as economies of scale often do. In the case of the latter, the marginal costs of serving the next customer decline until a market begins to be saturated with whatever product is on offer, and the difficulty of selling it then rises. At some point the returns to growing scale begin to diminish, and past a certain point there are no further economies of scale to be had. But could that ever be true of a learning system? In our electronically hyperconnected world, coordination costs are so low that, in many business realms, a single learning system serving all customers on the planet would constitute the best economic model.

Think, for example, about Salesforce.com, purveyor of Web-based tools for salespeople and sales managers to plan and keep track of their work. Because its software sits in the cloud, and not on isolated desktops or in local networks, the company has easy access to the experience of tens of thousands of diverse companies, all trying to learn how to manage a salesforce better. As MIT's Eric Von Hippel (who has written extensively about innovating based on the input of "lead users") would point out, this puts Salesforce.com in a position to gather new learning about best practices and unmet needs and incorporate it in the Salesforce offering for *all* its customers. This amounts to a textbook case of network-based increasing returns to scale: the more market share that Salesforce.com commands, the faster its offering can improve, and the bigger the performance gap that should open between its product and the second-place provider's. Once that dynamic becomes clear, why would any customer sign up with the vendor that is learning more slowly? In the absence of other differentiators, this dynamic sets up the now-familiar runaway, leading down the path to a monopoly provider.

Here's another illustration we like, and we introduce it with a quiz question: why would the former CEO of the world's leading CAD/CAM software company (Autodesk) ever have become CEO of Yahoo!? Here's the answer: it's because Carol Bartz was among the first to understand that a firm in a position to observe a distributed network of customers using its products could spot trends and innovations in their activity and find ways to profit from them. With tens of thousands of engineers using AutoCAD, the same Sundstrand hydraulic cylinder, say, was being rendered dozens of times by engineers around the world. Why not capture this work in a library and make it available to all users? And equipped then with the records of who checked out that cylinder's rendering, why not sell an analysis to Parker Hannifin, another hydraulics supplier, as a piece of competitive research?

This is the learning system established at Autodesk, and it both provided stickiness to AutoCAD and created an increasing returns situation. Stan Davis uses the term *information exhaust* for such meta information, noting how it can turbocharge a business. Yahoo! proved too great a challenge for Bartz as a turnaround CEO (she lost the job in September 2011), but the insight that it had to compete as a learning system to remain viable was sound. If that isn't obvious, we need only point to the success of Google, which exhibits the economies of adaptation better than anyone else. The products—information delivered to users, well-selected users delivered to advertisers—are created by continual refinement of knowing who wants what, all based on the customers' behavior. Each new Google offer is a bid to achieve unmatched capability to learn and adapt.

Here is our argument, then, in a series of short statements: with every passing year, businesses increasingly depend on innovation to succeed. Innovation is a process of adaptation based on feedback and learning. The opportunities for learning from feedback only grow with the number of customers served and activities observed. Taken to this logical conclusion, it's easy to envision how the bulk of economic activity will come to be organized into such learning systems. As Brian Arthur foretold, these businesses will have winner-take-all tendencies. They will become the twenty-first-century utilities, and there will be many of them. These utilities will have some of the same characteristics as their predecessors; they will favor dependability, for example, and even though they will be far more adaptable than in the past, they will not favor risk. How they will be regulated remains to be seen, but any such controls will have to be suitable for a global scale. In fact we will face at a global scale all the same questions that we faced at local and national scale when the telephone and train networks were created in the early twentieth century.

Note also that even though the most value-creating scale for many businesses will be planetary, it does not mean that the whole business must be run by a single economic entity. The world has learned, for the most part, that standards are valuable because they lead to interoperability, which allows different providers to, at a fundamental level, act as one. The Bell Telephone System needed to be a single system (although even it was not a single company) because in the early twentieth century creating an interconnected national telephone network was an extreme technical challenge. Today, servers owned by millions of entities work together to create an Internet that nobody owns, because Internet protocols made interoperability trivially easy. It was the ease of interoperability in the digital world that led to the deregulation of telephony. Now, particularly in Europe, power generation can be provided by numerous independent suppliers—including the solar panel on your roof—as long as distribution companies are regulated as common carriers.

In like fashion, the health care industry could adopt global standards for patient records and outcome reports and open standards for sharing learning. If a version of Partners HealthCare's POES existed at every hospital in the world, all could contribute data to a common learning system. And if that were to happen, it's not hard to imagine that regulators of drugs and health care around the world would then coordinate their actions in response to that growing knowledge base.

Ann-Marie Slaughter, who recently returned to Princeton from her role as director of policy planning at the U.S. State Department, sees the emergence of global networks of government agencies as the necessary next step to governance for global issues. Combining the trends of global scale and Internet-like interoperability, she foresees government roles—from drug licensing to international policing to financial management—increasingly being managed by networks of national agencies. These structures will coordinate across borders but will not require a new layer of global institutions. As an example, in June 2011, in São Paulo, the World Bank signed an agreement with forty large cities around the world to ease the financing of measures aimed at mitigating climate change.

This brings us back to Brian Arthur and increasing returns. His pivotal point was that information networks would favor a single standard for everything. What was left open was whether standards would be managed as one company's proprietary advantage, the way an early telephone company treated its geographic territory, or whether standards would be open, like physicists publishing the periodic table of the elements. Arthur argued passionately that proprietary standards would create monopolies that would rein in innovation and expropriate consumer surplus.

In other words, he feared that all the handshakes would be visible, bought, and paid for, as had happened in telephony. Since Arthur wrote, open source has thrived, and the learning system, not the operating system, has become the unit of monopoly. But will individuals contribute their genomes to a common database? (Not all of them, but enough.) Will drug companies pool their research? (Yes.) Will traders publish their algorithms? (No.) And will China control IP? (We think not.) Which handshakes will become invisible?

It's not clear which industries and companies might tend toward monopoly; that will depend on how they are currently structured and the ease of achieving interoperability. But it seems clear that there is some "utility" function to be performed in almost every value chain: sourcing, manufacturing, paying payrolls, customer relationship management. In addition, some of these utilities will be in surprising industries such as movies (entertainment in general, in fact) and drug therapies. We'll see branding, distribution, and management performed economically by large global studios and Big Pharma companies. But the movies and drugs will come from an economic sector having very different characteristics.

The Failure Sector and the Dynamic Economy

Operating in tandem with the utility sector we've just described will be another sector. We could call it the experimentation sector, or the innovation sector. Or, to name it for its salient characteristic, we might call it the failure sector. Whatever we call it, it doesn't operate by the same capital-intensive, zero-sum, risk-averse rules that the utility sector does. Instead, it is distinguished by its tolerance for risk and resilience in the face of failure.

Since at least the 1980s (that is, the era of deregulation) managers of big companies have been upbraided for their intolerance to risk. Certainly, that's a fair characterization. As Dick Morley—the MIT manufacturing innovator who inspired this book's title—once put it, "The trouble with big companies is that they take juicy, high-risk, high-return opportunities, then manage the risk out of them to the point that there's no return left." Knowing that mature firms must become more venturesome to continue growing, business gurus routinely advise them to embrace failure. Risk taking, they say, must be rewarded, even when it does not succeed.

Perhaps not surprisingly, managers of megacorporations remain largely unsold on that notion. Although select companies have seen the light, as a group global corporations remain too risk-averse to pursue the economy's high-quality opportunities for innovation. Yet the demand for innovation has only increased—and in the breach another source of it has emerged. This is what we're calling the failure sector.

What's new here is not that risk tolerance is important to innovation. It's that instead of thinking of the risk-prone people in a company, law firm, or investment bank, it's more helpful to think of all of them as making up a new component of the capitalist economy, working together. If you think about how new products and services are hatched and brought to market today, it isn't usually the work of only one entity—much less of the kind of R&D lab that major corporations once housed, such as Xerox PARC or Bell Labs. Instead, ideas, technologies, capabilities, and resources somehow organize themselves to meet the human and financial needs of new ventures.

Let's start with the people component of this sector we're alleging. As with any type of endeavor, there's a learnable skill to starting up a brand new business. The leaders who have gained this experience now constitute a kind of roving band that is an important element of the sector. "Serial entrepreneur" is among the most prestigious answers to "What do you do?"—and it's an answer that would have made no sense thirty years ago (back when "What's your business model?" was a question that would also have been met with blank stares).

Equally, investing in start-ups has its own quirks. So the sector features venture capital, which has grown from being an obscure corner of the financial industry to being its most potent part in funding economic growth. Even the once tiny community of angel investors has grown to include "super angels" and angel funds. Don't think of these investors—who accept their one-in-ten hit rate as a rule of their game—as at home in the financial industry. Ninety percent of the time, they're in the now more glamorous failure sector.

The sector has entities, too, to improve the flow of intellectual capital. InnoCentive is a network that brings together "seekers" who face technological challenges with "solvers" all over the world. Custom manufacturers enable innovators to see their designs fabricated without their having to create a factory (and soon, fab labs will distribute manufacturing capabilities to a more granular, global community of makers). Open source software enables entrepreneurs to stand up business capabilities quickly and cheaply; SourceForge, as mentioned, is the source of 260,000 open source software applications.

Noubar Afeyan, himself a serial entrepreneur, says that the skill can be not only learned but also codified. He teaches it at MIT's Center for Entrepreneurship, but, more significantly, after founding Flagship Ventures as a venture capital firm, he created a separate unit, Flagship VentureLabs, which "invents and launches transformative companies." It sounds like a founding position in a new sector to us.

The start-up sector even has its own growing newspaper (online, of course): it's called *Xconomy*. And no sector is complete without its own conference. FailCon takes place every fall in San Francisco.

All these elements have grown up on their own, but importantly, we're starting to appreciate that innovation takes off when these components are linked in fertile innovation ecologies. Kendall Square and Silicon Valley are the best-known places, but hardly the only ones, where we see rich interactions among serial entrepreneurs, VCs, law firms specializing in ventures, university technology transfer offices, and providers of physical incubator space. (Note that FailCon's sponsors include Silicon Valley Bank and a variety of business services firms.)

Do you need more convincing that the U.S. economy now features an innovation sector? How about the fact that policy makers from innovation-starved countries (where failure in a new venture still brings career ruin and even shame on your family) have spotted it and are trying to duplicate the same conditions in their economies? Although imitation might not be the best way to grow an innovation sector, the resources they're devoting to the goal are bringing them closer to solutions that will work for them.

No doubt we've got you sufficiently excited about this sector that you can't imagine why we would ever call it the failure sector.

It's time to remind you why we do: it's because most innovative ventures fail. The real strength of the system we've been describing is that it tolerates failure well—it constantly takes bets that more often than not don't pay off. Even though large firms haven't reconciled— perhaps can't reconcile—themselves to the risk–return crapshoot of innovation, the economy has adapted by developing an innovation sector to take on that role.

The resources we're describing mainly serve the risk-tolerant entrepreneur. (Who else would attend something called "FailCon"?) InnoCentive, for example, finds that its biggest hurdle in getting large corporations to use its services is not the challenge of proving that they are worth their cost. It's overcoming the legal objections raised by internal IP lawyers intent on managing risk and establishing control rather than speed. As for that very entrepreneurial question we mentioned—"What's your business model?"—can you imagine hearing one manager ask it of another in the hallway of a large company? (What, you didn't read the mission statement?) The biggest risks taken by entrepreneurs are not innovations in product, service, or process but in the business model. The fact that the Internet bust weeded out low-value business propositions is just what you'd expect from a sector investing with high risk tolerance.

Some large companies have squared this risk-aversion circle by finding portals to the innovation sector. Procter & Gamble's open innovation approach, widely written about, ably harvests the risks borne by others. Cisco's venture arm competes to fund promising companies, acquire technologies, and enlist talent. Firms like this have not so much developed their own risk tolerance as found a way to pay others for theirs. To return to Dick Morley's complaint, they allow a nice high-risk, high-return opportunity to be developed without all the risk being managed out of it—by someone else. Then they pay a boatload of appreciation. Rather than become tolerant of the risks of early-stage innovation, they resign themselves to paying more for the payoffs. Cisco Systems and Intel achieve similar results through their venture arms without having to change the attitudes of the managers of the mainstream business. It's not unlike real estate development— rich people aren't the "pioneers" moving into dicey neighborhoods— they are the ones paying developers to roll the dice first.

You get this. We know you get this. But we also bet it isn't your usual perspective on the world of VCs and IPO lawyers. From the usual point of view, all this apparatus is about producing lucrative "exits" and businesses built to flip. If you see it from another angle, though, it's an adaptation of a global economy confronted with more opportunities to innovate than the risk-intolerant institutions can manage. It's a whole sector primed to absorb all the failure that goes hand in hand with the new new thing. And it's an ingenious innovation that allows the economy to explore the new while exploiting the large-scale capital—human, physical, financial, social—already invested in the functioning economy.

From our view, standing on the sun, it now seems clear that the failure sector will continue to develop and will become a permanent element of the global economy. This sector operates over shorter cycle times, at higher levels of risk, and over greater distances—geographic, cultural, historical—than the industrial economy is accustomed to. It will continue to shorten the half-life of every technology, product, and market niche.

Biologists speak of a species' energy budget being divided between *exploiting* the ecological niche it inhabits and *exploring* for new niches, lest the current comfy one be disrupted. Big companies, our execution sector, have an enormous investment in protecting their niches, in part through investments that are difficult to pick up and redeploy. It's very difficult for them to take exploration seriously. That task falls to our experimentation sector.

Rather than view entrepreneurs as one-off innovators, large companies will come to see the failure sector as a part of their own ecologies, providing exploration services too risky for their more settled cultures, at a price they can afford. Increasingly, we will all come to realize that it takes a sector to raise an innovation.

And what of the emerging economies? They are shy on well-entrenched, world-class execution companies. They may acquire some—Lenovo comes to mind—or become parts of others (as with local mobile carriers being subsumed by the Vodafones of the world). But they are rife with risk-prone explorers.

To understand the emerging economies' natural advantages in the failure sector, listen to Abhay Havaldar, who started out in venture capital and then worked in operations for Tata. In 2002 he established the Mumbai office of General Atlantic, a private equity investor.

> When entrepreneurs discuss this in India, they have a very interesting perspective. They say that in California or Boston you've got so much stability in the ecosystem that you can't deal with the issue at hand. Whereas here, you've got so much uncertainty . . . there's uncertainty as to whether you can get to the office on time or not. So just people's willingness to deal with the degree of uncertainty is so much higher out here that you will not see plans being built to the degree of focus that you see in the West. They leave it open so that you can get it directionally, and they will have goals, but they will not fill it in to a financial model.

It sounds like a community primed for failure—and in a good way.

At the outset, we staked our claim that capitalism should and will recenter itself on innovation. The appearance of an innovation sector corroborates this conclusion. And the testimony of people like Abhay Havaldar and Sweta Mangal (remember her boredom with a country where everything "worked like magic"?), suggests it will grow fastest in the emerging economies. To thrive, execution-sector companies from rich economies will keep finding new ways to trade with this thriving sector. We describe GE's approach in chapter 9.

A Nonreceding Bliss Point and the Measurement of Happiness

Now let's turn to another major component of any economy: the people whose desires it must use resources to fulfill. Call them labor, call them consumers—they are both and more. The key point of interest to economists is the question of what drives them to engage in economic activity.

At some point in a first-year economics course you might have heard about the *bliss point*. This term refers to the fact that when economists analyze buyers' price elasticities, they can calculate the set of goods that should make those buyers completely satisfied. Satiated, in fact.

It's the quantity of consumption that is just right, so that having or being able to buy any less or any more would make a consumer less happy. Imagine that you had the means to gain just what you wanted and no more: then you could achieve your bliss point.

The problem is that for humans observed in the wild, this bliss point has the nasty habit of receding. You might think, in other words, that having a bigger house and a fancier car would make you satisfied. Unfortunately, though, if you manage to get those, almost as soon as you have them, you want more. French philosopher Denis Diderot described this phenomenon charmingly in his diary. His troubles began, he says, when a patron made him a gift of a beautiful smoking jacket. No sooner had he donned it, however, than he began to notice how shabby his other possessions were in comparison. The string of upgrades that followed, from clothing to furniture to real estate, may well seem familiar to you. If you'd rather sound more cultured than wonky about it, refer to your receding bliss point as the Diderot Effect.

To economists, and indeed to most Americans, it seems safe to assume by now that the bliss point will *constantly* recede. Our estimations put it within our grasp, but as we draw near, our expectations prove wrong. We start thinking, "For god's sake, why are we flying commersh?" Following the logic of runaways, this phenomenon suggests an ever fiercer competition to consume more, and more conspicuously, a continuation of the trend of the latest industrial economy.

McKinsey predicts that China's luxury-goods market will amount to $27 billion in 2015, some 20 percent of the world's total. Graff, retailer of the world's "most fabulous diamonds," has just set up shop in China. Certainly the huge demand for high-end luxury goods in the emerging economies would suggest that a consumption runaway is already in motion in the emerging markets as well.

But this is what makes a research finding by economics Nobel laureate Daniel Kahneman and his colleague Angus Deaton so interesting. In 2010 they published a paper based on a phone survey of 450,000 people in the U.S. It showed that rising happiness was correlated with rising income—but only up to a point. That point was $75,000.

Beyond that income level, there was no measurable increase in happiness. Kahneman and Deaton declared this to be the "specific dollar number, or income plateau, after which more money had no effect on day-to-day contentment." Does this suggest that the bliss point, at least with regard to financial buying power, might not be ever receding? Could it in fact be somewhat fixed—say, at the local purchasing power equivalent of a $75,000 income?

The bliss point research is early and controversial, but other work on happiness is less contested. It turns out that what makes people happiest is all in the realm of externalities—that is, not captured by whatever numbers they add up on their tax returns. In his recent book *The Social Animal*, David Brooks explains how much of it has to do with social connections. According to research he cites, belonging to a club that meets once a month has happiness-boosting power equivalent to doubling your income. Getting married increases happiness by the same amount as earning an extra $100,000 annually.

Of course we are back in the territory that we covered in our earlier chapter on accounting for happiness. All this is the reason that the U.K. prime minister David Cameron has instructed his Office of National Statistics (the British equivalent of the Census Bureau) to have citizens rate themselves on a 1–10 scale in response to four new questions:

- How happy did you feel yesterday?

- How anxious did you feel yesterday?

- How satisfied are you with your life nowadays?

- To what extent do you feel the things you do in your life are worthwhile?

Cameron and the others who are taking seriously the notion of gross national happiness seem to know that if we begin to measure GNH, then we will begin to take household happiness more seriously. Tracking the well-being of people is akin to tracking the external impact of corporations. It's off the balance sheet, but nothing could be more fundamental.

Speaking of the five-year planning period beginning in 2011, China Development Gateway states, "This year, instead of economic growth, improving people's happiness is on the top of [local governments'] agendas." In Chongqing, the provincial government has established a specific target for reducing the inequality of the income distribution.

It's too soon—because there isn't enough research, the happiness reporting tools don't exist to change people's behavior, and the world hasn't yet reached the critical level of income—to say what will happen and how fundamental a shift we might see. And it's easy to dismiss the idea that there will be some broad change in people's taste for ever more consumption. But here's an important example of the kind of change we might see more of. Consider that as incomes and education levels have risen, we have seen a shift in one feature that we might have thought to be a permanent element of the human condition: the number of children people have. The trend over the past three hundred years is toward fewer progeny. In colonial times in the United States it was not unusual to hear about families with children in the double digits, but by 1948 a book like *Cheaper by the Dozen* was clearly the stuff of comedy. In earlier times, having all those children was a key to prosperity. They were a form of insurance, because people were often lost to disease and accidents. And to a degree, given that you needed the extra hands on the farm, they were a form of capital. However, the economics flipped after the industrial age. Those teenagers didn't work in the fields; they required college tuition, and they didn't come back and support their families. Children became, in financial terms, liabilities instead of assets. Having fewer of them became the route to greater prosperity because raising them is expensive.

But only in financial terms. In most families, an extra child is an extra bundle of joy. In *Selfish Reasons to Have More Kids*, George Mason University economist Bryan Caplan argues that children are "consumption goods," not capital. Along the same lines, in conversation recently with friends, Julia learned that a mutual acquaintance, already a mother of three, was expecting a new baby. "You know," one friend archly commented, "that the fourth child is the new status symbol." Whether or not that's true, the thing to remark on is the joke's implication that the basis of competing with the Joneses has moved to a happiness yardstick.

The goods and services needed to keep body and soul together require ever less of the world population's work (thanks to the stunningly efficient new utilities discussed earlier), and there is a thriving industry in which those who wish to can express their creative talents (the failure sector). In this setting, there should be room and resources for people to pursue their desire to interact with others, whether through Facebook, fantasy leagues, or family. Ironically, in the emerging economies, one could imagine that birthrates will first decline as a function of education but then rise again as a function of affordability—and take a larger share of the "consumption" expenditure than those Graff diamonds.

Have we reached a sort of Maslovian level where we are no longer obsessed with consumption and will increasingly explicitly acknowledge nonmaterial sources of happiness? In particular, as consumption opportunities become more accessible and equally available around the world through rising incomes, will people everywhere start to outgrow an immature fixation on tangible property? To be sure, there were many predictions in the 1950s about the surplus of free time that would be achieved by "labor-saving devices" like kitchen appliances and how nobly it could be used. It doesn't seem to have played out that way. Perhaps none of what we are envisioning will happen, and the consumption race will prove as intractable as the arms race in getting a runaway under control.

On the other hand, maybe it will. Note that the median household income in the United States, at $50,000, still falls short of Kahneman's income plateau, to say nothing of the poorer populations of the world. But that point no longer seems unattainably distant. The day might be dawning when affluent people lose their appetite for ever more consumption and begin to reach for social goods, both at the individual level—friendships, for example—and at the society-wide level, such as social justice, rather than the next material ones.

What would this mean for individuals as workers in an economy? If greater social and emotional attainment constitutes "success," then clearly consumption should decline as a share of activity and resource allocation. This in turn means that it would cost the world fewer material resources to satisfy what makes an individual—and collectively all individuals—happy. There will be more exciting work available for those who have that drive to achieve. And in general, people will pay more attention to their social relations—and will have more time to enhance them.

As time goes on, it becomes increasingly clear that the mass orientation ushered in by the Industrial Revolution was an aberration.

Mass production, mass consumption, mass advertising made sense given its technologies, but the point and the effect of technologies was to put the production assets at the center of the picture. As usually happens, we have arrived at the point that we take for granted the distortions that grew out of the innovations of the Industrial Revolution. They are a prison we've chosen to live in. But the populations of emerging economies on the whole are not yet habituated to those confines.

There is a false dichotomy implied by the idea of "work–life balance": that you clock in to a job you don't enjoy to make enough money to go and do the things you do. The industrial-native battle for shorter hours and higher wages fought by twentieth century labor unions is all about this negative, work-to-live existence.

But today there is an elite for whom work is its own reward. Whether that work is science, music, blogging, or hedge fund trading, there are increasing numbers of people who marvel, like the Boys of Summer, that "you pay me to play this game." As incomes rise and the failure sector grows, an increasing percentage of people will be in this camp.

How might we observe this trend? We remember that in 2001, observing the growth of affluence around the world, the two of us staged a conversation about what would be scarce in the future. In this notional world of plenty, the group we convened concluded that attention—the very finite amount of focused time each of us has to spend—would be most precious, and added that the way it was spent was the largest determinant of how happy a person felt. Perhaps, in a kind of Maslovian leapfrog, some emerging nation will begin to measure the ratio of time people spend playing "a game they want to play" divided by time spent doing things they don't enjoy.

Of course the world will still have injustice, disease, and catastrophe, but measuring the fulfillment of desires rather than the fulfillment of orders should lead to a society doing more to alleviate these social problems. GDP, as we've noted, grows in response to the prisons, chronic illnesses, and cleanup efforts that accompany all that misery. And to return to one of our central themes, nothing is more powerful in bringing a system into a new line than adding a new feedback loop.

Faced with all this happy talk, the natural question for advanced economies now is where all the jobs will be. We can't quite imagine a society where grunt work is being done by robots and computers and where people are sufficiently economically enabled by that infrastructure to pursue the things they want and where we're not all relentlessly focused on the work–life question.

We can't help thinking of a dedicated entrepreneur we met recently: Ben Berkowitz, who started a Web site called SeeClickFix. It's a simple idea well executed. Any citizen who notices a nonurgent problem needing to be fixed in his community—a pothole, perhaps, or a deteriorating utility pole—logs on to the site and reports it. Now that need is publicized and also possibly part of an emerging pattern. For example, in Hartford, Connecticut, the fact that many citizens began noting where drivers tended to speed allowed traffic enforcement to focus its efforts. In other cases, citizens themselves decide to fix a reported problem out of civic pride.

Berkowitz told the story of why he created the business: it was in a moment of irritation at seeing yet another blighted patch of graffiti on what could have been a pleasing, pristine surface. He got a few friends together on a Saturday night and created the basic functionality of SeeClickFix. So you tell us: is devoting a precious weekend night to that effort a sign that Berkowitz's work–life balance is dangerously out of whack? The question is absurd.

Recently an audience member asked artificial intelligence guru Ray Kurzweil at an event in Cambridge, "If robots are doing all the work, then what will remain for people to do as jobs?" Kurzweil's response was reflective. "Let's imagine," he said, "that you had asked me that question a hundred years ago. Let's say I had told you that the percentage of people laboring on farms would drop to 3 percent of the population." Of course, the same question would have arisen. Freed from the daily chores of minding animals and crops, how could people possibly fill the day? How could they then be anything but a burden to society? But of course, as Kurzweil concluded, "We found new work to do."

In the emerging economies, more of it may be work people want to do. Fewer people work underground inhaling coal dust than a century ago, not because there is less coal used but because industrial technology let machines do the dangerous drudgery. Surely the global economy will similarly be clever enough to migrate away from jobs no one wants to activities people enjoy. Abhay Havaldar thinks he has a much better deal doing his work in Mumbai than he would in Mountain View.

Our second standing on the sun claim was that broad and subjective value would displace financial profit as the output society would maximize. In those terms, we don't believe the bliss point will stop receding. But in financial terms, it just might.

The Financial Sector and Externalities (Mostly Negative)

Certainly a whole book could be written—many already have been—on how the financial sector went off the rails and how it should be set straight. (Simon Johnson's *Thirteen Bankers* and Gretchen Morgenson's *Reckless Endangerment* are particularly fine.) We are not about to write that story. We can, however, address this vital sector of the economy in terms of the principles we've laid out so far, and this additional perspective may give greater force to certain ideas for reform.

Standing on the sun, it's possible to see the financial sector as another case of externalities ripe to be internalized. It also has its own well established basis for pseudocompetition. That would be the *efficient markets hypothesis*, which asserts that it is impossible to beat the market by stock-picking because the market is so good and quick at translating all relevant information about a company into its share price. In a perfect market with perfect information available to all omniscient parties, it is impossible, in other words, for investors to arrive at different conclusions about the right price for a capital asset. (The implication is that the way to make more than the average bear in the market is by taking bigger risks than others might be able to stomach. It can't happen through expert spotting of under- or overvalued securities.)

It's a sort of "best of all possible worlds" conviction that all that happens in financial markets must be for the best because it is the outcome of that best-of-all-possible arrangements, a market process. But this belief amounts to a myth—and a convenient one, as Justin Fox elucidates in *The Myth of the Rational Market*, because it helps to preserve the industry structure and its crony relationship with its regulators.

Even as we wrote our brief explanation of the efficient markets hypothesis, we couldn't help recalling the deep Israeli-accented voice of Yossi Vardi, a high-tech entrepreneur and venture capitalist. He told us once (and has probably said many times) that "everyone knows the capital asset pricing model is bullshit!"

Here's why we equate the insistence on efficient markets with the kind of pseudocompetitiveness you saw in chapter 5. In theory it is an argument for efficiency, but in practice it is an excuse for the concentration of power. Recall Keynes's cautionary wisdom: "Markets can remain irrational a lot longer than you and I can remain solvent." That's certainly true of you and me—but the bigger the biggest players in the market become, the less true it becomes for them.

So the financial industry has become one of the most visible handshakes of all. As former IMF Chief Economist Simon Johnson points out, one of the clearest signs was that in 2008, the proportion of profits of all U.S. business earned by just the financial services sector was— wait for it—42 percent. This money was not made doing the rightful job of the financial sector, which is to fund growth and innovation. Rather, it was a fee extracted from the greater economy by the financial sector in return for providing efficient markets—efficient, except for all that profit earned at the expense of the nonfinancial sectors. Less snarkily, George Soros, speaking at the Institute for New Economic Thinking, referred to the financial system as "swollen." "Obviously, we need financial services and obviously they are beneficial," he said. "But to have 7 or 8 percent of the [global] GDP—that may be too much . . . The financial markets produce the instabilities, the fluctuations, the volatility against which they also then provide the insurance."

A phrase that comes up often in discussions of the financial sector is, as mentioned earlier, *moral hazard*. It refers to the all-too-human tendency to not worry much about our behavior if we will not personally have to bear the consequences. A twenty-something who doesn't buy health insurance because he knows the emergency room will treat him in any case and doesn't care that it raises the costs for the insured has succumbed to moral hazard. If you think about it for a moment, you will appreciate that moral hazard is a particular case of negative externalities. Put another way, any business choosing to impose costs on others might be thought of as succumbing to moral hazard (whether regulations permit it or not).

In the case of financial institutions, the form of environmental pollution being spewed out is risk that they take but that others are obliged to bear, with no attractive return potential. Its most toxic form has been seen in the trading that financial institutions have engaged in for no purpose other than speculation for their own gain. (These classes of transactions are defensible only by the discredited "efficiency" argument.) Such trading entails risk that escapes the industry players and is borne by the rest of the players in the economy.

The various regulatory reforms contemplated and enacted since the financial crisis are all versions of getting large financial institutions to internalize their risk externalities. The fees paid by banks since the U.S. Depression to fund federal deposit insurance are just such a measure. To complain about the burden of a transaction tax on derivatives is to defend the right to externalize traders' risks to the larger society.

We need to be clear: we're speaking of two different kinds of externalized risk. The first has been written about a great deal—the burden of "too big to fail" institutions being bailed out at the expense of others. In a sense, this is of lesser importance because when taxpayers buy distressed assets they often make a profit on them. The downside, however, is clearly present: when bankers can take risks to enrich themselves with confidence that if things don't work out they will not suffer proportionately, moral hazard is hard to avoid.

The larger impact occurs when financial market issues create fear, uncertainty, and doubt among businesses and consumers. Whether this is manifested in households' concerns about foreclosure or retirement, or businesses' underperformance or workforce reductions for want of demand, it is a fact that outcomes in the financial casino have consequences for the real economy. This can come as a surprise: it's as if Caesar's Palace had a bad night, and all the air conditioners went off in Las Vegas. As with all negative externalities, workings that look efficient when they are ignored look a lot less so when their costs are counted. To defend the financial markets as efficient is to ignore their impacts on the economy at large.

Against this backdrop of the externalizing machine that the U.S. financial sector has become, it's interesting to note that in emerging economies, financing approaches have arisen that seem to be dominated by *positive* externalities. Microfinance is the one we explore in chapter 7. Although it's true that microfinanciers have figured out how to make a profitable business out of lending money in tiny sums to impoverished but enterprising people, much of the benefit produced by this activity has been through the economic development it enables. Social benefit was, in fact, the original impetus: Muhammad Yunus, who founded Grameen Bank, was moved to give the rural poor in Bangladesh access to credit so that they could lay the foundations to get beyond a hand-to-mouth existence.

Not everyone is an altruist, especially in the financial sector (or even, as recent exposés have shown, in the microfinance sector). There will always be people who just want to get rich, and there will even be benefits to the economy from their relentless entrepreneurialism. As we salute them, it is not unfair to ask that they internalize their externalities like every other respectable concern.

Unlike the other two sectors we've described—the new utilities and the innovation sector—which will naturally be moved by feedback, the feedback in the financial sector will probably continue to provide perverse incentives to actors within it. The big financial institutions around the world have an interest in keeping the game going. It will take some kind of earthquake—of greater magnitude than the Great Recession, apparently—to change the rules. Standing on the sun, this rigidity, or concentration of power, looks like the greatest obstacle to the evolution of capitalism.

What's Your National Model?

So let's talk about the rule changers themselves—government policy makers. What's our "standing on the sun" view on how their work might change?

Earlier we noted that, these days in the business world, it is an utterly commonplace question to ask, What's your business model? But until about a decade ago, that would have struck people as a strange thing to wonder about. Even in the highest ranks of organizations, few people thought about their businesses at that level of abstraction. In the 1970s it was a revelation to business school students that a business could choose between competing on price or competing on differentiation. It rarely occurred to managers that the business model they were laboring under was within their power to change or needed to be changed. No wonder the dot-com boom was so confusing.

A couple of decades of disruptive innovation, however, have taught business leaders that change unfolds at the level of business models and that it's much better to be the originator of such change than to be blindsided by it. Thus it has become a matter of very pragmatic interest for managers to understand what a business model is, how exactly their own is constructed, and what aspects of it a disruptor could contemplate changing.

What if we were to ask, then, the equivalent of, "What's your business model?" at the level of a country? We are taking that question, which is newly necessary at the corporate level, and proposing it at the country level.

When the Washington Consensus was the consensus and policy makers assumed that an emerging nation's mission was to get on the path toward G7-style capitalism, there were two orthodox growth strategies available. The first was *import substitution*, which meant that you should erect protective trade barriers around your "infant industries" to protect them from competition from established global companies while they served the home market to achieve scale. The model relies on local buying power, and hence governments were tempted to put stimulative policies in place to fuel local demand, often with inflationary consequences. Brazil and Argentina, for example, struggled to put themselves on a sustained growth path through import substitution, but in practice this resulted in high local prices, inefficient industries, and persistent inflation, as well as tariffs that were bad for trade.

Export-led growth worked somewhat better. This strategy relies on buying power abroad. The temptation for governments was to subsidize the local industry to provide attractive prices on the world market, once again shielding local producers in chosen industries from global competition. Of course, if you have commodities the world needs, as the OPEC countries do, export revenue can provide an economy's growth engine, assuming that the revenues are invested wisely. Norway owes some of its high prosperity scores to its effective use of oil revenues. At the opposite extreme, Japan (from 1960 to 1990) and Singapore, twenty years later, pursued export-led growth by focusing on adding increasing value in-country. Success requires governments to do an effective job of picking the industries to grow—and both of those countries succeeded.

Now, the technology and the rule changes discussed in part II have set the stage for a Cambrian explosion of development models.

Existing corporate business models have been disrupted, because technology has changed the trade-offs—what things cost, who pays for them, and how individuals interact with their work, to name a few. At the level of nations, comparable shifts are at work. Democracy is one arrangement for assembling the opinion of citizens—but now so is texting. Health care is a universal requirement—but provided in an array of models funded in different ways in different countries. In Brazil, corporations fund education as naturally as they fund health care in the United States; in India, a remarkable proportion of poor people's income is spent on private education. Polities are in a position to make choices.

Jeff Garten, former undersecretary of commerce for trade and dean of the Yale School of Management, was our first interview for this book. When we raised the question of the diversity of economic models, he pointed first to the question of state capitalism. When Airbus and Boeing compete, both the European Union and the United States put their respective thumbs on the scales, using economic and political means to tip global buyers toward products made on their soil. Garten pointed out, too, that the Chinese government's ability to act as a massive first customer could help make it a leader in developing industries such as electric vehicles and alternative energy.

We think that China's present success and likely future ability to deploy valuable infrastructure (such as the alternative to car ownership we describe in chapter 7) will erode the phobia of state capitalism in the West, or parts of it. Given that aversion, we want to emphasize that there are many dimensions of policy that often get lumped together when the discussion turns to economies as disparate as China and, say, Norway. These dimensions include not only the proportion but also the source of government revenues, which in Singapore come from state-owned enterprises, in Abu Dhabi, from natural resources (oil), and in Sweden, from high taxes (though not as high as they used to be). These sources are not necessarily correlated with a society's degree of income redistribution; Scandinavia tends to equalize wealth, Israel tends to concentrate it. The degree and method of intervention (for example, laissez-faire in Brazil versus Japanese direction of keiretsu) are other choices for arranging relationships in an economy. So "state capitalism" can cover a wide range of business models.

With more progress in more places, greater diversity of models, and the Washington Consensus in ruins, perhaps the world will become less dogmatic about these choices. Here, we sketch a few emerging economies that are pursuing unusual models.

As noted, Singapore probably deserves the title of best-managed economic development program of the twentieth century. In the eyes of the United States, overall, Singapore has sacrificed pluralism and some personal freedoms (usually cited are the penalties for spitting, bans on gum chewing, and draconian drug laws), but we'd focus on the record of 8 percent annual growth from 1965 to 2010. As the *CIA Factbook* rates GDP per capita—on a purchasing power parity basis—Singapore ranks fifth, at $62,100, putting it six rungs north of the United States, which ranks eleventh at $47,200. The "Singapore, Inc." model of state control of market-responsive businesses such as Singapore Airlines and the Temasek sovereign wealth fund bypasses the three-sector model; it's a nation run on the assumption of mixed value.

We acknowledge, of course, that replicating the story of Singapore is difficult; it's a bench-scale experiment in terms of area and population, and Lee Kuan Yew was an extraordinary leader. But some of its innovations are notable. First, the government puts strong emphasis on hiring for its own ranks only from the top of the nation's graduating classes. Second, the country has used its forcefully directive grip on the economy to execute strategy as effectively as any corporation could. When, for example, the city set its sights on becoming "The Intelligent Island" in 1980, the Economic Development Board realized it had only a handful of qualified IT people in the country and no university-level computer science courses. In response, the Board created university programs and pioneered the strategy of attracting returnees—Singaporeans with needed experience living abroad—who could be enticed by various incentives to come and lead the growth of the new capability.

Third, and perhaps most instructive, Singapore issued wage guidelines that would in fairly short order take it out of contention for low-value-added work like textiles. This policy ran directly counter to the development strategies of emerging economies at the time, but the country reasoned that with no resources other than its people (and a good location for a port), the only path to prosperity was to force the economy to employ them in increasingly valuable roles. Having reasoned thus, the country could have tried to achieve that goal by picking industries or providing incentives, but it didn't. By providing wage guidelines, it left it up to the private sector to figure out how to earn enough to pay people. As a result, when Singapore did exploit its one natural resource—the port—it became the first port to employ remote-controlled cranes, operated by workers in an office building. Since at any given moment only a fraction of the cranes are in use, it's far more productive for an operator to be able to switch from one to another.

In the United Arab Emirates, too, the state dominates economic activity. Leaders worry, rightfully, that the world is working hard to kick the oil habit. As David Scott, director of economic affairs at the Executive Affairs Authority, put it, "In the Middle East the game is musical chairs—the one with the least oil in the ground when the music stops wins." Given this perception, it is not surprising that the leaders of Abu Dhabi are intent on transforming the value of its petroleum into physical and human capital. The oil revenue is deployed in part through several sovereign wealth funds directed by the government. Some of these are directed purely at investing financially to diversify the nation's assets, but Mubadala Development Company is aimed explicitly at mixed value. Scott explained that Mubadala's investments must also contribute to Abu Dhabi's strategy for developing its infrastructure and capacity in industries it considers economic development priorities, from aerospace to information communications technology to real estate and tourism. But Mubadala does not invest unless foreign investors participate as well. This independent scrutiny helps protect against the risk that local favorites will get funding for investments that wouldn't pass muster in the global market. It's a well-founded concern as that risk is the Achilles' heel of import substitution strategies.

Our purpose in including these brief mentions of Singapore and Abu Dhabi is to establish that China is not the only economy, or the only successful one, with a strong state that takes business as a major part of its business, mixing social and economic goals as a matter of course. But now let's do turn to China.

We've mentioned Chris's visit to Expo. Visiting the China pavilion, he first attended a 360-degree movie projection depicting China's recent accomplishments and future opportunities. The key message was that growth would become "wiser," and "more harmonious" with nature, meaning, overall, less driven by material acquisitiveness. (We've shared our opinion that this is not so much a forecast as a message to the 140 million Chinese who attended Expo about the country's economic development plan.) Second, he encountered a stunning wall, perhaps a hundred yards long, depicting Chinese history in a beautiful, animated mural. Perhaps five hundred people were admiring it under the watchful gaze of a guard, who happened to be standing next to a "No Photos" sign. That gaze was taking in at any given moment fifty upraised cell phones, snapping away in violation of the dictum.

It's only an anecdote, of course, but we believe it's emblematic of an important element of China's economic strategy: it will build an information economy as determinedly as Singapore did, but it will not—yes, we're repeating this from chapter 7—it will not impose intellectual property laws along the lines that the West pushes it to. China will have both the insight that restriction inhibits innovation and growth and the clout to resist pressure to conform. In the meantime it will put up "No Photos" signs.

This approach to IP is of course only one element of China's strategy. Here might be how China would sketch its business model on the back of a napkin:

> Physical resources will be increasingly scarce, so we'll make
> arrangements with resource-rich countries immediately so as
> not to get caught short. But we'll also damp down demand
> for those resources by discouraging consumption and
> building mass transportation and solar infrastructures so that
> rising salaries are not associated with increased consumption,

as they have been in the West. Meanwhile, as a second pillar to the strategy, we recognize that information is an inexhaustible resource, and therefore we will not restrict its flow. This means that we will not crack down on violations of intellectual property law and copyright, and we will draw on the traditional cultural emphasis on education (which has not been universal). The combination of more-educated people and less-restricted flow of knowledge will yield continued growth and increasing productivity. We'll thrive on the positive externalities of knowledge and the resource efficiency of advanced technologies. And we'll keep politics under control through prosperity—and suppression when necessary.

India, on the other hand, might pursue a different model. It might stake out a differentiated position in the creation of social well-being and public health care and be the leader in the ratio of happiness to GDP. (This strategy has a historical precedent: when the British East India Company came to India, it was plagued by laborers who would work for a week, conclude they had earned enough to live on for a month, and not come back.) It might more deliberately leverage the unique cultural resource it has in its developing army of women entrepreneurs.

We were struck by a research finding by Anita Woolley and Tom Malone on the keys to high performance by a team. The study found that the teams that perform highest feature the most listening by team members to one another. In turn, it found that listening rises with the number of women on a team. That's one small example of how a cadre of women can be an economic advantage and why India may therefore hold a form of cultural leverage.

What is Russia's business model? For the next decade, we would liken it to a private equity turnaround. Investor and educator Vadim Makhov, who spent fourteen years improving the productivity of the Russian steel company Severstal before acquiring a U.S. steel company, points out that his country is blessed by natural resources but its talent has been developed in increasingly irrelevant industries. He described a slide he likes to project to the MBA classes he teaches at Moscow School of Management Skolkovo. It's a breakdown of GDP by industry. When he asks these well-informed students what he's showing them, they say, "It's our current GDP." That's when he surprises them. The slide is actually the U.S. GDP breakdown—from 1929. "It's the same structure," he says. "The same amount of oil and gas, steel and automobiles, the same amount of doctors, the same population. If you compare, you find only small differences." His point is that Russia's is still a resource-driven economy, or as he calls it a "rent economy." And the country is held back because this is the orientation of its older talent.

Thus, there is a tremendous amount of opportunity in Russia just in playing catch-up. According to a McKinsey study, Russia's overall productivity stands at only 30 percent of U.S. productivity. (It used to be worse: in 1998 it was only 20 percent.) That leaves a 70 percent gap to be closed. As Makhov notes, it's much simpler to catch up than to achieve an unprecedented breakthrough—and merely closing the gap "will double or triple our GDP."

He sees the youthful energy to accomplish that goal in the rising generation of entrepreneurs he meets. These young people see the opportunities and are hungry to go after them. Unwilling to accept the system as it is, their attitude says, "This is our country. We don't want to get out—we want to work here. The laws should work for entrepreneurship, for our business, for us." Makhov expresses wonderment at such a different mind-set taking hold, but at the same time he sees it as a natural overturning of the applecart by a group that is disenfranchised by the old crony system: "It's because they are too young to get to economic rent. Because all of the places are occupied with people who got to this economic rent. Now, this new wave of talent is coming in, and struggling and disrupting it."

What Russia needs to capitalize on its opportunities, Makhov says, is "a liquid network of entrepreneurs with high density, an open platform connecting them, and all the fundamental ingredients to work with." The only one of these missing is the platform, and that is a need he sees being recognized and addressed by Skolkovo and Skolkovo Innograd. So Russia can grow rapidly for a decade by rehabilitating its past investment in capabilities and infrastructure before charting new territory. By that time, there will be a new game, needing a new game plan. We're as skeptical about the chances for these changes as we are about the reform of the financial system—the forces arrayed against each are formidable—but the upside of success is so great that perhaps the society will find a way.

The foregoing descriptions are really caricatures, each emphasizing the most recognizable and salient features of a complex entity. And we have certainly glossed over important issues of corruption and the rule of law, which vary widely among the emerging economies, as well as many other important factors. The point we're trying to highlight is that in the days when capitalism was contesting with communism for hearts and minds in a zero-sum game, it was enough to classify a country by which side it was on. And capitalism was not much affected by the rules of the game in Russia, China, or Chile. Now there are many economic environments, each run according to its own rules. As with the second migration of homo sapiens out of Africa, capitalism is radiating to many different environments, and the species is diverging.

The Ecosystem of Emerging Economies

We've described five seeds of new forms of capitalism, including predicting the emergence of global utilities, the rise of an innovation sector, and a broad attainment of a bliss point by individuals. And we've described some of the many soils in which they will take root. As the results grow and mix, new rules of capitalism will arise, be tested, and spread or disappear.

The emergence of global infrastructure platforms—whether they emerge as some form of controlled monopoly or as independent, interoperable entities—will accelerate the emergence of the emerging economies. Mobile phone operators from around the world are eager to provide services. Express services are ready to deliver. Financial services, whether delivered by mobile phone or more traditionally, are easily extended. And increasingly, education services will be on offer. Even the delivery of medical services is becoming a platform-based business. Compared to any other time in history, the growth of the emerging economies is not likely to be impeded by a lack of infrastructure.

Likewise, regarding the innovation sector, it's now accepted that innovation accelerates when it is "open." The innovation sector we envision will increasingly be a global community and phenomenon. InnoCentive's "solvers" come from everywhere. And companies will see the emerging economies as a source of diversity and thus insight— as we describe in the next chapter.

Finally, as we contemplate the possibility of achieving bliss points, we can't help wondering, Do the people who have not become accustomed to the consumption hamster wheel have an advantage on their way to a happy life? In every chapter of this book, we note one fundamental advantage held by the capitalists of emerging economies: the green field opportunity they have relative to mature capitalist systems, with their installed bases and well-set ways. Perhaps a country doesn't have to live through its own robber baron era to arrive at a better way. There may be such a thing as Maslovian leapfrogging.

Recall from chapter 2 that the mechanism by which capitalism evolves is that capitalists choose some rules more often and other rules less often. Giving risk-seeking entrepreneurs access to global platforms will only enhance the emerging economies' growth opportunities and their opportunity to influence the connected capitalist system. And if indeed the next three billion are less concerned with competitive consumerism, that rule of capitalism will have every opportunity to compete in the ecology of capitalist rules around the world.

Richard Pascale, a Stanford professor of organizational behavior, pointed out two important lessons for business drawn from biology. First, a system that isn't changing very much is preparing to die. Second, the way to find the next new thing is to "cultivate the fringe." Western capitalism is ready for an infusion of change. It's likely to find it in the emerging economies.

Standing on the Sun

We began this chapter with a revered business leader, Narayana Murthy, pondering the question of which form of capitalism might ultimately take over the globe. In nominating the Scandinavian model, he and our other interviewees were attracted to what seemed to be sensible crossbreeding—in Murthy's words, the ability to combine "the power of capitalism with the concern that comes out of socialism."

The notion of convergence is tempting, especially when it involves a happy medium, but from our perspective it is not the right assumption. We're not counting on an Oslo Consensus to emerge—or any other end of capitalist history. There is too much evidence from biology that a diverse ecology keeps spawning new life, and each new form has effects on many others, leading quickly to consequences that can't be anticipated, triggering another round of adaptation. And that's in a closed system. The global economy is a system that's continually being perturbed by accelerating innovation. Combine that with the competition of different economic rules, and you have a recipe for continual innovations in capitalism.

Standing on the sun, it's clear that the future of capitalism is not a story of competing economic models ultimately producing a winner. It's an ongoing interbreeding of economic models, the result of which is a perpetually diverse and continually adapting set of arrangements for trade.

CHAPTER NINE

. . . And Move On

The new multinational as the vector of economic evolution

*When you try to rank priorities, when you look at market size, the U.S.
always comes out number one. Japan comes out number two. But that's not the
way the future goes—you're talking about the past.*

—Kay Eron, General Manager,
Performance Diagnostic Cardiology, GE Healthcare

When Oswin Varghese joined GE in 2001 as a senior design
engineer, he didn't expect to work on new-product
offerings conceived in and designed for his home market
of India. Although his team was located in Bangalore, that was only
because of India's attractive labor economics. The well-trained engineers employed there were executing refinements to the diagnostic
cardiology solutions GE sells to sophisticated health care providers
in mature economies. Varghese himself was focused on fine-tuning
the electronic subsystems that went into the company's electrocardiogram recorders.

By 2005, however, GE's worldview had shifted, along with the
world it was serving, and Varghese was helping to launch the first of its
Indian innovations developed "in country, for country." The product
in question—the low-cost MACi electrocardiogram machine—was
certainly created *for* a home-market opportunity. According to the
World Health Organization, cardiovascular disease in India has

> **To discuss these ideas on Twitter, use these hashtags:**
>
> *#NewDupont*   *#MNCvector*

quadrupled in the past forty years, and Indians have a propensity to suffer heart attacks on average six years earlier than is the global norm; if current trends continue, then by 2020, nearly 60 percent of the entire world's cardiac patients will reside in India.

Moreover, particular circumstances about the country led GE to believe the product should be developed *in* India. Most of the country's population resides far from urban areas and has little access to modern medical facilities; the skills and training of practitioners serving remote villages are uneven; medical environments can be far from pristine, and so any machines whose workings are susceptible to dust are sure to be unreliable; electrical power is dodgy; and the costs of health care are paid largely out of pocket by patients and their families, not insurers or government payers, making price sensitivity extremely high. All these design constraints could, of course, be communicated to an R&D lab halfway around the world, but the chances were higher that they would be reflected more deeply in the solutions of engineers for whom they were a lived reality.

Varghese's colleague Kay Eron, general manager of GE's Performance Diagnostic Cardiology business is certain of that. To understand the requirements of India's 700,000 general practitioners, she told us, "you need people in India who spend time in the field, side by side with these practitioners, visiting patients and hospitals, and understanding customer needs from the ground up."

Viewed from GE Healthcare's headquarters in London, the MACi machine Varghese and his colleagues created might not look like progress. The company's most sophisticated ECGs churn out pages saturated with data gathered from twelve channels of monitoring; buyers of the MACi device get only three. And although the MACi incorporates state-of-the-art diagnostic technology (the company's proprietary Marquette 12SL ECG analysis program), it in fact delivers less, not more, information to the user than the company's older, premium devices.

But from the perspective of a rural Indian practitioner, it is a triumph. The device is portable and battery operated, with each three-hour charge good for five hundred ECGs, or perhaps a month's worth of use in a remote village. The machine's simple interface makes it suitable for users with minimal training. It is ruggedly built to survive a dusty ride on the back of a scooter. And without forcing any compromise on the quality of basic diagnostic information, its price point is only Rs. 25000—about $500, an order of magnitude less than GE's top-of-the-line offering—making it a very feasible investment for a rural practitioner. For patients, in turn, the cost of an ECG procedure has gone way down, to Rs. 9, about the cost of a bottle of water. With the dramatic cost reduction, a major barrier to more widespread diagnosis and care has been removed.

All this sounds logical—what could make more sense?—and the sales numbers for the MACi and other in country, for country innovations prove the wisdom of the approach. But the thing to appreciate is how truly countercultural this activity is for a multinational, and especially for GE. Over the decades, the company has made a science of producing shareholder value and has become tremendously disciplined in driving the "GE way" of doing things through its managerial ranks. And that way has *not* been, for example, to invest in still-small markets with uncertain ROI prospects when there are plenty of other surer and more short-term opportunities out there. Kay Eron underscored this point for us, noting that GE's traditional approach to project prioritization based on market size and payback periods would not lead to innovation for emerging markets but to more resources being directed to products for the United States and Japan. It's not that an in country, for country investment could never clear the bar, and indeed, all proposals still need a solid business case. "But it's a little bit hard," Eron said, "because just on business size, we would lose. So there's also a *strategic* side, where we can say, okay, China is growing, we need to be strong in China, and this initiative is *for China.*"

That's only the beginning of the ways in which GE's managerial habits of mind are being challenged by a commercial landscape with a shifting center of gravity. The company is also fundamentally rethinking the assumption that the best business strategy is to design a world-class product once and then rack up the returns on it by pushing it into market after market around the globe. It has had to come to terms with the reality that creating "more products at more price points" (a current rallying cry) will necessarily involve cannibalization of its high-end sales. That's a conversation that GE CMO Beth Comstock assured us she has had with GE salespeople "many times"—and with good reason. Fully one-third of the revenues of the MAC400, the low-price ECG device launched for China, now come from Europe.

Comstock says GE is still experimenting to figure out how to retain the benefits of strong global product management while giving Kay Eron and her counterparts sufficient latitude for in country, for country entrepreneurship, and believes this process will continue for quite a while. Meanwhile, GE's chairman Jeff Immelt himself earmarks funds for projects that, as Eron observed, wouldn't get funding using the usual criteria but carry strategic importance.

Finally, one of our favorite aspects of the mind-set turnabout has to do with GE's traditional belief that any health product it brings to market should be wholly developed in-house. Varghese told us about the problem his team faced when it came to a peripheral but vital component of the MACi: its printer. He'd been puzzling about how to produce, at very low cost, a printer that would be both sturdy and capable of high-resolution output, when he noticed the machine spitting out his ticket at the railway station. That very device—inexpensive and easy to service, in contrast to the custom designed printers in GE's advanced models—has now been adapted for ECG output, saving the design team the work of reinventing it.

Again, this kind of pragmatism may seem only rational, but given GE's long history of elegant, total solution development, it's like asking a leopard to change its spots.

Fueled from the Sun, Planted in the Earth

And so we turn to the "So what?" territory for firms—the practical implications of the big-picture trends we've been describing. OK, so the environment of global business has shifted. All right, capitalism as a system is rapidly adapting. But at the level of the firm, what does it mean?

The big answer is that, like GE, firms will have to learn to succeed on new terms. Those changes in terms are the ones we've been outlining chapter by chapter. And the good news is that it is not that difficult to bring them down to Earth. In fact, just as all of the astronomers' calculations became less tortured after Copernicus put the sun in the center of their system, in many ways the conduct of capitalism will be less crazy and conflicted as capitalists internalize the reformulation of some basic rules.

Rule One: Learn to See Results in Color

Old formulation: *Measure financial returns to shareholders.*
New formulation: *Measure the real value sought by stakeholders.*

Let's start back in the territory we cover in chapter 3, where we note increased activity in measuring intangible and nonfinancial well-being. We liken it to the experience of moving from black and white to color film. Because we believe that everything we've described depends on getting full-color feedback to the firm, we give a more detailed prescription here than for the rules relating to the other chapters.

In GE's case, this means taking off the blinders that have kept managers relentlessly focused on maximizing shareholder value. By broadening its consideration of what constitutes a strategic opportunity beyond the question of what yields the highest number in a net-present-value calculation, we'd say GE is taking a more colorful view of value. We don't mean to imply that it is forgoing financial gains. Sales for GE's health care unit in India rose 20 percent in 2010 to $300 million, toward a projected $400 million in 2011, and a cool billion five years out. But listening to its team in India talk about GE's "Healthymagination" investments, we heard them stress the more fundamental return they're seeking: "better health for more people by lowering cost, increasing quality, and creating better access."

In other settings we've heard GE's top leaders say the same kinds of things, and their commitment to this nonfinancial goal seems sincere. But whether or not it is, they are certainly finding that the talent they need to recruit now demands a broader return on their efforts and will not be satisfied with only a generous paycheck. John Flannery, GE's president and chief executive in India, told the *Wall Street Journal* that, a decade ago, his HR function could count on the fact that top Indian talent wanted career experience working for a multinational. "But now," he said, "many see the action is right here in India, and we need to have a story that is competitive with Tata, Reliance" and other major Indian companies. Oswin Varghese described for us the positive change he saw in his colleagues' motivation when they switched from tweaking mature market products to creating transformational solutions for their own home towns: "It's more than working for GE and doing some product development. There is a passion beyond that, because we are taking the best thing available in the developed market and trying to deliver it in an affordable way in India and other emerging markets." That, he said, "is a big driving factor behind many people's work in the engineering team." Perhaps it's no surprise that, of the thirteen hundred engineers in GE's Bangalore development center, one-third are now devoted to ICFC programs. (One thing that will probably never change at GE is the instant conversion of a phrase such as "in country, for country" into an acronym.)

Other businesses starting to internalize this first new rule of capitalism—maximize real value—might follow a five-part prescription. As outlined here, it begins with developing a broader view of value and doesn't stop until the feedback loops are in place to make sure that understanding stays current.

Identify What's Really Important to Stakeholders

This is an exercise many businesses have already begun—engaging with their stakeholders and understanding what their expectations and desires are. Truly understanding what they are saying may require some retuning of managerial ears.

Bread & Circus was picking up on signals that other grocers were ignoring when it realized that customers cared about more than getting groceries at the lowest price. Their buying was also informed by the kind of world they wanted to live in. They cared about how food had been grown, what pesticides had been used or genetic modifications made to increase yields, and whether local farmers were making a living. That led Bread & Circus to support certain kinds of supply chain arrangements and to provide the kinds of commitments to its growers that other grocery chains shunned. The fact that Whole Foods Market, which bought the chain, is now a $9 billion business shows that Bread & Circus was on to something.

Whole Foods Market has continued to reassess the value its shoppers are looking for when they arrive in its aisles. Its 10-K statement not only lays out financial results but also defines a "Whole Trade Guarantee," which, in addition to spelling out quality standards for food, makes commitments to "provide more money to producers; ensure better wages and working conditions for workers; and utilize sound environmental practices." The company donates 1 percent of sales of Whole Trade products to the Whole Planet Foundation. Because its customers want more locally grown products, it has earmarked $10 million to lend to producers in its store locales to help them be better suppliers.

Meanwhile, remember Bhutan's singular focus on happiness? We were fascinated to discover a few years ago that the same emotion had become central to the thinking of Coca-Cola. It first struck us as a somewhat cynical marketing ploy. Given increasing concerns that empty calories, such as one gets from sugary beverages, lead to social ills like obesity, diabetes, and heart disease, the canny marketing message would probably be, Lighten up—don't we deserve some happiness in our day? But the company seems to take its message to heart. At the same time that it was launching the happiness marketing campaign, for example, it was changing its longtime stance toward suppliers, seeking to engage them as partners instead of using its scale to extract price concessions from them. It was acting on employees' input about the quality of their work lives. And it was sitting down with community representatives in locales from Atlanta to Albania to understand how they thought a business operating in their community could make them happier.

Look for Ways to Measure Those Things

Measurement of nonfinancial performance is often a tricky proposition, involving some assumptions and subjective calls, but it is not beyond the grasp of humankind. Business has made tremendous progress in the past few decades on measuring, for example, product quality, customer satisfaction, and employee engagement. The Balanced Scorecard pioneered by David Norton and Robert Kaplan is an exercise in assigning metrics to the many components of a business that, although lacking financial precision themselves, combine to yield the financial outcomes that business experiences. More recently, intangibles accounting guru Baruch Lev (he wrote *Intangibles: Management, Measurement, and Reporting*) has put forward his own version of a "value chain scoreboard."

When a company like Royal Dutch Shell decides to report on some kind of nonfinancial progress, its decisions on what to measure stem directly from its goals. In Shell's case, the sustainability report it has issued annually since 1997 begins with a simple statement: "Our aim is to help meet the energy needs of society in ways that are economically, environmentally and socially responsible." Accordingly it establishes metrics and related goals in each of those areas, such as its intention to raise its production of clean-burning natural gas to the point that it accounts for half of Shell's energy output in 2012. For Whole Foods, some specific objectives have to do with food quality, animal-compassionate products, and sustainable seafood practices, and the company has drawn up and published its own standards for measuring and monitoring those. So has Proctor & Gamble.

But in many cases, as businesses determine what's most important to measure, a little research will reveal that someone else is already working on how to measure it. This is where resources like TriplePundit.com—the site mentioned earlier that shares resources and builds community around measurement of intangibles—and the guidelines drawn up by the Global Reporting Initiative (a widely used sustainability reporting framework) come in handy.

Advocate—Even Agitate—for Standards

The real power of a set of measures is unleashed when there is broad agreement on them. Enterprises using the same yardsticks are able to benchmark performance and hold each other's feet to the fire. A firm's mission should be to arrive at systems of measurement that not only it but others in its industry (and beyond) can buy in to.

When companies develop their own definitions of success, they impose their own standards on their vendors, and sometimes their vendor's vendors, with the result that these suppliers must address a cacophony of disparate requests and demands. Meanwhile, the companies are also defining their own methods of reporting their efforts to reach their sustainability goals, meaning that the level of transparency is uneven.

Yvon Chouinard, founder of outdoor wear maker Patagonia, tells the story of how all this was going on in the global apparel and footwear industry and how that industry, collectively, is attempting to rise above it. In early 2009 Patagonia invited Walmart to join it in identifying and then inviting a select group of other industry players to make progress toward a unified "value chain index." By that fall, the two companies were sending out invitations to the CEOs of twelve companies. As an official of one of the recipient companies later said, "When you get a letter from Mike Duke and Yvon Chouinard, with the logos for Walmart and Patagonia side by side at top, it doesn't go to the round file."

In April 2010 those fourteen companies were in agreement on the goal, and by 2011 they, along with another eleven companies that joined their merry band, completed a prototype tool that was a mashup of an index Patagonia had already been using and another developed previously by Nike. By 2012 the tool will incorporate actual data on the total externalized costs of alternative operating decisions, and the Apparel and Footwear Coalition's membership will span more than fifty corporations.

Similar efforts are under way in the electronics and dairy industries, driven by people with the same passion and vision as Chouinard. The oil industry has its version in the guidelines drawn up by the International Petroleum Industry Environmental Conservation Association (to which Shell adheres). If the same kind of standard setting is not happening in some other highly-externalizing industry, maybe it only needs an impassioned manager to step up and drive it.

Track Performance

In one way or another, once a company determines how to measure which desirable outcomes, the imperative is to compile those results and gauge relative performance. This is a simple exercise in database building, plus ideally some imagination applied to its display.

We loved hearing about, for example, a new product being tested by engineering and architectural firm Arup. The company designs and builds high-rise office towers, among other large structures, and it realized that its customers—the real estate developers and owners—were facing new demands from their own customers, the businesses that would become tenants. Energy conservation had come to the fore, and at the same time these knowledge-intensive businesses, perennially in a war for talent, were concerned with employee engagement levels. Arup's innovation group proposed something called a "green screen" on every floor of a building. The green screen displays that floor's performance on environmentally minded goals, such as recycling to trash ratios, electricity use, and so on. Early tests affirm what has been proven in home monitoring of energy usage: that consumption drops when consumers' use is made visible to them. At the same time, businesses who invest in green screens will make a visible display of their corporate commitment to sustainability, a commitment their workers share and are happy to see.

Build Feedback Loops

Finally, the whole point of all this activity is to improve performance over time. The reason to install a green screen is that improvement happens most readily when a feedback loop allows managers and individuals to see the varying impact of different actions they take.

Along these lines, many devotees of the Balanced Scorecard have gone to some pains to create executive dashboards displaying performance information in as close to real time as possible. Just as with an automotive dashboard, the gauges do not serve simply as an FYI. Rather, they have immediate implications for action to intervene—hit the brakes, hit the gas, call for service—and correct the way things are going. Individual incentives and rewards are also inevitably part of the feedback picture. That's why many of the companies we interviewed in the course of writing this book have made bonuses contingent on achievement of some nonfinancial goals.

As we said in chapter 3, Brazil-based Natura is one of our favorites, because the system Marcos Vaz described explicitly makes nonfinancial performance an element of evaluation and compensation for everyone in the company, on par with financial performance. We were also impressed to see that environmental factors are not overweighted as the only kind of nonfinancial value; emphasis is also placed on developing workers' talents, adding value to communities, and enhancing customers' well-being. Our advice: when you open up the Crayola box, don't use only the greens.

In sum, this five-step regime is little different from what firms have traditionally done with financial measures. The only difference is that, when they started at step number 1, they excluded every party to value except the shareholder.

Rule Two: Internalize Externalities

Old formulation: *Externalize every cost you can.*

New formulation: *Own your impact, negative and positive.*

Measurement is the first step toward doing the important thing that capitalism's new environment demands—what we have called internalizing externalities. This is the simple, and at the same time complicated, matter of understanding the impacts an enterprise is having on the world, both good and bad, that don't redound to its income statement and balance sheet—and then taking steps to minimize and make up for the negative ones and to make the most of the positive ones.

In slightly more detail, the course of action for a management team is to begin *by performing an externalities audit.* We don't know of any accounting or consulting firm offering this service, but as standards and measures develop, it seems certain that assessments and then reporting requirements will follow, so getting ahead of the trend will save trouble later—and also offer stakeholder benefits now. This leads to the second step: *identify the affected parties.* Working with them, the goal should be to *codevelop a remediation plan.* In some cases, it will make sense to lobby for new regulations. That's a shocking statement to many ears, perhaps, but exactly what BP's John Browne saw as the way to enable responsible companies to do the right thing without being walloped by competitors that were less social minded.

And again, aligning incentives with the new behaviors they seek can only hasten the change.

In chapter 4, we describe and illustrate the exercise that firms might go through at the outset of this work. It begins with an intuitive image—a set of concentric rings like ripples emanating from a point of impact. The closest ring consists of direct impacts that, in the past, could not be measured with any precision and laid at any particular company's doorstep, but today can be. Particulates from a smokestack are the classic example. The imperative in this ring is that the company must now take ownership of the impact. Thus, for example, Shell's 2010 sustainability report announced that all of its major investment decisions would now factor in a CO_2 price of $40 per tonne.

In the next ring, by contrast, the advice is to take action. Impacts at this level, and in the third ring, too, are not directly attributable to a company's operations because the effects are indirect or the measurement capabilities do not exist to lay them at its doorstep (although that might change in the future). A firm's responsibility here is to be part of the solution, just as it is, in some indistinct way, part of the problem. What makes the difference between the second and the outermost ring? Only the firm's own capabilities. If it is equipped because of an internal competence to attack the problem and devise solutions, the onus is on it to do so. Chemists at Shell are not responsible for all of chemical impact, but by virtue of being chemists, they can advance the field of green chemistry. Companies that lack the particular competence to address indirect impacts can't take action to ameliorate any particular effect but should take an interest in those situations, helping to fund remediation through philanthropic contributions and raising awareness of the problem so that others with specific expertise will be drawn to help.

For a look at how even a small and long-in-the-tooth business can take this new level of responsibility seriously, check out Ellis Paint Company and Pacific Resource Recovery Services, a 125-year-old firm in Los Angeles. Its president and CEO, Sandra Berg, observed in a forum we hosted that Los Angeles would not strike many people as a natural home for an operation involving toxic materials. The community's ability to mount grassroots campaigns is strong, and its suspicion of business in general runs high. So how has Ellis Paint managed to survive there, and even thrive? "In a word," Berg explained, "we capitalized on externalities." She went on to provide more detail:

> Over the last thirty years we've simply recognized a market need—that our customers have environmental challenges to solve—and concluded that we could help them do that. For example, in 1979 (well in advance of hazardous waste laws) we developed a system to recycle our customers' paint-related waste. In the mid-1980s, we developed low-polluting products to keep our paint customers compliant with air quality rules and regulations. All along, we've been careful to respect our local community. In the early 1990s, for example, we needed an EPA permit to continue our recycling business. In applying for it, we chose to involve—rather than alienate—our activist East Los Angeles community and created an open dialog to discuss, understand, and resolve community concerns.

The mind-set here is instructive. Berg sees the externalities involved in her business as problems that she, her customers, and her community share, and her impulse is not the zero-sum one to make them all someone else's problem but rather to make them not a problem at all. Instead, they are a new line of business. Our message to managers is that the ability to make a positive difference where they can is one to be seized and not resisted at all cost. Management is the taming of the manageable, and the realm of externalities is the frontier of the manageable. That the scope of their managerial power grows is a sign of progress in the world. And in the emerging markets, without the habit of black and white vision, we expect that businesses will readily see these opportunities.

It took a long time and considerable legal wrangling for GE, by the way, to own its externalities with respect to pollution of the Hudson River—so long that the cod in the river evolved resistance to some of the pollutants. In 2009, the company began taking remedial action. We did not research the degree to which the "Ecomagination" priority has pushed the company in this direction. Looking at positive externalities, we consider that the company benefits by taking the positive impact on health and using it to attract the talent it needs.

And here's a case—and not a green one—from Apple. The story goes that Steve Jobs, when he tested a new Mac model, took his engineers to task because its start-up time was too long. He pointed out that Apple hoped to sell at least a million of the new machines and therefore that many people would boot up every day. Every second added to the process by bloated code would cost society more than four thousand man-days per year. For a group of engineers focused on system performance, that didn't matter. It was an externality. By pointing out a valuable resource that his company was failing to factor in to its decision making, Jobs internalized it.

To repeat what we explain in chapter 4, there really won't be a place for firms to hide from their externalities as capitalism adapts to ubiquitous, universally accessible measurement. The wise course of action, then, is for a company to find a way to take advantage of that.

Rule Three: Enjoy the Evolution

> Old formulation: *Gain the market power to extract monopoly rents in a zero-sum game.*
>
> New formulation: *Create new value through meaningful innovation.*

This new rule, as we've just stated it, sounds a little vague. Perhaps a better way to present what we have in mind is to repudiate what has been the rule: that firms should exploit their market power to get more, as fully as regulation permits (while fighting any regulation that might constrain them).

Or, let's make the new rule even more direct by using the shorthand term we introduce in chapter 5: they should stop engaging in pseudocompetition.

In our conversations with GE, a comment made by Munesh Makhija, the leader of technology development for GE Healthcare in India, was music to our ears. First, for context, the unmusical part: "In most of the world, we fight a market share battle," he observed. For example, in the United States, the annual growth of GE's markets, put together, is only in the low single digits, and its market share already hovers around one-third of those markets on average. "So really, the battle is around, How do I get a point from a competitor? What do I need to do to win the next set of deals? Knowing that each of those points is a lot of money, because those are big markets." Makhija was describing the conditions and mind-set that give rise to pseudocompetition.

Now here's the part we admired: "When it comes to India," he said, "we also have roughly 30 to 35 percent of share across the modalities we play in. But getting that next percent of share is really not a lot of money, because the markets are smaller. And so the mind-set is that it's not about a bigger slice of the pie, but about making the pie bigger. That's a mind-set we're learning, every day. If we want to be three times the size we are in the next five or seven years, it's not going to come from just gaining share points."

To be sure, it's hard to break the habit of fixating on current markets for current products and slugging it out with well-honed tactics for gaining market share. The easy mobility of talent, which means that many of a large company's workers at any given time are people who learned their trade at one of its competitors, probably doesn't help things. But a firm's ability to break that habit isn't only good for the world, which will therefore enjoy the fruits of more meaningful innovation, it's also good for that company's own survival. It seems it's always the bitter foes focused wholly on each other that fail to notice when a disruptor appears on the horizon with the potential to knock them both out of contention.

Of course, this kind of disruption is the story of Apple. If any industry can be called pseudocompetitive it was the music industry pre-Napster, marked as it was by seemingly intense battles between titanic players and yet somehow able to retain fat margins and churning out product that was ever more indistinguishable. Apple's genius was not only in seeing how music could be distributed differently but also in managing to assemble the ecosystem that would make that new way work.

Clay Christensen has built a career on teaching managers about the phenomenon of disruptive innovation, and he has provided plenty of advice to managers in incumbent firms on how to be a source instead of a victim of it. We think he's correct in his observation that the power dynamics within big companies leave them tripping over themselves. The positions of power—the big jobs that top talent historically gravitate toward in the execution sector—are all attached to big P&Ls, which is to say, mature business lines. The leader of an internal project to launch a disruptive offering, which by the way is often a scrappy "good enough" alternative to a premium offering, rarely stands a chance when push comes to shove in the budgeting process.

Hey, if it were easy, no one would have succumbed to pseudocompetition in the first place. The job of good managers is to stack the deck as much as they can in favor of the innovations that have the potential to break the mold. Back when Jack Welch was at GE, he was attuned to the opportunity and threat that the Internet presented sooner than most of his rank and file. To shake them out of their complacency, he launched something called Destroyyourbusiness.com. As Adrian Slywotzky and David Morrison recount in their 2000 book *How Digital Is Your Business?* the initiative inspired Welch to send a memo to his top managers, for the first time, via e-mail. "In the memo," the authors write, "he urged his unit heads to deploy under-25-year-olds whose sole task would be to figure out how the Internet could be used to destroy GE's existing businesses." As a result, every GE company's management was soon immersed in the study of business models and trying to imagine how theirs could be fundamentally altered to better meet customer needs.

Now, we don't think the average manager is going to wake up tomorrow and decide that his division is going to give up competing. What we're saying is that, to adapt to the next stage of capitalism, managers must find a way to orient themselves to customer value more than to their competitive set. Remember the old joke about the two campers who see a grizzly bear heading for them? As one of them scrambles to pull on his running shoes, the other regards him incredulously. "You can't outrun a grizzly, you idiot," he says. The first man answers, "I don't have to outrun a grizzly. I only have to outrun you."

Nothing could be intellectually easier than focusing on a competitor's performance and simply trying to do incrementally better. But it's an unattractive way to win, constantly looking over one's shoulder— and it probably doesn't buy much time in the end. And if there's one thing worse than spending your life selling sugar water, it's spending your life trying to sell slightly more sugar water than someone else whose only aim is to sell more than you. Instead of seeing competition as their purpose and salvation, firms will shift their perspective and see innovation as the point. As naïve as it may sound, they'll win in the new world of capitalism by ignoring competitors and focusing, relentlessly and creatively, on customers and the rest of their ecology. They'll be part of the rising tide. And they'll enjoy it.

Rule Four: Give It Away Until You Charge for It

Old formulation: *Focus on your particular value-adding capability and outsource all the rest (except where transaction costs are prohibitive).*
New formulation: *Pursue collaborative gains through invisible handshakes.*

Rule 4 goes hand in hand with rule 3, which we suppose is only appropriate because now we are into invisible handshake territory. If the old way to succeed as a capitalist was to negotiate aggressively within a zero-sum framework, then the new rule tells managers to seek to create more value for more stakeholders from collaborative rather than combative behavior.

The *visible* handshakes that characterize much of business today—the outsourcing arrangements, supply chain commitments, free-agent talent for hire—are the step that firms have taken toward acting by this new rule. They've recognized that the old saying "If you want something done right, do it yourself" is a dud. The tasks they choose to outsource aren't the low-value, who-cares stuff but rather the work that requires special expertise and offers a competitive advantage to be gained by putting it into the hands of world-class providers. (This, by the way, is why neither of us repairs our own house. Why settle for an amateur job?)

Now it's just another step to understand that not all such arrangements need be explicitly contracted. It's possible for companies, just as it's possible for individuals, to join forces on efforts that everyone sees as worth doing, without specifying exactly how the work will be distributed and the spoils divided.

This is not a brand-new thought. In 1963, University of Wisconsin law professor Stewart Macaulay published a seminal paper in the *American Sociological Review* citing ample evidence that, in fact, *most* business transactions were primarily noncontractual. Businesses, he observed, in their exchanges with other businesses, drew up many contracts and yet rarely seemed to legally enforce them or even refer to them, preferring to operate on good faith and with a shared commitment to a goal.

Based on that paper and the years of work that followed it, the late Grant Gilmore of Yale later declared Macaulay to be "the Lord High Executioner of the *Contract Is Dead* Movement."

Whether or not that movement went beyond the academy in the 1960s, it certainly has by now. Brad Wheeler, the driver of a successful open source initiative called Kuali, likes to make a similar point about legal action. Kuali is a collaborative project involving efforts of some five hundred software developers spread across more than sixty colleges, universities, and companies. Its aim is to create enterprise resource planning (ERP) systems for universities, as an open source alternative to the expensive proprietary systems sold by big vendors like SAP and Oracle. Wheeler reports that, as he talks to new parties interested in joining the effort, some of them ask, "Whom do I sue if there are problems?" The truth is, Wheeler says, "there is no entity to sue, or false comfort in the delusion of successfully ever doing so. The community itself is the guarantor of the systems, with full transparency to every line of software, every debate on features trade-offs, every bug and quality assurance test." Does that sound a little loosey-goosey in an area as mission critical as enterprise systems? Wheeler insists it's actually a highly resilient means to make sure that both features and security are attended to. "Institutions' continued engagement is bound by rational economics, not contracts," he says. "Anyone can walk away and take the full software code in a different direction, but the reward for doing so is inheriting the full costs to maintain it. The tension in this freedom and responsibility is a powerful attractor that holds the collaboration together."

Kuali's success, like the success of many current open source collaborations, suggests a basic template for dreaming up new invisible handshakes and then bringing together the parties to make them reality. First, managers should identify the innovations their ecology could create if it were one company (because, when you think about it, invisible handshakes are the norm within a company's walls). With a particular innovation in mind, leaders should then identify who could contribute what, and what would incent those players to play. And then they should ask, "What business models are possible?"

Returning to GE Healthcare, we learned that in India, physicians were proud to help the product development teams understand their needs; they felt pleased that GE was developing a product for their market, and they spent time helping the company understand their needs. So GE worked with them to co-create a distribution model. GE salespeople have partnered with AstraZeneca to provide training for their ECG line. Now the salespeople go to a village, explain the product, and leave it with the physician to try out for a few days. If the physician decides not to use it, they take it back—not unlike the rug dealers who urge you to try a carpet in your house, free of charge, for a while. If the physician keeps it, in some cases they help her establish a new business based on the device—the village phone lady of Bangladesh translated into cardiology.

If capitalism now depends most on innovation, innovation depends on collaboration. The old capitalism, bogged down by lawyers and zero-sum negotiations, slows down the process; collaborative innovation speeds it up. And worse, zero-sum players can't play with collaborators for very long, because after a few rounds the collaborators realize they're not collaborating. They're just taking.

Firms that want to be part of fruitful collaboration will start behaving generously. And as a result, they'll attract generous partners.

Rule Five: Operate for Benefit

> Old formulation: *Compartmentalize any support of social goals from the for-profit work of the enterprise.*
>
> New formulation: *Accept that every enterprise produces a mix of financial and other value types, and design your model to optimize it.*

In 2001, *Harvard Business Review* published a hypothetical story presenting a managerial dilemma and inviting real-world experts to offer advice on a problem of ethics and customer perceptions. At issue was whether the visitors to an amusement park would be morally offended by a pricing scheme that allowed higher-paying guests to get preferential treatment, such as the ability to jump on a ride without having suffered through a long, sweaty line. The story was somewhat heartwarming in its portrayal of a woman CEO named Jill Hoover, heir to the family business and wanting to honor her late father's profound democratic sensibilities and desire to make people happy.

For one of the commentators on the case, former American Airlines CEO and chairman Bob Crandall, the answer was clear cut. "As for the case's soupy discussion of her father's ideals, it's simply irrelevant. Jill needs to remember that she's running a business. Her purpose is not to run theme parks, but to make money for shareholders. If it turns out that the best way to maximize Paradise Park's value is to sell off the business for its real-estate value, that's what Jill should do. Come to think of it, Paradise Park would be a neat name for a gated community."

Clearly, Crandall is a capitalist of the old school. We don't mean to imply he was heartless. Under his leadership American Airlines gave generously to many worthy charities. But he honored the rule that business is business, and a company's social contributions should be isolated from its for-profit activity.

Increasingly we see men and women in positions of similar power to Crandall's voicing their frustration with a system that prevents them from honoring human needs and producing value for stakeholders other than those holding stock. Particularly in an era when investors have come to expect such immediate and sizable returns, they fear that U.S. corporate law compels them, if they are in a publicly traded corporation, to put the financial interests of shareholders above all other interests. But they resent that so much talent in their organizations is focused on maximizing shareholder value in the near term, even at great risk, and even when the means of achieving it might not be in the long-term interests of anyone—shareholders included.

For Sweta Mangal, looking to start businesses in India for India, mixed value comes naturally. But is it really possible for managers in publicly traded U.S.-based businesses to move their firms into the "fourth sector" territory we describe in chapter 7? As a first step, they might imagine that their government or the NGOs that serve their community are their customers, as well as the buyers they currently focus on. What would a business model look like that could serve the objectives of both kinds of stakeholders? That's the kind of thinking that led to the success of Shekulo Tov, the company outside Tel Aviv that sells decorative objects crafted by learning-disabled workers, even as it sells therapeutic services to the Israeli government. At the same time Shekulo Tov is paying its workers, it is being paid to employ them.

When Ben Cohen and Jerry Greenfield founded Ben & Jerry's Homemade Ice Cream in 1978, they began with a social-benefit mission, and their fourth sector thinking became so core to the company's DNA that it has survived more than a decade of ownership by multinational food giant Unilever.

So perhaps it's not surprising that an alumnus of the company, Will Patten, is now heavily involved in an initiative called the Vermont Benefits Corporation Act. It formally provides for a new class of organization—one that exists not simply "for profit" but "for benefit." With that term, it expands the definition of fiduciary responsibility beyond an exclusive obligation to shareholders to encompass the interests of all corporate stakeholders, including employees, the local economy, and the environment. Are the directors of a benefit corporation still obliged to act in the best interests of the company's owners? "Absolutely," Patten says. "But they have legal protection to make investments with an eye to the long term, aiming for sustainable returns, not fast paybacks for shareholders."

What if a firm had that "for benefit" status as a formal matter? What would that enable it to do? Whatever it is, we're inclined to say that firms should try to do it anyway. Far more constraining than the threat of shareholder lawsuits are the habits of mind that have made old-school capitalists forget to fight back.

If you've followed the argument so far, you understand that there's really no alternative for them. Every enterprise—for profit, nonprofit, governmental—already produces mixed value. Even hedge funds, which have come in for plenty of bashing here, give money to charity, provide employment, underwrite the arts, and so on. If they recognize, measure, and take responsibility for their externalities, they are de facto members of the fourth sector. So they should take pride in their positive externalities. They're not failing the shareholders by not turning them all into immediate profits; instead, they're helping the economy do its job.

The New Multinational Corporation

We've offered a first draft of a new rule set that firms can use to get ahead of the five curves described in chapters 3–7. We've told the stories of some pioneers and have provided examples of established companies in the West that seem to follow these directions. Humble as we are, though, we think it will take more than our saying so to impel change for many managers.

It may take a kick in the pants. After all, J. Edwards Deming, Joseph Juran, and their confreres were preaching about quality for decades to American businesses. The only ones listening were the Japanese, who were struggling to break into the economic big time and searching for new ideas. By the 1980s they were giving U.S. manufacturing industries a run for their money, the way the Chinese have more recently, and U.S. companies hastened to visit Toyota, Matsushita, Toshiba, et al. to see what quality, kanban, and kaizen were all about. (Along the way they learned about lifetime employment and keiretsu, which haven't proven so durable. Recombination and selection work hand in hand.)

But we don't think it's going to be China, or any other country, that sets the bar and provides the convincing examples this time. We think it will be a handful of very smart global companies that, yes, get it.

It's ironic: for a couple of decades now, pundits and many Silicon Valley garagistas have been declaring that big companies are too slow, too internally focused, too closed, too set in their ways, and irretrievably mired in the mind-set of twentieth-century capitalism. And indeed, it does take a long time to turn an aircraft carrier.

Once you do, though, you have a large, heavily armed weapon system going in the right direction.

Four factors favor this elite group of global companies. First, the best of them have been slowly *figuring out how connectivity, Web 2.0, and social networks can create value* in the MNC context. IBM, for example, conducts "jams" to gather opinions from all over the world and experiments with holding events in Second Life; P&G has instituted its Connect + Develop program to source innovation from everywhere. Movie studios have learned to open movies globally and adjust their ad campaigns based on what's being tweeted around the world. These companies—we don't claim to have an exhaustive list—have been studying (or learning osmotically from employees) how new connectivity, diversity, and recombination of new ideas and behaviors can make them better businesses and have taken significant steps to incorporate them in their ways of doing business.

Second, *the winner-take-all, "natural monopoly" economics described in chapter 5 favor the global company that has a head start on creating a planet-scale learning system.* Partners Healthcare has a great model but lacks the clout to transplant it to every hospital in Boston, let alone the world. Autodesk may dominate the CAD/CAM space in most of the world, but it has powerful competitors in other closely allied spaces like manufacturing process control. But consider IBM's Smarter Planet initiatives. IBM began with the insight we mention in chapter 4—that sensors were proliferating in every corner of the globe and of people's lives, and the data sensors produce will be made available to improve the management of every process people care about at every scale, from blood circulation to traffic circulation to air traffic control. IBM set out to establish the framework for gathering, analyzing, and acting on real-time information. And as it creates solutions for smarter cities, smarter retailers, smarter buildings, and smarter public health (the "Smart" Web page lists twenty-seven domains to be smartened up), it has a great shot at creating the mother of all learning systems.

It's important to note that IBM is doing this without trying to create a closed, proprietary system. It is creating the App Store for the real world, establishing a core platform that others in a specific ecology can contribute to. This is particularly impressive given that, not long ago, this aircraft carrier was sailing in the opposite direction. In the days of SNA (IBM's proprietary standard for data networking that dominated the pre-Internet infrastructure), IBM fought hard to resist an open, international standard. Then Linux came along, and IBM embraced it—perhaps largely to support a competitor to Microsoft's hegemony at the time. But since then, IBM has released numerous patents into the commons and made many canny choices to become more open. (Remember the story of Microsoft's Kinect in chapter 5? This is the same story, writ much larger.)

So IBM, like GE, is exemplifies the bifurcation of the economy we describe in chapter 8. It has the scope, capabilities, and resources to create a global learning network that will yield increasing returns. And it has a sufficiently open system and attitude to play well with the experimentation sector, ensuring that the IBM ecosystem will continue to attract users and developers.

A third advantage of this handful of companies is *the ability to act decisively, globally, swiftly*. This statement is paradoxical, we realize, coming from us. Our point of view has been that success is an emergent outcome and not something that can be managed directly—and we're not abandoning that conviction. But the outcomes that emerge, whether from biological, social, or economic activities, depend on the environment that hosts them: giant lizards arise in the rain forest, polar bears in the tundra.

In any organization, no decision is more embattled than one that changes the rules. Whether those rules have to do with sales commission structure, the paths to the top, or the rearrangement of decision rights, the fact is that every individual in the organization has already adapted to them as they are, and each has an opinion about the impact of a proposed change. In a democracy, this makes it hard to alter, say, government spending priorities. Or anything else. Lee Kuan Yew and many other Asian commentators deride the resulting indecision of Western democracies.

Companies are not democracies, especially the well-established global leaders we're discussing here, and every employee knows it. So even though empowerment, latitude, and entrepreneurship can be genuinely encouraged and celebrated in a large company (and after thirty years of trying, in a generation of management), it's still true that when a Sam Palmisano declares Smarter Planet the course to be set, or a Jeff Immelt sets aside funding for ICFC, the environment changes. The internal entrepreneurs reevaluate their opportunities and understand the new constraints. In a well-run company with the right kind of talent, resources—in particular the attention of talented people—start pursuing the new direction in thousands of ways no one can anticipate.

In his 1993 book *The Twilight of Sovereignty*, Walter Wriston anticipated that corporations would become more powerful than nations.

He was speaking from his experience in building Citicorp into an organization that could move more money around the world than any central bank save the U.S. Fed. We think that this combination of being the world's fastest learners and most decisive actors fulfills this prophecy, if only for a handful of companies. But they have discovered something Wriston didn't anticipate.

Wriston once told Chris it had taken him thirty years to build a cadre of managers he could send anywhere in the world and trust they'd do the job as Citicorp would want it done. (Interestingly, another lionized manager of the 1990s, ABB's Percy Barnevik, told Chris almost verbatim the same thing.) But Beth Comstock, GE's CMO, gave us a different slant: "We had to find someone who knew water, and knew strategic marketing and innovation. That person had to know India, and ideally you'd want them to know the company. And that person doesn't exist. So we've had to shift. Maybe they *don't* know the industry, but they know the market really well. It's taken us five to eight years to get to that point." Now, though, it gives them an advantage in moving rapidly.

Underscoring this point, Comstock continues:

> Over the past three years we've come up with a leadership
> and growth training series for our [global] business unit CEOs
> and their teams. Now we're taking it and saying, "How do
> I take all those innovation tools and apply them locally?"
> Pretty much every business is going to be doing this in the
> next year. Once you get your toolkit, you get your few pilots,
> and you know it works, then you have the ability to mobilize
> the whole company and say, "Everyone has to go in that
> direction." I think we do that pretty well. There are parts of
> us that are slow, but once we make up our minds, we go with
> incredible speed and scale, and we're trying to decrease the
> time it takes to get buy-in.

The fourth and final force that will create these dominant MNCs combines their learning network and decisiveness advantages. As far back as 1994 Jack Welch claimed that, following the quarterly meetings of all the GE business heads, the shared knowledge of world markets across business lines made it "the smartest management team in the world, for a couple of months." Now the connectivity isn't physical and quarterly; instead, it's continual and virtual. *Global companies are sensing networks*, not only picking up the latest market trends but also learning internally what works. They can pilot incentive systems, training tools, and marketing programs, obtain feedback, and decide what tools are valuable and should be made available throughout the company.

We conclude that these companies will emerge from a couple of decades of lagging in their uptake of new management approaches and principles to being the leaders. They will discover new approaches first, codify them most thoroughly, and disseminate them fastest. Thus they will be the primary vectors for promulgating the new practices of capitalism.

As they do, they will moderate the threat of stagnation in the G7 nations as the emerging economies take the growth and innovation lead. Most of the MNCs reinventing themselves as we've described are Western-based companies. They are moving swiftly both to participate in the successes of the emerging economies and to learn from them. As important players in their native economies, they will strengthen growth and accelerate innovation there.

The New DuPont Equation

We've described five new rules we expect these leaders to internalize. And all along, we've said that the shifts in capitalism won't occur because of any ideological scolding or hand-wringing but because capitalists will find it valuable to do different things. Our discussion of pathfinder MNCs suggests how that path will be beaten.

Once the vanguard has shown the way, others will pave it. In chapter 3, we describe how the DuPont equation arose from an attempt to codify how visible hand capitalism could be managed. Is it too soon to look for the formula that could replace it?

It probably is, but we're standing on the sun, so we won't let that deter us. Recall that the original equation was a formula that helped manage for maximum return on investment, depending on margin, sales-to-asset ratio, and financial leverage. Aside from the damaging runaways this perspective produced, some flaws need to be fixed for a new capitalist formula:

- Most fundamentally, the objective of business should be broadened beyond ROI. Too narrow an objective function leads to runaways, in particular the fetishizing of financial return and measurements. There is no longer a need to make the most of financial investment; there's more money available than can be productively invested.

- The definition of value creation should take into account the benefits perceived by all stakeholders and should be broad enough to take into account variations in valuation around the world.

- As a management guideline, any prescription must move the corporation from a mind-set of managing a static equilibrium to acting on and adapting to a dynamic ecology.

- Accordingly, the guideline should help enterprises plan for the growth of their ecologies not solely the growth of their entities. Business models for extracting one's share of the value created are hard to prescribe, because the interests of different entities vary.

So here's our candidate: consider that the contribution to growth is driven by the value of a typical innovation, the number of people affected by each innovation, and the frequency with which innovation occurs. Arithmentically:

$$\frac{\text{Change in value created}}{\text{Time}} = \frac{\text{Change in value from the average innovation}}{\text{Person}} \times \frac{\text{Persons}}{\text{Innovation}} \times \frac{\text{Innovation}}{\text{Time}} = \text{Growth}$$

A dynamic economy requires growing companies—those that increase their value-added contribution over time. To maximize this, a company should prioritize the innovation that leads to the greatest value. This sounds obvious. But consider the change in the tone of voice we heard when GE engineers spoke of their work developing life-saving solutions for their home markets; at one point, in describing GE's in country, for country incubator product, Ravi Kaushik exclaimed to us, "There are people in villages, still, now, who are using light bulbs to warm up babies! . . . That's the market creation opportunity, where we migrate people to baby warmers, which are safer and clinically better." Now note the contrast with how most marketers talk about their work and how many of our economy's resources are allocated to pseudo-competitive innovations that add very little value. Second, an innovation should have the widest possible market. As the late C. K. Prahalad pointed out, the "bottom of the pyramid" is a market and not a social problem, and entrepreneurs like Varun Sahni are treating it that way. So is GE, with its "more products at more price points" strategy, bringing billions of people into its target markets.

And third, the battleground of competitiveness now goes beyond time to market, to include the frequency with which a firm brings valuable innovations to market. GE, by creating independent local development teams, is adding to the diversity of ideas and the opportunity to recombine them, and hence the likelihood of having innovations to bring to market more often.

Looking at Apple, you'd conclude it had been using this equation for a long time. It has focused on building an ecology, earning its fair share of the rewards but leaving plenty for others who can earn them (at the expense of those who have historically extracted margin from market power by restricting the market). Apple's offers are more highly valued than its competitors'—largely for intangible reasons ranging from design to sustainable disposability—and have extremely broad appeal globally. And it has brought true innovation to market more frequently than perhaps any other consumer products company in recent decades.

If we were running the economy from our warm place on the sun, we'd want companies to use this formula to allocate their attention and capital. We readily acknowledge that we have described only the first of the three phases of adaptation that would occur if a new feedback loop were put in place: the one in which managers take seriously the objectives it's intended to achieve and start trying to make themselves as good as Apple and GE. In the next step, enterprises— and this formula applies equally to businesses, government agencies, and NGOs, because it's about mixed value and not profits—would find ways to organize around these concepts. Eventually, it could become a somewhat mindless game of its own and possibly even give rise to runaways. Then we'll have to go back to the sun and take a new look.

Standing on the Sun: Capitalism Adapts

This book emerged from a question, asked before the onset of the Great Recession: what's next for capitalism? It was motivated by the then obvious facts, some of them enumerated in chapter 1, that pointed to a future that will be different from the past as economic power shifts to younger, faster-growing emerging economies and as information technology creates a kind of globalization never seen before.

The events during the gestation of our thinking suggested that the question was far from academic. The global financial crisis, political upheaval in the Middle East, sharpened concerns for energy and climate, and the debates in the West about health care, social services, and debt are independent events—to a point. But with the exception of the actual tectonic event in Japan, all of them can be related to tectonic shifts in the way the world organizes to fulfill people's desires. As happened during industrialization, power is shifting across geographies, classes, and cohorts.

If we were historians, we'd throw up our hands at the challenge of predicting the next world order. And as businesspeople, we know that the business perspective is too narrow, short term, and self-interested to let us make reliable predictions about something as broad as the form of capitalism.

But drawing on the lessons of evolutionary biology, we have a model for parsing the situation. As we say in chapter 2, we're at the dawn of a Cambrian Explosion. In the real one, an innovation—multicelled animals—is believed to have given rise to most of the phyla we see today, during a period in which biological innovation accelerated by an order of magnitude.[1] Today, global connectivity in its many present and future forms is the multicellular innovation, and will give rise to uncountable experiments. Many will fail, following in the path of the

five-eyed *Opabinia*. That's why we need the experimentation sector.
And all successes will stand on the shoulders of successful past accomplishments (hence the execution sector); by analogy, all multi-celled
animals use mitochondria and DNA. Private ownership and markets
are the mitochondria of economics, and we don't expect these core
elements of capitalism, now embraced not only by formerly commu-
nist societies but by virtual communities online, will disappear.

Rather than theorize about what might come next, we visited some
of the hotter spots of economic innovation and found five trends that
we are confident point to directions of economic evolution. And in the
preceding chapter and this one, we've hazarded some opinions about
how they would drive economic models. We would count ourselves
successful if we got as far as predicting mammals; we certainly don't
think we've identified *homo sapiens*.

But if you travel to India, China, Brazil, Israel, and the many other
places we've been in the past three years, you won't doubt that every
country on Earth is adapting, and the West, perceiving it has everything to lose and short-sighted about what it might gain, is adapting
more slowly than most. This conservatism will be particularly costly
at a time when innovation and change are accelerating. But connectivity provides the diversity and recombination that fuel evolution;
instant reaction from global markets accelerates selection.

Standing on the sun, we don't see a coming battle of ideologies but
a natural and inevitable process of evolution.

We worry that the United States in particular will suffer from the
innovator's dilemma—the inability to let go of its past successes. This
would be catastrophic, because the innovative talent that has made
the U.S. economy resilient to change in the past is now sufficiently
mobile that the country would lose its attractiveness as a place to innovate, just as India and other economies are becoming more hospitable.
Already, many innovators from abroad who learn their trade in Silicon
Valley and Kendall Square and formerly would have remained there
return to Mumbai, Shanghai, or Singapore to work and live.

If the leaders of China are ready to see what works, to call it communism, and move on, the West should be equally wise. The world
economy is going to be less about competition, more about innovation, less about individual people or companies, more about groups

and ecologies, and less about concentration of power and wealth and more about sustainable social systems. This is hard to see on the ground, but quite evident on the sun. Capitalism will adapt, with us or without us. Whatever works, let's call it capitalism and move on.

We leave you with another bit of wisdom from Tom Stoppard, one we've come to embrace as we've tried to make sense of all we've seen during our research. In the play *Arcadia*, the mathematician Valentine marvels at recent developments in the mathematics of adaptive systems.

"It's the best possible time to be alive," he says, "when almost everything you thought you knew is wrong."

Epilogue

In any given country, we benefit from living around well-off neighbors,
and we trade and share many things with them, and we can as a
species spread all of these things around the world . . . with one proviso:
we will have to keep updating rules.

—Paul Romer, New York, September 15, 2010

Economics has been seen as separated from the rest of human learning,
divorced from religion or ethics, because it's all about "rationality." But
[in India] I see everyone is rational, but it's not always about in-the-moment
profit maximization. By rationality I mean a concept of self which is about
fulfillment, a much bigger concept. And I don't know when or how that is
going to clash with the "capitalist economic system."

—Nikhil Ojha, Mumbai, October 6, 2009

Here you have one American macroeconomic perspective, and one Indian business leader's view from the ground up. We hope the book you've just read integrates the two: capitalism can, and will, move in the direction of providing a "broader sense of fulfillment," not through a clash of systems but through the interbreeding and continual selection of rules.

To stand on the sun is to see that connectivity and globalization will put this process in motion. The rules of competition and innovation will change, and property rights will be redefined to exploit the unique economics of information. And although we acknowledge that adaptive systems will always surprise us, we see many benefits in these developments.

You may be wondering how you can help.

We've said that capitalism is what capitalists do. These choices of behavior are shaped by rules at every level—social mores, regulations, tax incentives, compensation plans, personal principles—and they coevolve with one another. The choices individuals make, in other words, influence the rules that operate in the system. Without the peahen's insistence on fancy tails, there wouldn't be a runaway.

In 2009, Chris spoke to an executive of a credit card company about how his business was enduring the downturn. "Well," he responded, "you have to remember that most of our business is getting people to spend money they don't have on crap they don't need." Chris, emboldened by the crisis atmosphere of the time, asked him why he would abet such an activity. "We're a profit center," he said. "This is what they pay me to do." And indeed, the company had written the rules that way.

Our point here is not to join the chorus newly hating on debt-financed consumerism. It is that in Washington Consensus capitalism, the explanation "This is what they pay me to do" has carried great authority.

Standing on the sun, it does not. Each of us is a part of the environment that selects the rules. Around the world, as measurement, reporting, and transparency affect the rewards, individuals will decide not to ask for, or pay, bribes, decide not to dump their waste, decide not to abuse laborers because they have few choices of employment, decide not to sell people mortgages they can't afford, decide not to trade credit default swaps with taxpayer money—and choose not to accept financial incentives as an unquestioned rationale for action. Yes, there are incentives to do all of those things. But as Nikhil Ojha says, there are other rational incentives as well. All you have to do is give greater weight to nonfinancial colors, and you will be part of the selective pressure that is choosing the rules for the next form of capitalism.

A peahen doesn't know any better. But you do.

Notes

Chapter One

1. Ken Favaro, Per-Ola Karlsson, and Gary L. Neilson, "CEO Succession 2010: The Four Types of CEOs," *Strategy & Business* 63 (Summer 2011): 123–456.

2. World Bank, "World Development Indicators Database, 1 July 2009: Gross Domestic Product (2008)," January 7, 2009, http://siteresources.worldbank.org/DATASTATISTICS/Resources/GDP.pdf.

3. Economist, *Pocket World in Figures, 2010 Edition* (New York: The Economist Group, 2010).

4. Second Republic, "India Mobile Service ARPU Declined by Up To 37% in 2008," http://www.secondrepublic.in/StoryDescription.aspx?mainid=1&storyid=276. The article reports on the Telecom Regulatory Authority of India data.

5. Telefonica, "Key Figures," http://www.telefonica.com/en/about_telefonica/html/magnitudes/magnitudes.shtml.

6. "A Special Report on Innovation in Emerging Markets," *Economist*, April 17, 2010.

7. Ibid.

8. In *BLUR* (*BLUR: The Speed of Change in the Connected Economy* by Stan Davis and Christopher Meyer [April 1, 1999, Perseus Books]), Chris's first book (coauthored with Stan Davis), this approach to continual evolution in place was called "downloading the upgrade."

9. Associated Press, "Man's Quest to Trade Paper Clip For House Successful," http://www.foxnews.com/story/0,2933,202842,00.html.

10. The first GUI was released by the National Center for Supercomputing Applications at the University of Illinois in 1993.

11. And six of the world's top ten national growth rates from 2000 to 2009 were in Sub-Saharan Africa.

12. As we discuss in chapter 2, this instant connectivity guarantees occasional, unpredictable avalanches.

13. Christopher Meyer, "The Next Bubble: Eyeballs," Now, New, Next blog, September 16, 2009, http://blogs.hbr.org/now-new-next/2009/09/the-eyeball-bubble.html.

14. See http://en.wikipedia.org/wiki/List_of_countries_by_number_of_mobile_phones_in_use.

Chapter Two

1. Plus or minus a couple of years—it was a long relationship.

2. Converts call this kind of thing a *meme*, a word coined by geneticist Richard Dawkins to signify an idea that spreads through a population of minds in the way that a gene can penetrate a population. In effect, he's applying the same kind of adaptive systems thinking we've adapted for capitalism to the process Keynes described by which today's actions are driven by yesterday's ideas. See John Clippinger, ed., *The Biology of Business*.

3. Chris already wrote one: *It's Alive* (Crown Business, 2003).

4. Paul Romer, "A Theory of History, with an Application," presentation to the Long Now Foundation. http://fora.tv/2009/05/18/Paul_Romer_A_Theory_of_History_with_an_Application.

5. John Maynard Keynes, *The General Theory of Employment, Interest and Money* (1935), 383.

6. Bacteria have more than two parents. If you're not a mammal, skip this section.

7. See Christopher Meyer, "The New Facts of Life," *Wired*, February, 2004.

8. This is a simplification, of course—many elements of an ad's design affect whether web users actually get to see it. The new field of search engine optimization is aimed at designing ads for this aspect of fitness.

9. Affinnova, http://www.affinnova.com/press_releases/06-16-08_optimize08.html.

10. Richard Preston, *American Steel* (1992), describes in mesmerizing detail an accident in which blobs of molten steel rained down on a factory floor. If that's not enough, where it landed the moisture in the concrete instantly turned to superheated steam, turning the plant into a minefield.

11. It can be argued that when economists describe the search for, say, an equilibrium price in a market, they are describing a kind of feedback; if the price is too high, the market buys too few, and the producer lowers the price until the optimum point is reached. But in practice, economists are taught to calculate the optimum not through simulations of individual choices but through methods of calculus that assume a static world and a stable answer.

12. "Elasticities" are a kind of dumbing down of partial derivatives. Much of postwar economics in the United States, led by Robert Samuelson, focused on the application of differential calculus to the core ideas of economics. In itself, this focus was productive, but it paved a road for the profession to rewarding technical ingenuity more than practical insight. This meant that the profession itself evolved from "political economy" to a technical exercise in finding soluble equations.

13. Joshua Epstein, director of the Brookings Institution's Center for Social Dynamics, has applied ABM to a wide variety of economic and social questions. In 2009 he received the Pioneer Award, the most prestigious grant given by the National Institutes of Health, to support research into epidemiology and inoculation strategies using these techniques.

14. In a weird and happy coincidence, Chris drafted this chapter on a plane returning from a meeting in Brazil. His seatmate on the plane was another speaker from the conference: Edward Prescott.

15. Eric Beinhocker, *The Origin of Wealth: Evolution, Complexity, and the Radical Remaking of Economics* (Boston: Harvard Business School Press, 2007), 47.

16. Ironically, the common use of war metaphors in business arose in part from a similar effort. General Von Clausewitz, the nineteenth-century German general who articulated many of the principles of war still taught in war colleges, was fascinated with the new insights of physics, and he set about trying to understand and express what they meant for his profession. Today, the Marines, led by Lt. Gen. Paul Van Riper, have been pioneering the application of complexity insights to war fighting. Some of his success was described in Malcolm Gladwell's *Blink*.

17. The extinction of the dinosaurs and subsequent proliferation of mammals came hundreds of millions of years later than the Cambrian, but it is another episode of rapid evolutionary change.

Chapter Three

1. Facebook's first index measured only English speakers residing in the United States, but it is working to expand its coverage. Current tidbit: Canadians are happier on the day before Canadian Thanksgiving, it turns out, than on the day itself.

2. *Report by the Commission on the Measurement of Economic Performance and Social Progress*, 2009, http://media.ft.com/cms/f3b4c24a-a141-11de-a88d-00144feabdc0.pdf.

Chapter Five

1. Dissenting opinion of Justice Douglas in *United States v. Columbia Steel Co.*

2. Ankush Chopra is also assistant professor of strategy and management at Babson University. Examples shared in personal communication, November, 2008.

Chapter Six

1. We must acknowledge the inspiration to the whole maker movement provided by Neal Stephenson, who in his 1995 book *The Diamond Age* imagined a device called a matter compiler. The user fed a design—a digital file that could be expensive if it had been custom made—into the compiler, which drew the recycled atoms it needed at commodity prices.

2. Technically, economists distinguish between the minimal profit needed to keep firms in the market—akin to the highest price consumers will pay for a product—and "economic rent," profits above this minimum. If a business creates positive externalities, they will be divided between consumer surplus and economic rent.

3. Quoted from Professors Dennis Crouch and Jason Rantanen, posted on Patently-O, a patent law blog, commenting on the work of Michael Meurer and Jim Besson on July 15, 2007. In 2008, Princeton University Press published Meurer and Besson's *Patent Failures*.

Chapter Seven

1. Disclosure: Chris is a partner of The Monitor Group.

Chapter Eight

1. A favorite in this line is *The Lady Eve*, a classic 1941 Preston Sturges comedy starring Barbara Stanwyck and Henry Fonda. In it, a character named Muggsy indulges in some comic business in a tycoon's mansion, trying to determine which of the phones on a table is ringing.

Chapter Nine

1. See http://en.wikipedia.org/wiki/Cambrian_explosion.

Bibliography

Introduction: The Center of Capitalism?

Baumol, William J., Robert E. Litan, and Carl J. Schramm. *Good Capitalism, Bad Capitalism, and the Economics of Growth and Prosperity*, 1st ed. New Haven, CT: Yale University Press, 2007.

Ferguson, Niall. *Empire: The Rise and Demise of the British World Order and the Lessons for Global Power*. New York: Basic Books, 2003.

Halper, Stefan A. *The Beijing Consensus: How China's Authoritarian Model Will Dominate the Twenty-First Century*. New York: Basic Books, 2010.

Herman, Arthur. *The Idea of Decline in Western History*. New York: Free Press, 1997.

Huang, Yasheng. *Capitalism with Chinese Characteristics: Entrepreneurship and the State*. New York: Cambridge University Press, 2008.

Kang, David C. *Capitalism: Corruption and Development in South Korea and the Philippines*. Cambridge, UK/New York: Cambridge University Press, 2002.

Kelly, Kevin. *Out of Control: The Rise of Neo-Biological Civilization*, 1st ed. New York: Perseus Books, 1994.

Lessig, Lawrence. *Free Culture: The Nature and Future of Creativity*. New York: Penguin Press, 2004.

Mahajan, Vijay. *Africa Rising: How 900 Million African Consumers Offer More Than You Think*. Upper Saddle River, NJ: Pearson Prentice Hall, 2008.

Schumpeter, Joseph A. *Capitalism, Socialism and Democracy*, 2nd ed. New York, London: Harper & Brothers, 1947.

Sobel, Dava. *A More Perfect Heaven: How Copernicus Revolutionized the Cosmos*. New York: Walker & Company, 2011.

Stoppard, Tom. *Rock 'n' Roll*. London: Faber and Faber, 2006.

Chapter One: Capitalism's New Center of Gravity

Anderson, Chris. *Free: The Future of a Radical Price*. New York: Hyperion, 2009.

Benioff, Marc, and Carlye Adler. *Behind the Cloud: The Untold Story of How Salesforce.com Went from Idea to Billion-Dollar Company—and Revolutionized an Industry*. San Francisco: Jossey-Bass, 2009.

Erickson, Tamara. *Plugged In: The Generation Y Guide to Thriving at Work*. Boston: Harvard Business Press, 2008.

Friedman, Thomas L. *The World Is Flat: A Brief History of the Twenty-First Century*. New York: Farrar, Straus and Giroux, 2005.

Garten, Jeffrey E. *The Big Ten: The Big Emerging Markets and How They Will Change Our Lives*. New York: Basic Books, 1997.

Gifford, Rob. *China Road: A Journey into the Future of a Rising Power*. New York: Random House, 2007.

Gupta, Anil K., and Haiyan Wang. *Getting China and India Right: Strategies for Leveraging the World's Fastest Growing Economies for Global Advantage*. San Francisco: Jossey-Bass, 2009.

Jha, Prem Shankar. *The Twilight of the Nation State: Globalisation, Chaos and War*. London/Ann Arbor, MI: Pluto Press, 2006.

Kelly, Eamonn. *Powerful Times: Rising to the Challenge of Our Uncertain World*. Upper Saddle River, NJ: Pearson Prentice Hall, 2005.

MacDonald, Kyle. *One Red Paperclip: Or How an Ordinary Man Achieved His Dream with the Help of a Simple Office Supply*. New York: Three Rivers Press, 2007.

Magnus, George. *Uprising: Will Emerging Markets Shape or Shake the World Economy?* Chichester, UK: Wiley, 2010.

Mahbubani, Kishore. *The New Asian Hemisphere: The Irresistible Shift of Global Power to the East*. New York: PublicAffairs, 2008.

Martin, Chuck. *The Third Screen: Marketing to Your Customers in a World Gone Mobile*. Boston: Nicholas Brealey Publishing, 2011.

Moody, Glyn. *Rebel Code: Linux and the Open Source Revolution*. New York: Basic Books, 2002.

Palfrey, John, and Urs Gasser. *Born Digital: Understanding the First Generation of Digital Natives*. New York: Basic Books, 2008.

Prahalad, C.K. *The Fortune at the Bottom of the Pyramid: Eradicating Poverty Through Profits*, rev. and updated 5th anniversary ed. Upper Saddle River, NJ: Pearson Prentice Hall, 2009.

Rosen, William. *The Most Powerful Idea in the World: A Story of Steam, Industry, and Invention*. New York: Random House, 2010.

Shapiro, Carl, and Hal R. Varian. *Information Rules: A Strategic Guide to the Network Economy*. Boston: Harvard Business School Press, 1998.

Shirky, Clay. *Here Comes Everybody: The Power of Organizing Without Organizations*. New York: Penguin Press, 2008.

Spence, Michael. *The Next Convergence: The Future of Economic Growth in a Multispeed World*. New York: Farrar, Straus and Giroux, 2011.

Subramanian, Arvind. *Eclipse: Living in the Shadow of China's Economic Dominance*. Washington, DC: Peterson Institute of International Economics, 2011.

Sullivan, Nicholas P. *You Can Hear Me Now: How Microloans and Cell Phones Are Connecting the World's Poor to the Global Economy*. San Francisco: Jossey-Bass, 2007.

Tapscott, Don. *Grown Up Digital: How the Net Generation Is Changing Your World*, 1st ed. New York: McGraw-Hill, 2008.

Useem, Michael, Peter Cappelli, Harbir Singh, and Jitendra Singh. *The India Way: How India's Top Business Leaders Are Revolutionizing Management*. Boston, Mass: Harvard Business Press, 2010.

Wriston, Walter B. *The Twilight of Sovereignty: How the Information Revolution Is Transforming Our World*. New York: Scribner, 1992.

Zakaria, Fareed. *The Post-American World: Release 2.0*. New York: W. W. Norton & Company, 2011.

Chapter Two: Cambrian Capitalism

Arthur, W. Brian. *The Nature of Technology: What It Is and How It Evolves*. New York: Free Press, 2009.

Beinhocker, Eric D. *The Origin of Wealth: Evolution, Complexity, and the Radical Remaking of Economics*. Boston: Harvard Business School Press, 2006.

Cronin, Helena. *The Ant and the Peacock: Altruism and Sexual Selection from Darwin to Today*. Cambridge, UK/New York: Cambridge University Press, 1992.

Darwin, Charles. *The Origin of Species*. 1859. 150th anniversary ed. New York: Signet Classics, 2003.

Dawkins, Richard. *The Extended Phenotype: The Gene as the Unit of Selection*. Oxford/San Francisco: W.H. Freeman & Company, 1982.

Eberhart, Russell C., Yuhui Shi, and James Kennedy. *Swarm Intelligence*. San Francisco: Morgan Kaufmann, 2001.

Enriquez, Juan. *As the Future Catches You: How Genomics & Other Forces Are Changing Your Life, Work, Health & Wealth*. New York: Crown Business, 2001.

Epstein, Joshua M., and Robert L. Axtell. *Growing Artificial Societies: Social Science from the Bottom Up*. Cambridge, MA: MIT Press, 1996.

Fisher, R. A. *The Genetical Theory of Natural Selection*. New York: Oxford University Press, 2000.

Frank, Robert H. *The Darwin Economy: Liberty, Competition, and the Common Good*. Princeton, NJ: Princeton University Press, 2011.

Godin, Seth. *Survival Is Not Enough*. New York: Free Press, 2002.

Graeber, David. *Debt: The First 5,000 Years*. Brooklyn, NY: Melville House, 2011.

Kauffman, Stuart A. *At Home in the Universe: The Search for the Laws of Self-Organization and Complexity*. New York: Oxford University Press, 1995.

Keynes, John Maynard. *The General Theory of Employment, Interest and Money*. 1936. Rep. London: Macmillan and Co., Ltd., 1964.

Meadows, Donella. *Thinking in Systems: A Primer*. White River Junction, VT: Chelsea Green Publishing, 2008.

Meyer, Christopher, and Stan Davis. *It's Alive: The Coming Convergence of Information, Biology, and Business*. New York/London: Texere Publishing, 2003.

Miller, John H., and Scott E. Page. *Complex Adaptive Systems: An Introduction to Computational Models of Social Life*. Princeton, NJ: Princeton University Press, 2007.

Mitchell, Melanie. *Complexity: A Guided Tour*. New York: Oxford University Press, 2009.

Resnick, Mitchel. *Turtles, Termites, and Traffic Jams: Explorations in Massively Parallel Microworlds*. Cambridge, MA: MIT Press, 1997.

Romer, Paul. *Endless Frontiers: How Ideas Shape Economic Growth*. Princeton, NJ: Princeton University Press (forthcoming).

Stokey, Nancy L. Robert E. Lucas Jr., and Edward C. Prescott, *Recursive Methods in Economic Dynamics*. Cambridge, MA: Harvard University Press, 1989.

Chapter Three: Capitalism in Color

Alonso, William, and Paul Starr, eds. *The Politics of Numbers*. New York: Russell Sage Foundation, 1987.

Anderson, Ray C. *Confessions of a Radical Industrialist: Profits, People, Purpose—Doing Business by Respecting the Earth*. New York: St. Martin's Press, 2009.

Bok, Derek. *The Politics of Happiness: What Government Can Learn from the New Research on Well-Being*, 1st ed. Princeton, NJ: Princeton University Press, 2010.

Brooks, Arthur C. *Gross National Happiness: Why Happiness Matters for America—and How We Can Get More of It*. New York: Basic Books, 2008.

Caplow, Theodore, Louis Hicks, and Ben Wattenberg. *The First Measured Century: An Illustrated Guide to Trends in America, 1900–2000*. Washington, DC: American Enterprise Institute Press, 2000.

Chandler, Alfred Dupont, Stephen Salisbury, and Adeline Cook Strange. *Pierre S. Du Pont and the Making of the Modern Corporation*. New York: Harper & Row Publishers, 1971.

Diener, Ed. *Happiness: Unlocking the Mysteries of Psychological Wealth*. Malden, MA: Wiley-Blackwell, 2008.

Easterlin, Richard A., Holger Hinte, and Klaus F. Zimmerman. *Happiness, Growth, and the Life Cycle*. Oxford: Oxford University Press, 2011.

Frey, Bruno S. *Happiness: A Revolution in Economics*. Munich Lectures in Economics. Cambridge, MA: MIT Press, 2008.

Graham, Carol. *Happiness Around the World: The Paradox of Happy Peasants and Miserable Millionaires*. New York: Oxford University Press, 2010.

Igo, Sarah E. *The Averaged American: Surveys, Citizens, and the Making of a Mass Public*. Cambridge, MA: Harvard University Press, 2007.

Kahneman, Daniel. *Well-Being: The Foundations of Hedonic Psychology*. New York: Russell Sage Foundation Publications, 1999.

Leonsis, Ted. *The Business of Happiness: 6 Secrets to Extraordinary Success in Life and Work*. Washington, DC: Regnery Publishing, 2010.

Porter, Michael E., and Mark R. Kramer. "Creating Shared Value." *Harvard Business Review*, January 2011.

Sachs, Jeffrey D. *The Price of Civilization: Reawakening American Virtue and Prosperity*. New York: Random House, 2011.

Savitz, Andrew W. *The Triple Bottom Line: How Today's Best-Run Companies Are Achieving Economic, Social, and Environmental Success—and How You Can Too*, 1st ed. San Francisco: Jossey-Bass, 2006.

Stiglitz, Joseph E., Amartya Sen, and Jean-Paul Fitoussi. *Mismeasuring Our Lives: Why GDP Doesn't Add Up*. New York: The New Press, 2010.

Chapter Four: Embracing Externalities

Aaker, Jennifer, and Andy Smith. *The Dragonfly Effect: Quick, Effective, and Powerful Ways to Use Social Media to Drive Social Change*. San Francisco: Jossey-Bass, 2010.

Begole, Bo. *Ubiquitous Computing for Business: Find New Markets, Create Better Businesses, and Reach Customers Around the World 24-7-365*. Upper Saddle River, NJ: FT Press, 2011.

Brooks, David. *Bobos in Paradise: The New Upper Class and How They Got There.* New York: Simon & Schuster, 2001.

Campbell, Greg. *Blood Diamonds: Tracing the Deadly Path of the World's Most Precious Stone,* 1st ed. New York: Basic Books, 2002.

Chouinard, Yvon. *Let My People Go Surfing: The Education of a Reluctant Businessman.* New York: Penguin Press, 2005.

Esty, Daniel C., and Andrew S. Winston. *Green to Gold: How Smart Companies Use Environmental Strategy to Innovate, Create Value, and Build Competitive Advantage.* New Haven, CT: Yale University Press, 2006.

Fine, Allison. *Momentum: Igniting Social Change in the Connected Age.* San Francisco: Jossey-Bass, 2006.

Finkelstein, Eric A., and Laurie Zuckerman. *The Fattening of America: How The Economy Makes Us Fat, If It Matters, and What to Do About It.* Hoboken, NJ: Wiley, 2008.

Hawken, Paul. *The Ecology of Commerce: A Declaration of Sustainability.* New York: Harper Business, 1993.

Hofmeister, John. *Why We Hate the Oil Companies: Straight Talk from an Energy Insider.* New York: Palgrave Macmillan, 2010.

Hollender, Jeffrey, and Bill Breen. *The Responsibility Revolution: How the Next Generation of Businesses Will Win.* San Francisco: Jossey-Bass, 2010.

Humes, Edward. *Force of Nature: The Unlikely Story of Wal-Mart's Green Revolution.* New York: Harper Business, 2011.

Kurtzman, Joel, and Glenn Yago. *Global Edge: Using the Opacity Index to Manage the Risks of Cross-border Business.* Boston: Harvard Business School Press, 2007.

McDonough, William, and Michael Braungart. *Cradle to Cradle: Remaking the Way We Make Things.* New York: North Point Press, 2002.

Reynolds, Glenn H. *An Army of Davids: How Markets and Technology Empower Ordinary People to Beat Big Media, Big Government, and Other Goliaths.* Nashville, TN: Nelson Current, 2006.

Rivoli, Pietra. *The Travels of a T-Shirt in the Global Economy: An Economist Examines the Markets, Power, and Politics of World Trade.* Hoboken, NJ: Wiley, 2005.

Schultz, Howard. *Onward: How Starbucks Fought for Its Life Without Losing Its Soul.* New York: Rodale Books, 2011

Shepard, Mark. *Sentient City: Ubiquitous Computing, Architecture, and the Future of Urban Space.* Cambridge, MA: MIT Press, 2011.

Watson, Tom. *CauseWired: Plugging In, Getting Involved, Changing the World.* Hoboken, NJ: Wiley, 2008.

Weeden, Curt. *Smart Giving Is Good Business: How Corporate Philanthropy Can Benefit Your Company and Society.* San Francisco: Jossey-Bass, 2011.

Chapter Five: Pseudocompetition

Arthur, W. Brian. *Increasing Returns and Path Dependence in the Economy.* Ann Arbor, MI: University of Michigan Press, 1994.

Chandler, Alfred D., Jr. *The Visible Hand: The Managerial Revolution in American Business.* Cambridge, MA: Belknap Press, 1977.

Cohan, William D. *Money and Power: How Goldman Sachs Came to Rule the World.* New York: Doubleday, 2011.

Deans, Graeme, Fritz Kroeger, and Stefan Zeisel. *Winning the Merger Endgame: A Playbook for Profiting from Industry Consolidation*, 1st ed. New York: McGraw-Hill, 2002.

Friedman, Milton. *Capitalism and Freedom: Fortieth Anniversary Edition*, 1st ed. Chicago: University of Chicago Press, 2002.

Hannaford, Stephen G. *Market Domination! The Impact of Industry Consolidation on Competition, Innovation, and Consumer Choice*. Westport, CT: Praeger, 2007.

Kiechel, Walter. *The Lords of Strategy: The Secret Intellectual History of the New Corporate World*. Boston: Harvard Business Press, 2010.

Leibenstein, Harvey. *Beyond Economic Man: New Foundations for Microeconomics*. Cambridge, MA: Harvard University Press, 1976.

Litan, Robert. *Rules for Growth: Promoting Innovation and Growth Through Legal Reform*. Kindle ed., Amazon Digital Services, 2011.

Lynn, Barry. *Cornered: The New Monopoly Capitalism and the Economics of Destruction*. Hoboken, NJ: Wiley, 2010.

Markopolos, Harry. *No One Would Listen: A True Financial Thriller*. Hoboken, NJ: Wiley, 2010.

Moon, Youngme. *Different: Escaping the Competitive Herd*. New York: Crown Business, 2010.

Mueller, Milton L. *Universal Service: Competition, Interconnection and Monopoly in the Making of the American Telephone System*. Washington, DC: AEI Press, 1998.

Ogle, Maureen. *Ambitious Brew: The Story of American Beer*. Boston: Houghton Mifflin Harcourt, 2006.

Porter, Michael E. *Competitive Advantage: Creating and Sustaining Superior Performance*. New York: Free Press, 1998.

Reich, Robert B. *Supercapitalism: The Transformation of Business, Democracy, and Everyday Life*, 1st ed. New York: Alfred A. Knopf, 2007.

Schulz, Eric. *The Marketing Game: How the World's Best Companies Play to Win*. Holbrokk, MA: Adams Media Corp, 1999.

Schwartz, Barry. *The Paradox of Choice: Why More Is Less*, 1st ed. New York: Ecco, 2003.

Smith, Adam. *An Inquiry into the Nature and Causes of the Wealth of Nations*. 1776. Hamburg, Germany: Management Laboratory Press, 2008.

Stalk, George, and Rob Lachenauer. *Hardball: Are You Playing to Play or Playing to Win?* Boston: Harvard Business School Press, 2004.

Wu, Tim. *The Master Switch: The Rise and Fall of Information Empires*. New York: Knopf, 2010.

Chapter Six: The Invisible Handshake

Benkler, Yochai. *The Penguin and the Leviathan: How Cooperation Triumphs over Self-Interest*. New York: Crown Business, 2011.

Berners-Lee, Tim. *Weaving the Web: The Original Design and Ultimate Destiny of the World Wide Web by Its Inventor*. New York: HarperOne, 1999.

Bessen, James, and Michael J. Meurer. *Patent Failure: How Judges, Bureaucrats, and Lawyers Put Innovators at Risk*. Princeton, NJ: Princeton University Press, 2008.

Bingham, Alpheus, and Dwayne Spradlin. *The Open Innovation Marketplace: Creating Value in the Challenge Driven Enterprise.* Upper Saddle River, NJ: FT Press, April 11, 2011.

Botsman, Rachel, and Roo Rogers. *What's Mine Is Yours: The Rise of Collaborative Consumption.* New York: Harper Business, 2010.

Carver, Raymond, "Gravy." In *All of Us: The Collected Poems.* New York: Knopf, 1998.

Chesbrough, Henry, *Open Innovation: The New Imperative for Creating and Profiting from Technology.* Boston: Harvard Business School Press, 2003.

Coase, Ronald. "The Nature of the Firm" *Economica* 4, no. 16 (1937): 386–405. Rep. in Coase, R.H. *The Firm, the Market and the Law.* Chicago: University of Chicago Press, 1988.

Gansky, Lisa. *The Mesh: Why the Future of Business Is Sharing.* New York: Portfolio Penguin, 2010.

Gershenfeld, Neil. *FAB: The Coming Revolution on Your Desktop—From Personal Computers to Personal Fabrication.* New York: Basic Books, 2005.

Godin, Seth. *Free Prize Inside: The Next Big Marketing Idea.* New York: Portfolio, 2004.

Hayes, Tom. *Jump Point: How Network Culture Is Revolutionizing Business.* New York: McGraw-Hill, 2008.

Howe, Jeff. *Crowdsourcing: Why the Power of the Crowd Is Driving the Future of Business.* New York: Crown Business, 2008.

Lessig, Lawrence. *The Future of Ideas: The Fate of the Commons in a Connected World.* New York: Random House, 2001.

———. *Republic, Lost: How Money Corrupts Congress—and a Plan to Stop It.* New York: Twelve, 2011.

Lerner, Josh, and Mark Schankerman. *The Comingled Code: Open Source and Economic Development.* Cambridge, MA: MIT Press, 2010.

Marshall, Alfred. *Principles of Economics.* Nabu Press, 2010.

Meyer, Peter B. *The Airplane as an Open Source Invention.* Office of Productivity and Technology, U.S. Bureau of Labor Statistics, October 15, 2007. www.hbs.edu/entrepreneurship/pdf/Meyer-summary.pdf.

Nowak, Martin A. *Evolutionary Dynamics: Exploring the Equations of Life.* Cambridge, MA: Belknap Press of Harvard University Press, 2006.

Ross, Jeanne W., Peter Weill, and David Robertson. *Enterprise Architecture as Strategy: Creating a Foundation for Business Execution.* Boston: Harvard Business School Press, 2006.

Saxenian, AnnaLee. *Regional Advantage: Culture and Competition in Silicon Valley and Route 128.* Cambridge, MA: Harvard University Press 1994.

Shenkar, Oded. *The Chinese Century: The Rising Chinese Economy and Its Impact on the Global Economy, the Balance of Power, and Your Job.* Upper Saddle River, NJ: Pearson Prentice Hall, 2004.

Shirky, Clay. *Cognitive Surplus: How Technology Makes Consumers into Collaborators.* New York: Penguin Press, 2010.

Shreeve, James. *The Genome War: How Craig Venter Tried to Capture the Code of Life and Save the World.* New York: Knopf, 2004.

Stephenson, Neal. *The Diamond Age, or, A Young Lady's Illustrated Primer.* New York: Spectra, 1995.

Sterling, Bruce. *Distraction*. New York: Bantam Spectra, 1998.

Thall, Peter M. *What They'll Never Tell You About the Music Business: The Myths, the Secrets, the Lies (and a Few Truths)*. New York: Billboard Books, 2002.

Tisch, Jonathan M., with Karl Weber. *Citizen You: Doing Your Part to Change the World*. New York: Crown, 2010.

Torvalds, Linus, and David Diamond. *Just for Fun: The Story of an Accidental Revolutionary*. New York: HarperBusiness, 2002.

Von Hippel, Eric. *Democratizing Innovation*. Cambridge, MA: MIT Press, 2005.

Washington, Harriet A. *Deadly Monopolies: The Shocking Corporate Takeover of Life Itself—and the Consequences for Your Health and Our Medical Future*. New York: Doubleday, 2011.

Weber, Steven. *Success of Open Source*. Cambridge, MA: Harvard University Press, 2004.

Wilson, Edward O. *Consilience: The Unity of Knowledge*. New York: Knopf, 1998.

Chapter Seven: The Fourth Sector

Brest, Paul, and Hal Harvey. *Money Well Spent: A Strategic Plan for Smart Philanthropy*. New York: Bloomberg Press, 2008.

Bugg-Levine, Antony, and Jed Emerson. *Impact Investing: Transforming How We Make Money While Making a Difference*. San Francisco: Jossey-Bass, 2011.

Casanova, Lourdes. *Global Latinas: Latin America's Emerging Multinationals*. New York: Palgrave Macmillan, 2009.

Cassidy, John. *How Markets Fail: The Logic of Economic Calamities*. New York: Farrar, Straus and Giroux, 2009.

Chutani, Sailesh, Jessica Rothenberg Aalami, and Akhtar Badshah. *Technology at the Margins: How IT Meets the Needs of Emerging Markets*. Hoboken, NJ: Wiley, 2010.

Crutchfield, Leslie R., John V. Kania, and Mark R. Kramer. *Do More Than Give: The Six Practices of Donors Who Change the World*. San Francisco: Jossey-Bass, 2011.

Crutchfield, Leslie R., and Heather McLeod Grant. *Forces for Good: The Six Practices of High-Impact Nonprofits*. San Francisco: Jossey-Bass, 2007.

Elkington, John, and Pamela Hartigan. *The Power of Unreasonable People: How Social Entrepreneurs Create Markets That Change the World*. Boston: Harvard Business School Press, 2008.

Hirshberg, Gary. *Stirring It Up: How to Make Money and Save the World*. New York: Hyperion, 2008.

Karamchandani, Ashish, Michael Kubzansky, and Paul Frandano. *Emerging Markets, Emerging Models*. March 2009. http://www.monitor.com/Portals/0/Monitor Content/imported/MonitorUnitedStates/Articles/PDFs/Monitor_Emerging_ Markets_NEDS_03_25_09.pdf.

Liberman, Varda, Steven M. Samuels, and Lee Ross. Determining Prisoner's Dilemma Game Moves, *Personality and Social Psychology Bulletin*, September 2004.

London, Ted, and Stuart L. Hart. *Next Generation Business Strategies for the Base of the Pyramid: New Approaches for Building Mutual Value*. Upper Saddle River, NJ: FT Press, 2010.

Lublin, Nancy. *Zilch: The Power of Zero in Business*. New York: Portfolio, 2010.

Mehta, Pavithra K., and Suchitra Shenoy. *Infinite Vision: How Aravind Became the World's Greatest Business Case for Compassion.* San Francisco: Berrett-Koehler, 2011.

Neff, David J., and Randal C. Moss. *The Future of Nonprofits: Innovate and Thrive in the Digital Age.* Hoboken, NJ: Wiley, 2011.

Novogratz, Jacqueline. *The Blue Sweater: Bridging the Gap Between Rich and Poor in an Interconnected World.* New York: Rodale Books, 2009.

Sabeti, Heerad. "The For-Benefit Enterprise." *Harvard Business Review,* November 2011.

Tierney, Thomas J., and Joel L. Fleishman. Give Smart: Philanthropy That Gets Results. New York: PublicAffairs, 2011.

Ury, William L., Roger Fisher, and Bruce M. Patton. *Getting to Yes: Negotiating Agreement Without Giving In,* 2nd ed. Boston: Houghton Mifflin Harcourt, 1992.

Yunus, Muhammad. *Banker to the Poor: Micro-Lending and the Battle Against World Poverty.* New York: PublicAffairs, 1999.

Chapter Eight: Call It Capitalism . . .

Atarnon, Yuvai, Vinay Dixit, Glenn Liebowitz, and Cathy Wu. *Understanding China's Growing Love for Luxury.* McKinsey Insights China. 2011. http://www.mckinsey.com/locations/greaterchina/InsightsChina_LuxuryGoods.pdf.

Brooks, David. *The Social Animal: The Hidden Sources of Love, Character, and Achievement.* New York: Random House, 2011.

Brown, Phillip, Hugh Lauder, and David Ashton. *The Global Auction: The Broken Promises of Education, Jobs, and Incomes.* New York: Oxford University Press, 2010.

Caplan, Bryan. *Selfish Reasons to Have More Kids: Why Being a Great Parent Is Less Work and More Fun Than You Think.* New York: Basic Books, 2011.

Chandler, Alfred D., with the assistance of Takashi Hikino. *Scale and Scope: The Dynamics of Industrial Capitalism.* Cambridge, MA: Belknap Press, 1990.

Davenport, Thomas H. *Thinking for a Living: How to Get Better Performances and Results from Knowledge Workers.* Boston: Harvard Business School Press, 2005.

Davidson, Christopher M. *Dubai: The Vulnerability of Success.* New York: Columbia University Press, 2008.

Davis, Stanley M. *Future Perfect,* 1st ed. Reading, MA: Addison Wesley, 1987.

Diamond, Jared. *Collapse: How Societies Choose to Fail or Succeed,* 1st ed. New York: Viking, 2004.

Diderot, Denis. "Regrets for My Old Dressing Gown, or A Warning to Those Who Have More Taste Than Fortune." 1772. http://www.marxists.org/reference/archive/diderot/1769/regrets.htm.

Draper, William H. H. *The Startup Game: Inside the Partnership Between Venture Capitalists and Entrepreneurs.* New York; Palgrave Macmillan, 2011.

Enriquez, Juan. *The Untied States of America: Polarization, Fracturing, and Our Future.* New York: Crown, 2005.

Fox, Justin. *The Myth of the Rational Market: A History of Risk, Reward, and Delusion on Wall Street.* New York: HarperBusiness 2009.

Gawer, Annabelle, and Michael A. Cusumano. *Platform Leadership: How Intel, Microsoft, and Cisco Drive Industry Innovation.* Boston: Harvard Business School Press, 2002.

Gompers, Paul A., and Josh Lerner. *The Money of Invention: How Venture Capital Creates New Wealth*. Boston: Harvard Business School Press, 2001.

Hagel. John, III, and John Seely Brown. *The Only Sustainable Edge: Why Business Strategy Depends on Productive Friction and Dynamic Specialization*. Boston: Harvard Business School Press, 2005.

Harford, Tim. *Adapt: Why Success Always Starts with Failure*. New York: Farrar, Straus and Giroux, 2011.

Hoffman, David E. *The Oligarchs: Wealth and Power in the New Russia*. New York: PublicAffairs, 2002.

Johnson, Simon, and James Kwak. *13 Bankers: The Wall Street Takeover and the Next Financial Meltdown*. New York: Pantheon, 2010.

Kahneman, Daniel, and Angus Deaton. "High Income Improves Evaluation of Life but Not Emotional Well-Being." *Proceedings of the National Academy of Sciences Early Edition*, August 2010. http://www.princeton.edu/~deaton/downloads/deaton_kahneman_high_income_improves_evaluation_August2010.pdf.

Kaletsky, Anatole. *Capitalism 4.0: The Birth of a New Economy in the Aftermath of Crisis*. New York: PublicAffairs, 2010.

McGregor, James. *One Billion Customers: Lessons from the Front Lines of Doing Business in China*. New York: Free Press, 2005.

Michel, Serge, and Michel Beuret. *China Safari: On the Trail of Beijing's Expansion in Africa*. New York: Nation Books, 2009.

Morgenson, Gretchen, and Joshua Rosner. *Reckless Endangerment: How Outsized Ambition, Greed, and Corruption Led to Economic Armageddon*. New York: Times Books, 2011.

Murthy, NR Narayana. *A Better India: A Better World*. New York: Penguin Global, 2009.

Pascale, Richard, Mark Milleman, and Linda Gioja. *Surfing the Edge of Chaos: The Laws of Nature and the New Laws of Business*. New York: Crown Business, 2000.

Prestowitz, Clyde. *The Betrayal of American Prosperity: Free Market Delusions, America's Decline, and How We Must Compete in the Post-Dollar Era*. New York: Free Press, 2010.

Rachman, Gideon. *Zero-Sum Future: American Power in an Age of Anxiety*. New York: Simon & Schuster, 2011.

Ries, Eric. *The Lean Startup: How Today's Entrepreneurs Use Continuous Innovation to Create Radically Successful Businesses*. New York: Crown Business, 2011.

Rodrik, Dani. *One Economics, Many Recipes: Globalization, Institutions, and Economic Growth*. Princeton, NJ: Princeton University Press, 2007.

Serra, Narcís, and Joseph E. Stiglitz, eds. *The Washington Consensus Reconsidered: Towards a New Global Governance*. Initiative for Policy Dialogue Series. New York: Oxford University Press, 2008.

Skorman, Stuart. *Confessions of a Serial Entrepreneur: Why I Can't Stop Starting Over*. San Francisco: Jossey-Bass, 2007.

Sims, Peter. *Little Bets: How Breakthrough Ideas Emerge from Small Discoveries*. New York: Free Press, 2011.

Slaughter, Anne-Marie. *A New World Order*. Princeton, NJ: Princeton University Press, 2004.

Soros, George. *Open Society: Reforming Global Capitalism*. New York: PublicAffairs, 2000.

Yew, Lee Kuan. *From Third World to First: The Singapore Story: 1965–2000*. New York: Harper, 2000.

Chapter Nine: . . . And Move On

Bower, Joseph L., Herman B. Leonard, and Lynn S. Paine. *Capitalism at Risk: Rethinking the Role of Business*. Boston: Harvard Business Review Press, 2011.

Christensen, Clayton M. *The Innovator's Dilemma: When New Technologies Cause Great Firms to Fail*. Boston: Harvard Business School Press, 1997.

Govindarajan, Vijay, and Chris Trimble. *Reverse Innovation: Create Far From Home, Win Everywhere*. Harvard Business Press, 2012.

Gupta, Anil K., and Haiyan Wang. *Getting China and India Right: Strategies for Leveraging the World's Fastest Growing Economies for Global Advantage*. San Francisco: Jossey-Bass, 2009.

Hamel, Gary. *Leading the Revolution: How to Thrive in Turbulent Times by Making Innovation a Way of Life*. New York: Plume, 2002.

Haque, Umair. *The New Capitalist Manifesto: Building a Disruptively Better Business*. Harvard Business Press, 2011.

Heckscher, Charles. *The Collaborative Enterprise: Managing Speed and Complexity in Knowledge-Based Businesses*. New Haven, CT: Yale University Press, 2007.

Kanter, Rosabeth Moss. *SuperCorp: How Vanguard Companies Create Innovation, Profits, Growth, and Social Good*, 1st ed. New York: Crown Business, 2009.

Kelly, Eamonn. *Powerful Times: Rising to the Challenge of Our Uncertain World*. Upper Saddle River, NJ: Wharton School Publishing, 2005.

Lager, Fred. *Ben & Jerry's: The Inside Scoop: How Two Real Guys Built a Business with a Social Conscience and a Sense of Humor*. New York: Crown, 1994.

Lev, Baruch. *Winning Investors Over: Surprising Truths About Honesty, Earnings Guidance, and Other Ways to Boost Your Stock Price*. Harvard Business Review Press, 2011.

Macauley, Stewart. "Non-Contractual Relations in Business: A Preliminary Study." *American Sociological Review* 28, no. 1, February 1963.

Slywotzky, Adrian J., Karl Weber, and David J. Morrison. *How Digital Is Your Business?* New York: Crown Business, 2000.

Stoppard, Tom. *Arcadia*. New York: Doubleday Books, 1996.

Taylor, William C. *Practically Radical: Not-So-Crazy Ways to Transform Your Company, Shake Up Your Industry, and Challenge Yourself*. New York: William Morrow, 2011.

Toffler, Alvin. *The Adaptive Corporation*. New York: McGraw-Hill, 1984.

Watts, Duncan J. *Everything Is Obvious: *Once You Know the Answer*. New York: Crown Business, 2011.

Index

Acknowledgments

It's easy, in the final throes of finishing a book, to think that the ideas and inspirations are your own. Standing on the Sun, it's obvious that, like Copernicus, we have relied on the data and ideas gathered by many others to find our models.

Standing on the Sun had an unusual origin. During the summer of 2008, before the financial collapse, three members of the Harvard Business Review Press editorial staff dropped in on Chris to discuss the trends that would be shaping business in the next few years. He'd been focused on building a new company, Monitor Talent, not spending time on these kinds of questions, and didn't have a ready answer. But he did have a point of view: that capitalism is an adaptive system whose environment has changed, so to see its future you need to observe what's happening at the leading edge of those changes—the emerging economies. It was Jacque Murphy, then editorial director of Harvard Business Press, who said "You've got to write a book about that."

Next, HBR agreed to a proposal by Julia that she and Chris work together on the book. Since we'd collaborated a decade earlier on *Blur: The Speed of Change in the Connected Economy*, we knew this would be a productive and successful arrangement—but we weren't sure Harvard would agree. Thanks to Adi Ignatius, they did.

We were like the dog that catches the car—now what? We thought it prudent to consult a set of extraordinarily experienced and qualified people about the premise of the book: that capitalism could change if it found itself in an environment that rewarded different approaches to value creation. Jeffrey Garten, Seth Godin, Simon Johnson, Kevin Kelly,

Joel Kurtzman, Iqbal Quadir, Clay Shirky, and James Wolfensohn all were kind enough to entertain a mass of untested ideas and suggest how they might be developed. In the same category, years ago, conversations with Walter Wriston and Percy Barnevik planted important seeds about building global institutions.

Our hypothesis sharpened but intact, we needed access to facts on the ground—people doing business and making policy in the emerging economies—who could describe for us firsthand the way their worlds work. Ashish Karamchandani, Ruth Lande (gracious beyond reason), Chris Malone, Anand Raman, and above all Ethan Zuckerman were recklessly generous with their contacts, introducing us to dozens of insightful, engaged people. We are grateful also to the Bankinter Foundation of Innovation, particularly Mónica Montes, Rita Arrojo, and Juan Rosas, and to Gil Forer of Ernst & Young. Both organizations' activities brought us into contact with thoughtful business people from around the world. A memorable conversation with Michael Schrage was one result.

The cliché is that "everything looks like a mess in the middle." Over a year's time, we interviewed an array of business leaders and practitioners, policy makers and analysts, and in one case in Delhi while waiting for an interviewee who didn't show, a gentleman bringing repeatable business processes to Indian orphanages. We spoke with former or sitting CEOs and CMOs of world-class companies, including Mauicio Botelho, Jeffrey Hollender, Marc Mathieu, Narayana Murthy, and Luiz Seabra, who with Gabriela Callil and Marcos Vaz helped us understand Cosméticos Natura. Beth Comstock, GE's CMO, and Stacey Tank introduced us to Kay Eron, Munesh Makhija, Ravi Kaushik, and Oswin Varghese, who shared compelling details of their business with us.

Writers like Atanu Dey, Bernie Avishai, Suchitra Shenoy, Dina Mehta, and Amy Ye provided more perspective and more contacts. Policy makers like Feras Abu Ibrahim, Eli Opper, and David Scott, and investors like Abhay Havaldar, Ravi Moorthy, Yuval Cohen, and Yossi Vardi spent longer than they should have with us. Members of Monitor's Inclusive Markets Team—Naina Batra, Mike Kubzansky, Nabomita Dutta, and Prashant Lalwani—provided their own thinking as well as introductions to many pathfinding entrepreneurs in India.

Monitor partners Chris Malone, Rogerio Rizzi, Francisco Salazar, and Gustavo Zevallos found time to help, and Nikhil Ojha, head of Monitor's Mumbai office, was personally engaged and unusually thoughtful.

Dozens of practicing business people (for profit and for benefit) took the time to explain their work to us. Among them were Sunil Abrahim, Shuja Ali, Reshma Anand, Rajni Bakshi, Amit Kumar Banerjee, Anat Bernstein, Shraga Biran, Irad Eichler, Chris Flynn, Itzhak Forer, Jack Hidary Henry (from Huawei, whose last name we can't retrieve), Pankaj Jain, Dan Kennedy, Sweta Mangal, Steve Meller, Will Patten, Heerad Sabeti, Kamal Quadir, Jerry Rau, Paolo Rossi, Manish Sabharwal, Varun Sahni, Joe Silva, Murad Tahboub, Don Taylor, Yoram Tietz, Aviv Wasserman, Chris West, Harry West, and Paul Van Zyl. And in various parts of the world, Diogo Yamamoto, Zarine Commissariat, and Roselle Smit were invaluable in keeping the blizzard of appointments and rescheduling under control.

We amassed an inchoate, intractable, intriguing set of observations. But the facts on the ground didn't fit the commonly accepted principles of capitalism. We understood we needed a model with something new at the center: hence the allusion to Copernicus in the title. We were fortunate to have the help of patient and thoughtful people to serve as sounding boards for the conclusions we reached—and often, with their help, discarded. Mel Blake, Stephen Forth, Mark Fuller, Bob Litan, Miranda Meyer, Mary Rivet, and Rafe Sagalyn provided unvarnished feedback. As our ideas took shape, we posted many of them on our HBR blog, where hundreds of people around the world helped us see their flaws and merits. We are grateful to our anonymous peer reviewers for their efforts to keep us from overreaching; we hope they were successful. The project was greatly advanced by our interns: Kyle Dionne-Clark added a dose of analytical thinking, and Kathleen Pope pulled our hundreds of snippets into retrievable and elegant form.

Tim Sullivan, our editor, who joined HBR Press in 2010 and found himself with a project he had never vetted, let alone volunteered for, embraced it as his own and provided just the right level of skepticism and guidance (though why the image of him saying "This is me being enthusiastic" lives in our memory deserves some attention). Very late in the game, when we pushed hard for some bending of the design process, the design team, led by James de Vries, deployed talent and tenacity to help us. They produced, we think, a beautiful book.

And it took the work of Erin Brown and her team, Jennifer Waring, Rimjhim Dey, and Stephanie Gerson to help get this book into your hands—thanks!

Finally, we want to acknowledge how much we've each valued our own collaboration. Chris gained from Julia's panoptic perspective on and insights into what others are thinking, her conviction that ideas, no matter how pretty, must fit together in a consistent argument useful to you, dear reader, and her ability to make them do so while tactfully discarding the rest. Julia, for her part, appreciated anew the never-dull experience of following Chris's mind where it took him, figured she gained the equivalent of a graduate degree in the process, and enjoyed Chris's bright wit and constant good cheer as an extra benefit. We're lucky to have had two years of sharing discoveries and epiphanies almost daily. And we're mutually grateful for an extraordinary chance to explore each other's ideas about a world evolving more rapidly than ever before.

About the Authors

Chris Meyer has spent his career anticipating and shaping the future of business, as an economist, entrepreneur, author, and think tank leader. His most recent entrepreneurial venture is Monitor Talent, which he founded as a unit of Monitor Group based on insights developed in an earlier book, *Future Wealth* (coauthored with Stan Davis). Chris coauthored two other books with Stan Davis: *It's Alive: The Coming Convergence of Information, Biology, and Business* and *Blur: The Speed of Change in the Connected Economy*. The books have been translated into thirteen languages; *Blur* was a *BusinessWeek* bestseller.

Chris's ideas have been shaped by consulting work with many clients, including Microsoft, Texas Instruments, Citicorp, the Singapore Economic Development Board, and the Chairman of the U.S. Joint Chiefs of Staff. More broadly, he engages with executive audiences through his writing for *Harvard Business Review*, *Sloan Management Review*, *Fast Company*, *TIME*, the *Wall Street Journal*, and *BusinessWeek*, and through his speaking engagements at APEC, TED University, the World Economic Forum, and many other events.

Chris founded the Information Industries practice at Mercer Management Consulting and, while director of the Ernst & Young Center for Business Innovation, the Bios Group, a venture to apply early adaptive systems theory to business.

He holds BAs in both mathematics and economics from Brandeis University and earned his MBA from Harvard Business School. At the University of Pennsylvania, he held a University Predoctoral Fellowship in economics. He lives in Boston with his wife and, from time to time, his daughter.

Julia Kirby has been an editor at *Harvard Business Review* since 2000 and has collaborated with hundreds of scholars, executives, and consultants to bring their best ideas to its pages. Passionate about improving the practice of management, she acquires and develops content across the full range of organizational challenges, from strategy to operations to leadership development, and for presentation in print, digital, and live formats. Prior to joining HBR, Julia worked for more than a decade in the management consulting industry.